The Business
Models Handbook

Second edition

The Business Models Handbook

The tools, techniques and frameworks every business professional needs to succeed

Paul Hague

First published in Great Britain and the United States in 2019 by Kogan Page Limited
Second edition published in 2023

2nd Floor, 45 Gee Street	8 W 38th Street, Suite 902	4737/23 Ansari Road
London EC1V 3RS	New York, NY 10018	Daryaganj
United Kingdom	USA	New Delhi 110002
		India

www.koganpage.com

© Paul Hague, 2019, 2023

The right of Paul Hague to be identified as the author of this work has been asserted by him in accordance with the Copyright, Designs and Patents Act 1988.

ISBNs

Hardback   978 1 3986 1177 1
Paperback   978 1 3986 1175 7
E-ISBN   978 1 3986 1176 4

British Library Cataloguing-in-Publication Data
A CIP record for this book is available from the British Library.

Library of Congress Cataloging-in-Publication Data
Names: Hague, Paul N., author.
Title: The business models handbook : the tools, techniques and frameworks
   every business professional needs to succeed / Paul Hague.
Description: Second edition. | London ; New York, NY : Kogan Page, 2023. |
   Includes bibliographical references and index.
Identifiers: LCCN 2023017463 (print) | LCCN 2023017464 (ebook) | ISBN
   9781398611757 (paperback) | ISBN 9781398611771 (hardback) | ISBN
   9781398611764 (ebook)
Subjects: LCSH: Strategic planning–Handbooks, manuals, etc. | Business
   planning–Handbooks, manuals, etc. | Management–Handbooks, manuals,
   etc. | BISAC: BUSINESS & ECONOMICS / Strategic Planning | BUSINESS &
   ECONOMICS / Marketing / Direct
Classification: LCC HD30.28 .H332 2023 (print) | LCC HD30.28 (ebook) |
   DDC 658.4/012–dc23/eng/20230413
LC record available at https://lccn.loc.gov/2023017463
LC ebook record available at https://lccn.loc.gov/2023017464

Typeset by Integra Software Services, Pondicherry
Print production managed by Jellyfish
Printed and bound by CPI Group (UK) Ltd, Croydon, CR0 4YY

CONTENTS

Online resources to accompany this book can be accessed at:

www.koganpage.com/TBMH

or at:

www.b2bframeworks.com

PREFACE

I am a market researcher. It has been a lifelong career for me. Many years ago, as a cub researcher, I sat in a training session when the trainer introduced the subject of a SWOT – strengths, weaknesses, opportunities and threats – analysis. It was simple stuff. He was making the point that the SWOT model helped locate data within a context. The business model brought the data to life. It pushed it into action. It gave it purpose. The guru trainer said, 'there are dozens of these frameworks and you should familiarize yourself with them'. I couldn't believe him. I could only think of the 4Ps – product, place, price and promotion – and the SWOT. I felt sure he was exaggerating.

Little by little, over the years, these tools, models and frameworks have made themselves known to me. They became friends, helping me to analyse data and giving a direction to the intelligence I had collected. I became fascinated by the inventors of these frameworks. They had eponymous names. The Ansoff matrix. The Boston matrix. Porter's five forces. Kano's customer requirements. Who were these people? The models had made them famous, at least in the eyes of business people and analysts. Many of the founders were academics whose teaching and writing included books and articles, but it is their models that we remember them by. The models have become their moment of glory.

As I am approaching the end of my working life I was looking for a project. As an avid user of models, particularly those used in marketing and business strategy, I was familiar with the many websites that describe them. Wikipedia is wonderful in this respect but the models are scattered throughout its 5 million articles. Mind Tools (www.mindtools.com) brings together frameworks of all kinds and is a brilliant website. However, there is a charge and you need to be online to use it. Michael Porter has written some great books that sit on my shelves but their focus is largely on competitive intelligence. I wanted something in hard copy, something that would sit next to my computer and be a ready reference book. I floated the idea to Kogan Page and they liked it. Before I knew it, I had the go-ahead.

The excitement of receiving the commission soon evaporated as I faced the task of researching and writing about each of the models. Which models should be included? Is conjoint a model or a tool and does it matter? How many models should I cover? Pragmatism provided the answers. I would include any tool or model that I thought would be useful to someone in marketing as I figured that, in the main, it will be marketers who will find the book useful. I would limit the book to 50 models, chosen for the only reason that they are my favourites.

I wanted the chapters to have the same balance, approximately the same number of words and a similar structure. This was not easy. Some models are so big and complicated they have books written about them, while others are simple and self-explanatory. What should the structure be? On the one hand I could see the logic of starting with a description of the origins of the model, and on the other hand, I sensed that the user of the model would want to get straight into what it is and how it works. Some models remain pure and unadulterated, others have changed over time.

I know the importance of providing examples and case studies and this can be a challenge as some of the best business strategies never come to light, remaining hidden in the companies that develop them. I scoured the internet for good case studies. These I have referenced for anyone who wants to look at the original source. In addition I have been privileged to have access to the many projects that I have carried out as a consultant. I have drawn upon these, often masking the identity of the companies to maintain confidentiality.

For those of you who want PowerPoint templates to apply the models, updates and the latest thinking on frameworks, visit my website at **www.b2bframeworks.com**

Four years have now passed and I have been surprised and gratified by the success of the *The Business Models Handbook*. Alongside the book, my website, www.b2bframeworks.com, has grown in popularity and from it I am able to see which frameworks are most visited. It shows some popular frameworks that were not included in the book. It shows that it is time for a second edition to rectify these omissions.

This is a book that does not need to be read from cover to cover. I hope you will dip into it and see it as a friend that is there to help when you are looking for a way forward. I hope that it will help you improve your strategic thinking and deliver that competitive edge you are seeking.

Introduction 01

An overview of business and marketing models

People in business often talk about their 'business model'. By this they mean the way that their business is organized to make money. Business models also have another meaning. They refer to the frameworks and analytical tools that are used in strategic planning. These are the business models that are the subject of this book. They are the methods by which people in business plan their strategy. They are generic models, tool kits if you like, that structure how we think about and find a solution to a business problem.

We use models all the time. If we are faced with a problem we try to answer the question 'Where are we now?' At this stage we lay down our understanding of the problem and what has caused it. We then turn to the next question, 'Where are we going?' We set ourselves goals that will solve the problem. Finally, we ask 'How are we going to get there?' We work out what we are going to do, who is going to do it, what resources we need and how long it will take.

Business models give us a sense of confidence. They are a sort of map; a plan of where we are and where we can go. Just as we would never attempt to walk up a mountain without a map, we should never address a business problem without a model.

There are hundreds of models and frameworks to help us develop our business strategies. There are models for our overall strategy such as SWOT, Porter's five forces and PEST (political, economical, social and technological). There are models that help us to find a competitive edge such as Porter's four corners, Porter's generic strategies and USP analysis. There are models that help develop marketing strategies such as customer journey mapping, Maslow's hierarchy of needs, Rogers' diffusion curve and the 4Ps.

It is important to familiarize ourselves with the different models. They each play to their strengths. Successful business models have a simplicity about them. Once someone is introduced to the model, it makes perfect sense. It is a formula that explains a situation. It is a tool kit for the user. Often the model includes templates that, once completed, clarify the subject. The models eventually become a shorthand that makes it easy to have a conversation with colleagues. We refer to 'our USP' and everyone knows it is our unique selling proposition – the thing that distinguishes us from the competition.

Useful as they are, business models should not be regarded as the holy grail. Just as we can get tired of the use of *SmartArt* in PowerPoint, we should be careful not to use models as cookie cutters. They are there to be adapted. Each chapter contains a note on the development of the models and how they have changed. Indeed, you are encouraged to think of your own model. Some years ago my company was commissioned to carry out a market research survey for a house builder to find out the satisfaction of customers who had bought one of their properties. The analyst who worked on the project presented the findings in the framework of a snakes-and-ladders board. Buying a new house had its ups and downs. The building society or bank could provide a ladder or a snake depending on the financial circumstances of the buyer. Some builders offered a part-exchange deal that could move the buyer higher up the board. Then there was the building phase, which could be a ladder or a snake and determined whether the house would be ready on time. Moving day was another critical moment and when the keys were passed to the householder they could see if their new house was pristine or had a list of snags that needed sorting. The die that determined how quickly and easily someone moved up the board was the sales agent. A good sales agent helped the customer progress quickly onwards and upwards while a poor one left them languishing. The graphic image of the model was very powerful and was remembered long after the hard facts of the survey were forgotten.

Companies have been in existence forever. The Industrial Revolution brought many innovations, including mass production, but it was not until we entered the 20th century that business models were developed. In fact, most of them are a product of the last 40 to 50 years. Spurred by increasing levels of competition, more demanding customers and new forces that put pressure on companies, solutions were found by consultants and academics. Models were born. The first models often focused on some aspect of marketing.

The AIDA – attention, interest, desire, action – model is a rare example of a framework created in the early 1900s. After the Second World War the development of models came in a rush following Theodore Levitt's teaching on the basic principles of marketing. This was a period during which business schools were opened throughout the United States and Europe. Their professors were inspired to make their name with new business structures and tools. Michael Porter's name is synonymous with a number of business models on competitive strategy. He was joined by Ansoff, Maslow, Kano, Kotler, Rogers, Mintzberg and Greiner. Consultants got in on the act too. McKinsey developed a number of famous models. The Boston Consulting Group gave its name to the matrix for portfolio management. Arthur D Little made a contribution.

Latterly Edward de Bono has provided us with models to inspire lateral thinking. Daniel Kahneman has introduced the world to System 1 thinking, which is quick, emotive and often subliminal; and System 2 thinking, which is slower and more logical. Many of the consultants are still practising and we can expect that the development of models has not finished.

Knowing which model to choose is half the problem. In part our choice is narrowed down by the type of problem that we face. Are we seeking help in the development of a new product? Do we face new competitive threats? Are we planning a high-level strategy for the business? We can look within these categories for a model that could be appropriate. This second edition has been expanded and now covers 63 popular frameworks. They are laid out in Table 1.1, classified according to whether they are mainly used for business strategy, innovation, fighting the competition, pricing, product management, improving company efficiency, promotion and branding or understanding the customer. Many of the models can be used in more than one application.

Table 1.1 Business models and frameworks covered in this book

Strategic frameworks	
Chapter 2	3Cs
Chapter 3	4Ps
Chapter 4	ADL matrix
Chapter 6	Ansoff matrix
Chapter 10	Boston consulting group (BCG) matrix
Chapter 13	Business model canvas
Chapter 22	Directional policy matrix
Chapter 25	EFQM excellence model
Chapter 28	Greiner's growth model

(*continued*)

Table 1.1   (Continued)

Strategic frameworks

Chapter 31	Kay's distinctive capabilities
Chapter 33	Market sizing
Chapter 35	McKinsey 7S
Chapter 36	Mintzberg's 5Ps for strategy
Chapter 37	MOSAIC
Chapter 41	PEST
Chapter 43	Porter's generic strategies
Chapter 53	Strategy diamond
Chapter 54	SWOT analysis
Chapter 56	Tipping point
Chapter 62	VMOST

Frameworks for better understanding the customer

Chapter 17	Customer activity cycle
Chapter 18	Customer journey maps
Chapter 19	Customer lifetime value
Chapter 20	Customer value proposition
Chapter 27	Gap analysis
Chapter 30	Kano model
Chapter 32	Kotler's five product levels
Chapter 34	Maslow's hierarchy
Chapter 38	Net Promoter Score®
Chapter 40	Personas

(*continued*)

Table 1.1 (Continued)

Frameworks for better understanding the customer	
Chapter 48	Segmentation
Chapter 50	SERVQUAL
Chapter 55	System 1 and System 2 thinking
Chapter 57	Unique selling proposition (USP)
Chapter 61	Value-based marketing
Frameworks for fighting the competition	
Chapter 14	Competitive advantage matrix
Chapter 15	Competitive intelligence
Chapter 26	Four corners
Chapter 42	Porter's five forces
Chapter 60	Value net
Frameworks for pricing	
Chapter 16	Conjoint analysis
Chapter 39	New product pricing (Gabor-Granger and van Westendorp)
Chapter 44	Price elasticity
Chapter 45	Price quality strategy
Chapter 51	SIMALTO
Chapter 59	Value equivalence line
Frameworks for communications and branding	
Chapter 5	AIDA
Chapter 11	Brand audit
Chapter 12	Bullseye for brand positioning

(*continued*)

Table 1.1 (Continued)

Frameworks for product management	
Chapter 46	Product life cycle
Chapter 47	Product service positioning matrix
Frameworks for innovation	
Chapter 9	Blue ocean strategy
Chapter 21	Diffusion of innovation
Chapter 23	Disruptive innovation model
Chapter 52	Stage gate new product development
Frameworks for improving company efficiency	
Chapter 7	Balanced scorecard
Chapter 8	Benchmarking
Chapter 24	Edward De Bono's six thinking hats
Chapter 29	Importance-performance matrix
Chapter 49	Service profit chain
Chapter 58	Value chain
Chapter 63	Weisbord's six box model

3C framework   02

Maximizing a company's strength relative to the competition

What the model looks like and how it works

It is natural to wish that we didn't have any competitors. Life would be much easier if we had the marketplace to ourselves. However, in the real world this is hardly ever the case. We could look on competitors as a force for good. Copying a competitor is not a good idea as it would result in a 'me too' offer. A competitive environment is likely to promote more innovation, faster responses and an all-round improvement in customer service. It follows therefore that in developing a business strategy we should fully understand the competitive environment.

Kenichi Ohmae began life as a nuclear scientist and subsequently became an organizational theorist and management consultant. He developed the Japanese theory of balancing people, money and things into a three-part strategy for business. He has shown us how to see the competitive environment within the context of our customers, competitors, and the company itself. When these 3Cs are taken into account, a business strategy can be developed. Ohmae proposes an industry framework in which three elements are in balance:

Company

If a company is to be successful in fighting or defeating the competition it is important that it understands its strengths and weaknesses. It is likely that the company will have a range of different strengths. One of the strengths should be developed into a competitive advantage. Ohmae recognizes that there are some things that companies find it difficult to do, in which case they could be outsourced. If activities are outsourced it may be necessary to manage in-house costs in order to ensure there is no loss of competitive advantage.

Customers

Customers have a choice and will buy from companies that they believe offer them better value, better service or in some way a competitive edge. Not all customers are the same and Ohmae recommends segmenting them according to their different needs and behaviours. This requires considerable understanding of the customer base – who they are, how they use the products, where they live, their age, interests and use of competitive products.

Competitors

As always, it is important to understand competitors' strengths. For some firms it may be a cost advantage while for others it could be their reputation and brand strength. Where possible it is important to understand how the players in the market collect value and make profits. In developing a strategy it is important to work out which are the competitors that we are aligned against – the ones that we need to beat. Crucial to this is determining exactly how we are going to beat them. In making this decision it is important to fully understand the business strengths and weaknesses and the customers' views. It is not unusual for a company's sales force to say that the only way to beat the competition is to be more aggressive with prices. On the other hand, a survey of customers may show that they value other things such as ease of use, length of life, or customer service.

The strategy to beat the competition can only be devised after balancing the strengths of the company and its unique selling points, and understanding customers and what they value and the way in which the company's offer is better than the competition. Focusing on just one or two of these 'Cs' would not be sufficient to be successful in the marketplace.

The origins of the model

Ohmae is an academic, business consultant and organizational theorist. In 1991 he published a framework on competitive strategy in his book *The Mind Of The Strategist: The art of Japanese business.*[1] After starting life as a nuclear scientist, in the early 1970s Ohmae took the lead in McKinsey's Tokyo office and from this point became known for his views on globalization.

He threw light on how major Japanese business leaders used vision and intuition to turn their ideas into action and weren't exclusively driven by rational analysis as most Westerners believed. He made the point that many large and successful Japanese companies achieve their strong position without an army of corporate planners or strategists. They have a visionary leader whose views are accepted by the company as the way forward.

Ohmae, known as Mr Strategy, said that the first step in developing a strategy is to focus on just one thing – the thing that matters most. From there it is necessary to think about competitive advantage and to achieve it at a reasonable cost. Having understood the competition it should be possible to recognize a relative strength as perceived by customers.

A company's strategy should have three legs. One leg is what the company should focus on, taking into account its resources and what it does best. The second leg is the customer-based strategy in which the focus is on a segment of the market that is served best by the company's products. The third leg of the strategy is competition based. This is where the company seeks to exploit whatever superiority it has over its competitors.

Developments of the model

As with most frameworks, the triangle concept is simple but the intelligence required to achieve the balance between customers, competitors and company could be complex and thorough. It shouldn't be based just on internal perceptions. Customer surveys, benchmarking metrics and objective data are vital if an appropriate strategy is to be devised. It is a framework in which other frameworks could help, such as segmentation, competitor intelligence and the competitive advantage matrix. At every stage of the analysis it is important to ask the question, 'why?'. This may point to a number of small advantages which collectively offer a significant advantage over the competition.

The model in action

Ohmae tells a story of a competitive battle between Fuji and Sakura, two suppliers of photographic film to the Japanese market. Sakura was losing market share to Fuji, which was the bigger company with a better-known brand. It examined Fuji's strengths, which were the quality of its film for sharp colours and contrasts. However, customers were becoming more concerned about cost. Sakura didn't want to create a price war by simply reducing its ticket price. Instead, it responded to the economic need by launching a 24-exposure film at the same price as Fuji's 20-exposure film. This allowed Sakura to maximize its resource in cost efficiency, meet the needs of price-sensitive customers, and obtain a competitive advantage over Fuji.

Some things to think about

- What is the critical success factor within your company?
- How could you make better use of your resources?
- Why do people buy your competitor's products?
- What above all else do your customers value from the products you supply?
- What is your company's single relative strength versus the competition?

Note

1   Ohmae, K (1982) *The Mind of the Strategist*, McGraw-Hill

The 4Ps 03

How to design your marketing mix

What the model looks like and how it works

There is an old saying that marketing is about getting the right product at the right price in the right place with the right promotion. The 4Ps (Figure 3.1) is an extension of this simplistic view. It describes the four essential components of the marketing mix:

Figure 3.1   The 4Ps

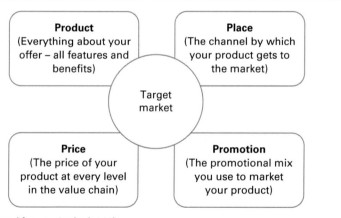

SOURCE Adapted from McCarthy (1960)

Product

This is what a company has to sell. It may not be a physical product; it could just as easily be a service or a product accompanied by a service. It is nevertheless what the company offers. Arguably, the product is the most important part of the marketing mix. It defines who will buy it, how much they will pay, what features they will find appealing and where it could be sold.

Questions that need to be answered to determine that the product is right for its market are:

- What benefits does the product provide to the customer? How do these benefits solve the customer's problem?
- What type of customers are the most likely targets for the product? What are their demographics, their behaviours, their attitudes and their psychographic profiles? How would they be described as a segment?
- How will the customer use the product? How frequently will they use it? When will they replace it?
- What would the customer do if the product was not available?

Price

Price is the component of the 4Ps that collects revenue. The other 3Ps incur costs. The price that someone is prepared to pay for a product is the 'bargain'. From the customer's point of view it is a figure that is worth paying to obtain the product and, from the supplier's point of view, it is a figure that covers the costs of production and collects (hopefully) sufficient revenue to make a profit.

Questions that need to be answered to determine that the price is right for its market are:

- How do customers perceive value in the product? What are the key benefits that they value? What monetary value is put on each of these benefits?
- How sensitive are customers to the price of the product?
- To what extent do customers perceive the lifetime value of the product (how long it lasts, the degree of maintenance that is required, any resale value, etc)?
- What are competitors' prices for a similar product? To what extent is the product perceived to be better or worse than competitors' products?

Promotion

People need to be aware of the availability of products and they need to be convinced of their value. Promotion is the means by which this communication takes place. The promotion could be any part of a mix that includes adverts in social media, the internet, newspapers, magazines, journals, the TV and radio. It could also include direct marketing such as flyers or emails.

Exhibitions, public relations and point-of-sale material are part of the promotional mix.

Questions that need to be answered to determine that the promotion is right for its market are:

- Which promotions are successful in getting through to people? How are different promotions performing? How should the promotional mix be changed to make it more effective?

- What is the reach of the promotion? How many customers/potential customers will see it?

- What is the impact of the promotion? To what extent will it stop people in their tracks and capture their interest?

- What is the relevance of the promotion? Is it something that the customer is interested in? Do the messages resonate?

- What is the call to action? What will potential customers do next?

Place

The product (or service) is made available somewhere for the customer. This could be in a shop, online or direct from the manufacturer. It is the channel (or channels) by which the product is distributed.

Questions that need to be answered to determine that the place is right for its market are:

- What are the channels that are most used by the customer for this type of product?

- How are the channels changing in terms of importance?

- What penetration of the channels can be achieved?

- What are the opportunities for finding new routes to market – i.e. alternative channels?

- What does each of the organizations in the channel require in terms of margin and service support?

- How will the product stand out from competitive products in the channel?

It should be clear from the above that the 4Ps are not aimed at just anyone; they are aimed specifically at a target audience. The four essential ingredients of the marketing mix are often referred to as hygiene factors. If the company fails on any one of them, the marketing strategy will fail.

The origins of the model

The 4Ps were coined by Edmund Jerome McCarthy, an American marketing professor. McCarthy's aim was to bring science and structure to marketing as befitted his training as a statistician and mathematician. He launched the framework in 1960 in a book entitled *Basic Marketing: A managerial approach*.[1] The book became a bestseller on the subject of marketing and the simple mnemonic of the 4Ps was quickly accepted.

Developments of the model

Still holding with the mnemonic of the 4Ps, other authors have added three more elements to the mix:

- **People**: it is argued that, in many businesses, people are a critical part of the offer. They make the product. They sell the product and create relationships with customers. They service the product and they deliver it. They deal with enquiries and problems. People are an essential component in any offer.

- **Process**: the process by which the product is made is part of the offer. A company has other processes that are relevant to customers such as the way it deals with enquiries, carries out credit checks, handles complaints, etc. These are all part of the offer.

- **Physical evidence**: in some situations the physical environment is an important part of the offer. This would especially be the case for a supermarket where the width of the aisles, the layout of the store, the colours, the smells and the ambience of the place can all have a big influence on the marketing.

In 2013, Richard Ettenson, Eduardo Conrado and Jonathan Knowles wrote an article in *Harvard Business Review* entitled 'Rethinking the 4Ps'.[2] They argued that the original 4P model is not suited to the business to business (B2B) world. They claimed that the old 4P framework stresses product technology and quality, and these they said are hygiene factors and do not differentiate. In an attempt to shift the focus from products to solutions, they suggested the SAVE framework. SAVE is an acronym for solution, access, value and education:

- **Solution** (rather than product). This places the emphasis on solving the problem rather than selling the product.

- **Access** (rather than place). It is important to have access to customers wherever they are and whatever they are doing. This means that bricks-and-mortar distribution outlets are far less relevant today than, for example, the internet.

- **Value** (rather than price). People care far less about the price than what they get for their money – it is value that matters.

- **Education** (rather than promotion). Promotion can be seen as manipulative and, in many B2B markets, trust and reputation are more important. Trust is built up over time in an educative way.

The model in action

The 4P model (or one of its derivatives) can be used whenever a marketing plan or business case is being considered. It is particularly useful in two business scenarios: launching a new product and entering a new market.

Launching a new product

New products are the lifeblood of all companies. Successful companies continuously modify or introduce new products to meet the changing needs of their customers, and it is said that a successful company has over one-third of its products that are less than three years old. This proportion could vary considerably, and companies that make confectionery – for example – are more likely to have a greater proportion of new products in their port-folio than those that make steel components. Whether the product in ques-tion is a new doughnut or a new alloy, the discipline of checking out the 4Ps is still worthwhile:

- Does the new product better meet the needs of customers than existing products?

- How much are the features and benefits of the new product valued over and above those of existing products?

- Will the new product fit into the distribution chain alongside existing products?

- What promotion will be required to launch the new product?

Entering a new market

Growth can often be achieved by taking a product into a new geography or launching it to a new group of customers. The questions to be answered must be:

- Where does the product sit against competing products that are already available?
- In the new geography or the new segment, what will people pay for the product?
- What channel to market will be successful within the new geography?
- What are the messages that will work in the new geography?

Western companies selling into China have had to modify their product portfolios. KFC offers Peking duck, Starbucks has added green and aromatic teas and Coca-Cola sells carbonated fruit drinks (as well as Coke) to the Chinese. Manufacturers of workplace gloves sell smaller sizes to fit the smaller hands of the Chinese workforce.

The price that is charged in a country has to be appropriate for the income in that country. This is often referred to as purchasing power parity. It is why a Big Mac may cost three or four times as much in Norway or Switzerland than it does in India.

The channel to market varies enormously across different countries. In China and in many Asian countries the open market is still a major outlet for all types of products – both consumer and industrial. Small and specialist shops abound in the East while megastores are dominant in the West.

The promotion of products differs considerably across the world. In the East, great significance is placed on the name of the product, the design of the logo and possibly the colour of the pack.

When IKEA opened stores in China, it could not afford to support them with the big catalogues that were a standard promotion in the West. They used smaller brochures that could be sent out several times during the year. They also communicated with a softer message. Instead of positioning the company as a proud rebellious brand – as it does in the West – they communicated how small changes would make life better, a more humble approach aimed at young Chinese women of 25–35 years of age.

Some things to think about

- Consider using a 4P structure when developing a marketing plan. It is particularly useful when entering a new market, launching a new product or developing a new customer segment.
- When analysing your 4Ps, keep in mind the target customers. Build personas for the customers (see Chapter 40) and build the 4Ps around them.

Notes

1 McCarthy, EJ (1960) *Basic Marketing: A managerial approach*, Richard D Irwin, Homewood
2 Ettenson, R, Conrado, E and Knowles, J (2013) Rethinking the 4Ps, *Harvard Business Review*, January–February

ADL matrix 04

Strengthening a product portfolio or strategic business units

What the model looks like and how it works

The ADL matrix from the consultants Arthur D Little is a tool that helps managers work out a strategy for their business (or product portfolio), depending on whether it is newly formed or ageing and whether it is strong or weak in its market. Young and dominant businesses favour strategies that push aggressively for market share, while old and weak businesses suggest exiting the market.

The life cycle phases

The ADL matrix recognizes four stages to the life cycle. The company in the youthful or embryonic stage of the life cycle is likely to be less profitable than one in the stage of maturity. In the youthful stage there will be a requirement for heavy investment in the company, whereas in later stages of the business's life cycle it will be a cash generator. ADL describes the four stages as:

Embryonic

The business unit is new and in its youthful stage. This is a period when a business needs strong financial support because profits are not yet being realized. The market has not yet begun to settle down and there are many fragmented suppliers.

Growth

The business unit has taken off and is showing rapid growth. A company that is growing fast may not know if it is ahead or behind the growth of the market, as the frenetic pace means that there is a high level of confusion. The focus is on rapid expansion and making sure that there is sufficient production to meet the needs of customers.

Maturity

Growth is slowing for the business unit. Rationalization begins to take place and the shape of the competition and the structure of the market becomes more recognizable. A business unit that previously was focused on producing as much as possible now becomes interested in brand positioning and segmentation in order to maximize profits.

Ageing

The ageing business sees sales fall away. This can be a period during which profits can be harvested if the business is managed well. Competitors may exit the market. Those that remain may have learned to play by the rules and follow a market leader. It is nevertheless a difficult time for the business and the decision must be made as to whether there is scope for rejuvenation or if it would be better to exit the market.

The strength of the company

The strength of the strategic business unit (SBU) is measured according to the business's competitive position. This is dependent on its market share, its financial performance relative to the competition, any hold it has over customers or the value chain, the strength of the brand, its pricing strategy and so on. The competitive position has five classifications:

Dominant

A company in this category is a market leader and could be a monopolist. Its high market share brings with it the ability to maintain high prices and strong profits.

Strong

A company in this category is possibly an oligopoly, sharing a strong position with a small number of other companies. There is competition between the large suppliers but usually good opportunities to divide up the market and make money.

Favourable

A business in this position operates in a fragmented market where there is no dominant player. Although there may be a number of rivals, there is no clear leader. A business could have a competitive advantage in a certain segment of the market.

Tenable

A company in this category serves a niche, for example a limited geographical area or with a special product.

Weak

A company in this position has poor financial performance and a small position within an aggressive market. The business may be too small to survive within the market.

Six strategies for any business

ADL suggests that there are six strategies that could be followed by a business unit, especially one that is in a weak or ageing position:

1 **Market strategies:** moving into a new geography or developing different segments. Building brands.

2 **Product strategies:** launching new products, finding ways of differentiating the products, positioning the products against the needs of specific segments.

3 **Management and system strategies:** finding processes that give a competitive advantage such as production at a lower cost, better customer service.

4 **Technology strategies:** investing in research and development to ensure that the product portfolio is full of new products with high market appeal.

5 **Retrenchment strategies:** building on customer loyalty to rebuild the business and obtain a greater share of wallet or higher prices.

6 **Operations strategies:** improving logistics and gaining a competitive advantage through faster deliveries or more efficient operations.

The origins of the model

The ADL matrix was developed in the late 1970s by the Arthur D Little consulting company. It follows the product portfolio matrix developed by the rival Boston Consulting Group in 1970 (see Chapter 10). The Boston matrix is based on two dimensions – the attractiveness of a market and the competitive position of a business within that market. The ADL matrix also plots the competitive position of the business and it does so against the life stage of that business. The ADL matrix has not achieved the popularity of the Boston matrix.

Developments of the model

Any business model that involves life cycles struggles to define how these can be recognized. The difference between a youthful company and an ageing company is obvious, but it is sometimes hard to see when a business moves from one life-cycle phase to another. There is no standard length to the life cycle and they vary enormously, being relatively short (just a matter of a few years) in the case of electronic products to very lengthy in the case of many raw materials.

The model in action

A company with a portfolio of products or a number of different business units would use the ADL matrix in three steps:

Step 1: determine the position of the business in its life cycle

This is not always easy, for as has been pointed out, there are no clear lines between the different phases of the life cycle. It is very obvious when a business is in an embryonic or an ageing stage. Questions that might help clarify where a company sits in the life cycle are:

- How big is the market?
- How many companies supply the market?
- How big are these companies?
- How old are these companies?

A large number of small and young businesses indicate an embryonic stage while a small number of large companies suggest maturity and old age.

Step 2: determine the competitive position of the business

This should be easier than determining the life stage. A company in a strong competitive position will have a distinctive product offer, command premium prices, enjoy a significant market share, good growth and high profitability.

Step 3: plot the position of the business on the matrix

In theory this should be easy. In practice, a business might find itself straddling two or three different positions. If this is the case, it is worth returning to steps 1 and 2 and revisiting the questions. It should now be possible to position the business in one of the appropriate strategy boxes:

- **New or growing company with a strong or dominant position** – aim to defend this position and where possible improve market share.
- **Mature or ageing company with a strong or dominant position** – aim to defend this position and grow with the market or consider harvesting profits.
- **New or growing company with a weak position in the market** – find a niche in which you can survive or, if the business is not profitable, consider withdrawing from the market.
- **Mature or ageing company with a weak position in the market** – if it isn't possible to improve the competitive position, consider withdrawing from the market.

Some things to think about

- The ADL strategies for growth are worth thinking about for every strategic business unit or product.
- Although positioning a SBU/product in the matrix can be difficult, it is worth attempting as it will be a good pointer for the long-term strategic direction.

AIDA   05

A business model for improving marketing communications

What the model looks like and how it works

The AIDA framework (Figure 5.1) is one of the most familiar in the world of communications. It is widely used in advertising and promotions to describe how communications are made effective in four important steps. As with any marketing framework, the AIDA model should be targeted at a specific audience who are interested in the product in question.

Figure 5.1   The AIDA model

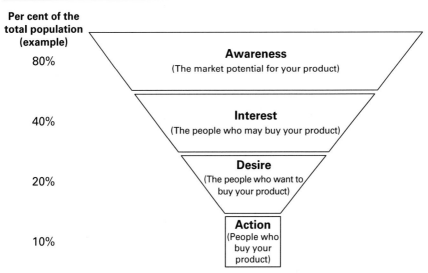

Awareness

The starting point of all effective communications is to be noticed. If people are not aware of a product, they cannot be interested in it and no action can be taken. Typically the promotional opportunities include mass media such as websites (and search engine optimization (SEO)), TV, radio, newspapers, journals, billboards, public relations, direct marketing (such as flyers, emails, personal calls from salespeople), point of sale, packaging and social media.

Achieving awareness is critical to all promotions. The components of the promotional mix that are selected to build awareness will depend on the target audience and the product or service that is being advertised.

Most promotional campaigns comprise a mixture of different media. Promotions that hit consumers from many directions make it hard to say exactly how awareness was created. This gave rise to the famous saying credited to both John Wanamaker (1838–1922) and Lord Leverhulme (1851–1925): 'Half the money I spend on advertising is wasted; the trouble is I don't know which half.'

In general, the greater the amount that is spent on promotion, the greater will be the level of awareness – bearing in mind the above comment about much of it falling on stony ground. As a rule of thumb, companies allocate around 2 per cent of revenue for their promotional budget.

The amount spent on promotion is not the only driver of awareness. Awareness is built up over time through the repetition of a message. It is also heavily influenced by headlines, images and colours – all generating impact of one kind or another in an attempt to win attention.

Word of mouth is important in building awareness. Social media fulfils this role today. Just a few years ago it was literally one person talking to another. The UK retailer Marks & Spencer carried out hardly any above-the-line advertising for 100 years, relying on its customers to recommend the brand.[1]

Interest

Achieving a healthy awareness of a product is not in itself enough. There has to be an interest in the offer if the promotion is to generate action. The promotion will need to resonate with the target audience. The audience must feel that it is relevant to them and offer something that will satisfy their needs and wants.

The offer, which could be a product or service, will have features and benefits. The way these are portrayed determines how interested someone will be in moving forward to consider making a purchase. This portrayal of the offer is the customer value proposition (CVP). As the term suggests, the proposition must be valued by the potential customer if interest is to be generated. What is more, the language that is used to interest the customer should be colloquial – the language of the consumer; the language in which they think and speak.

Desire

The promotion must now generate a desire for the offer. The potential customer will have considered the CVP with all its features and benefits. Effective promotions focus on the one or two parts of the value proposition that are most appealing to the potential customers. Finding things in an offer that are unique, distinctive and alluring – and communicating them in an advert – is not easy. Promotions often fail because they try to cover too many benefits and so dilute the message.

At this stage, the potential customer may be considering a number of alternative offers. These alternative offers make up 'the consideration set'. A potential customer may start with a handful of products that are given consideration, whittling them down according to their perceived value and perceived benefits until a choice is made. The final decision may be based on emotional or subjective factors such as a predilection for a particular brand.

Action

At its conclusion, the AIDA model looks for action. The action could be the purchase of a product or it could be something less commercial such as a visit to a website or a request for a brochure – whatever are the goals of the promotion.

AIDA is a sequential model in which the proportions of people at each level decline significantly. For example, if 80 per cent of a target audience are aware of a promotion, we can expect that the proportion who are interested in the offer will be much less, maybe just 40 per cent. This proportion declines again as the promotion builds desire for the product – perhaps only 20 per cent of the total target audience. Finally, we reach the small proportion who take action as a result of the promotion. A 10 per cent conversion to action is, by most yardsticks, highly commendable.

The origins of the model

In 1904, Frank Dukesmith, an American pioneer in the art of salesmanship, suggested that there are four steps leading up to a consumer trialling a product or making a purchase decision.[2] Following Dukesmith's sequence, the AIDA acronym was coined in an article by CP Russell in 1921.[3] As a cultured man he recognized that AIDA is also the name of an opera and he suggested that this would make it memorable.

Developments of the model

The principle of achieving action through a series of steps was not just limited to advertising. In 1911 the book *Successful Selling* by Arthur Sheldon[4] promoted the AIDA model for sales teams. He added the dimension of satisfaction, emphasizing the importance of keeping the customer happy in order to generate repeat purchases. His modified model was known as AIDAS.

Others have added their nuances. In 1961 RJ Lavidge and GA Steiner proposed a slightly different model for predicting advertising effectiveness,[5] though not one that lends itself to a catchy acronym. Like the AIDA model, theirs was also stepwise but with more stages in the conversion process:

- **Awareness**: as before.
- **Knowledge**: deepening the awareness to a point where people had information on what they were considering.
- **Liking**: triggers are pulled as people learn more about the product to the point that they like certain features and benefits.
- **Preference**: in the consideration set made up of products from different suppliers, a preference is built up for one in particular.
- **Conviction**: at some stage in the buying process there has to be a move beyond simple preference to one that is convinced the product is the right one.
- **Purchase**: the build-up of knowledge, liking, preference and conviction leads ultimately to action in the form of purchasing the product.

The model in action

The challenge in today's overcrowded world, where we are bombarded with communications, is grabbing attention. People are programmed to pay attention to things in which they are interested. If you are not a drinker, you are less likely to take note of an advert for alcoholic drinks than someone who enjoys a tipple. Mothers-to-be will take note of communications about babies, gardeners will notice ads for garden centres and children will pay great attention to television ads for toys.

The timing of the communications affects the noise. The vast majority of toys that are bought each year are purchased at Christmas. In theory, it makes sense to advertise toys when people are buying them. However, in the cacophony that takes place around Christmas, when all the other toy suppliers run their promotions, the share of voice (the level of awareness that is achieved) may be quite low. One major toy manufacturer avoided the drowning out of their adverts by beginning their campaign early in October when the competitive environment was less fierce.

Whenever the ads are launched, they have to have impact. Strong colours, powerful images and compelling headlines may get the ads noticed, although these all have to be within the brand guidelines. The creative teams that design the ads know how to draw the reader from the top of the page with an eye-catching image to a headline and, ultimately, to the body copy. Creating impact, interest and building conviction is the name of the game. It is not always obvious what will work. Air Products, a manufacturer of industrial gases, showed a number of sample ads to potential customers. The ads that tested best for impact and relevance were those that featured people. The ads that were creative and stylish but did not feature people were rejected.

David Ogilvy, the ad man who established Ogilvy & Mather, made an astute point in his book on advertising (1983).[6] He said, 'When I write an advertisement, I don't want you to tell me that you find it "creative". I want you to find it so interesting that you buy the product.' Finding those triggers of interest makes promotions effective. This father of advertising went on to say, 'Write great headlines and you will have successfully invested 80 per cent of your money.' He knew that 8 out of 10 people only read the headline.

Some things to think about

At each stage of the AIDA sequence, ask yourself four questions:

- Who is my product (or service) aimed at – who is the target audience?
- Will the promotion grab the attention of the target audience?
- Is the promotion relevant to the target audience?
- Does the promotion drive to a course of action?

Notes

1 MacRury, I (2008) *Advertising*, Routledge, Abingdon
2 Dukesmith, F (1904) Three natural fields of salesmanship, *Salesmanship*, January, **2** (1), p 14
3 Russell, CP (1921) How to write a sales–making letter, *Printers' Ink*, June
4 Sheldon, A (1911) *Successful Selling, Part 1*, Kessinger Publishing, Montana
5 Lavidge, RJ and Steiner, GA (1961) A model for predictive measurements of advertising effectiveness, *Journal of Marketing*, **25**, October
6 Ogilvy, D (1983) *Ogilvy on Advertising*, Vintage, New York

Ansoff matrix   06
How to grow your company

What the model looks like and how it works

Most businesses have an appetite for growth. A company that grows is seen as successful. Success attracts more customers and creates a virtuous circle. It attracts good staff and presents new opportunities that keep them engaged. Consistent growth is not easy to achieve, especially when a business matures.

The Ansoff matrix provides a model for growth that is based on four strategic premises: market penetration, market development, product development and diversification, as set out below.

Market penetration: selling more existing products to existing markets

This situation offers opportunities for:

- obtaining a greater share of wallet from existing customers;
- finding new customers within the markets currently served.

Most companies do not have 100 per cent share of wallet of their customers. Business is nearly always shared with one or two competitors. A customer that has chosen a supplier has already become convinced of their merit. It should, therefore, be easier to sell more to this customer than to acquire a brand-new customer. You may have noticed that if you make a donation to a charity you very quickly receive more requests from the same charity for further funds. The charity knows that it is easier to persuade an existing donor to make a further donation than it is to acquire a new donor.

This very obvious source of new business is often ignored. A company that has a strong 'hunting DNA' will be more fired up to look for new business from new customers than one that has a strong 'farming DNA'. Farming existing clients and selling them more products is always to be encouraged as the first growth opportunity.

Market development: selling existing products to new markets

This situation offers opportunities for:

- selling to new customers in new geographies;
- selling to new customers in vertical segments not previously served.

Businesses need a good blend of new customers as well as the development of existing customers. Inevitably some existing customers will stop buying for one reason or another, either because they have no further use for the product or they have found what they think to be a better alternative. These lost customers need replacing. Replacing lost customers with new customers will result in a static position. New customer acquisition has to more than replace the churn if growth is to be achieved. Market development is about finding: 1) new customers in new geographies; 2) new customers in existing geographies.

With regard to the second of these options, the opportunity for finding new customers in existing geographies is through segmentation. Most companies segment their customers, targeting a particular demographic in the case of consumer companies, or a particular industry vertical[1] in the case of B2B companies. New customers can be found in a new segment. Gillette made small modifications to its disposable razors aimed at men in order to make them more appealing to a female audience. Guinness used to be an older person's drink and it famously built a huge demand for its stout amongst younger people by positioning itself as cool, intelligent, original and different to the wide array of light beers and lagers.

Acquiring new customers is not easy. If it was, companies would simply press the promotional button and enjoy the flood of new revenue. New customers need to be taken through a number of steps before they commit to a purchase. First they need to build up familiarity with the new supplier; they need to develop an interest in its products to the point where they have a strong desire to buy them. This is described in the AIDA model (see Chapter 5).

Product development: selling new products to existing markets

This situation offers opportunities for:

- selling new products to existing customers;
- finding and satisfying unmet needs within existing markets.

The trust and relationship that exists with a supplier puts them in a strong position to offer new products. The brand and its reputation is known and stands for something. It is an opportunity to offer additional products that the customer may want. It may be that the new products are developed in-house or they could be brought into the portfolio under licence.

These brand extensions are more likely to be successful if they satisfy the needs of the customer (an obvious point) and are closely related to the brand that the customer is already buying. Let's take some simple examples. A baker of bread could readily sell meat pies or confectionery products to its customers. An airline may be able to offer holidays to the loyal customers who choose to fly with it. An industrial company supplying machinery could consider offering contract maintenance to its customers. All these are closely associated offers to the original brand. Once a brand moves beyond its core values, it becomes more difficult to sell the product. Virgin created an extremely strong brand in the music industry and positioned it as a challenger to some long-established and often stuffy brands. This worked well in airlines and trains. It has been less successful in wines, cola, condoms and bridal gowns.

Diversification: selling new products to new markets

This situation offers opportunities for:

- developing new products for new geographical markets or segments;
- the acquisition of companies in a different field of activity.

The grass on the other side of the fence often seems greener. Companies look around and believe there must be easier and better ways of making money. The dream of selling new products to new customers is powerful and yet it is the most difficult route to growing a business. In effect, selling new products to new customers is a business start-up. The products have to be proven, the company has to be positioned as a viable source in the minds of potential customers, and an existing network of competitors has to be defeated. When a company is successful in selling new products to new customers, it is big news. The Swedish company, Husqvarna, is famous today for its chainsaws and lawnmowers. However, over the course of a few centuries, it has produced a large range of different products, aimed at quite different audiences. It originally produced muskets, bicycles, motorcycles, kitchen equipment and sewing machines. In more recent times Apple diversified beyond the manufacture of computers to become a business heavily dependent on the iPhone.

For every success a company has in selling new products to new customers, there are dozens of failures that are never recorded. It is the hardest of the four Ansoff strategies for growth, but when it is achieved, it is the most spectacular.

The origins of the model

The Ansoff matrix is named after Igor Ansoff. Ansoff was born in Russia in 1918 to an American father and Russian mother. His family moved to the United States in 1936 where he studied engineering and mathematics. He gained business planning and strategy experience working for the Rand Corporation and Lockheed Aircraft.[2] It was in this corporate stage of his career that he published 'Strategies For Diversification' in *Harvard Business Review* in 1957.[3] Shortly after this, he moved into academia and enjoyed a number of positions at US and European universities until his death in 2002.

Developments of the model

The Ansoff matrix is a tool for guiding the strategic growth of a company. It may not be sufficient on its own. Each of the four strategies requires a deeper consideration of the external environment. For example, it may not be possible to say whether there are growth opportunities for more market penetration unless data exists on the share of wallet, the nature of the competition, attitudes of customers to buying more from a company and so on. The tool is best used in conjunction with others such as PEST (looking at the external environment), AIDA (determining the difficulties of communicating with a new market) or SWOT (establishing a company's strengths and weaknesses).

The model in action

The Ansoff matrix is a useful tool for determining where growth can be achieved. It will help a company to establish which is the best option for long-term growth by indicating where the greatest impact can be achieved at the lowest risk. In order to make best use of the Ansoff matrix it is necessary for a company to gather and analyse a huge amount of information.

Ansoff himself recognized this to be a potential problem and led to the phrase 'paralysis through analysis' – the danger of having too much information such that it is difficult to see the way forward.[4]

The Ansoff matrix is a useful model for carrying out a marketing audit. It forces a company to consider different strategic options on the basis of facts. As a result, it is liked by boards and stakeholders that need to see options for growth as well as the risks that are entailed.

The Coca-Cola Company has successfully achieved growth over the last 100 years. This can be recognized within the matrix described by Ansoff.

Market penetration: selling existing products to existing customers

Coca-Cola knows that if it can persuade existing customers to drink an extra can of Coke per week, it will have a huge impact on its sales. Much of the company's promotional strategy over the years has majored on it being a refreshing drink and persuading us to drink more of the beverage.

Product development: selling new products to existing customers

The original portfolio of the sarsaparilla-based drink has grown over the years. The company has successfully launched new flavoured colas such as cherry in 1985. It was the company's first extension beyond the original recipe. Since then other variants have been added, including lime, lemon and vanilla.

Market development: selling existing products to new markets

Diet Coke has a long history and was launched in the 1970s. Although Diet Coke found a market over a wide demographic, it had a much higher penetration amongst females. Coke repackaged the exact same product in a black can and called it Coke Zero. Launched in 2005, it had a more masculine appeal and established the low-calorie product in the male market.[5]

Diversification: selling a new product into a new market

The Coca-Cola Company has diversified beyond cola drinks into health drinks of various kinds. It has added dairy and juice companies. It has acquired Vitaminwater[6] and has started selling coffee and tea in Brazil.[7]

Some things to think about

- For most companies, the easiest and often the most fertile place to look for growth opportunities is to sell more of the same to existing customers. This means you need to know your share of wallet with each customer so you can assess the potential to sell them more.

- The next place to look for growth is to sell your existing products to new customers. What new segments could you attack? Which countries where you do not sell at the present could be attractive markets for your products?

It is tempting to want to sell new products into new markets. Be very careful with this strategy. Before going down this road you need to be convinced that there are no opportunities worth pursuing with existing products and in existing markets.

Notes

1 Vertical markets refer to the industry classification that governments often call Standard Industrial Classification, or in the US, NAICS (North American Industry Classification System).

2 https://en.wikipedia.org/wiki/Igor_Ansoff (archived at https://perma.cc/3LLC-ATJF)

3 Ansoff, I (1957) Strategies for diversification, *Harvard Business Review*, 35 (5), pp 113–24

4 www.economist.com/node/11701586 (archived at https://perma.cc/3HAD-W9T8)

5 https://en.wikipedia.org/wiki/Coca-Cola_Zero (archived at https://perma.cc/T7KL-WL2U)

6 www.investopedia.com/articles/markets/081315/vitaminwater-has-been-cocacolas-best-purchase.asp (archived at https://perma.cc/27AV-4T59)

7 www.reuters.com/article/brazil-coca-cola-coffee-idINL1N1A01AV (archived at https://perma.cc/T89E-F4EQ)

Balanced scorecard

07

Measures and targets for achieving a strategy or improving performance

What the model looks like and how it works

Companies have forever used measures to run their business. It would be unthinkable if a company didn't know its revenue, profit, cash flow, bank balance and the like. Most businesses also want to compare these metrics with other organizations to see how they are performing. This is benchmarking and it is described in Chapter 8.

The Balanced Scorecard framework makes use of these metrics. It is based on measures taken in four areas of a business:

- **Financial:** the finances of a company are its pulse and blood pressure. They show its health. Typically, they would include revenue, net profit, gross margin, fixed costs, variable costs and cash in the bank.

- **Customers:** these metrics show to what extent a company is performing well in the eyes of its customers. They include basic statistics such as numbers of customers, numbers of new customers, sales per customer as well as customer satisfaction scores, Net Promoter Scores® and the like.

- **Learning and growth:** innovation is vital if a company is to grow. Knowledge is an asset which offers a competitive advantage. There are many measures here that can be tracked. These could include numbers of patents, amount spent on research and development, numbers of training days per employee, the skills of employees, productivity and employee satisfaction.

- **Internal processes:** these measures are a determination of the efficiency of a company in using its resources to maximum advantage and delivering value to customers. They could include numbers of complaints, deliveries on time and in full, inventory levels, speed of decision making, the percentage of new products in the portfolio and so on.

As the name suggests, there has to be an optimum balance between these four areas that will result in a vision and strategy for the company.

The balanced scorecard is not simply an abacus. The measures in the four areas of business are chosen to ensure improved customer satisfaction, improved profits, improved internal processes, and innovations that will future-proof the company.

The balanced scorecard is much loved by consultants. It is the invention of David Norton (a business consultant) and Robert Kaplan (a professor at Harvard Business School). It is a set of measures by which the performance of a company can be tracked both financially and in customer satisfaction and organizational efficiency.

The beauty of the balanced scorecard is that any measures can be built into it that are relevant for the vision and strategy of the company.

In one form or another most large organizations use the balanced scorecard. They have objectives that must be met and key performance indicators (KPIs) to keep track of them. The balanced scorecard framework has been selected by the editors of the *Harvard Business Review* as one of the most influential business ideas of the past 75 years.

The origins of the model

The idea for the balanced scorecard was set out in an article by Robert Kaplan and David Norton in the 1992 edition of *Harvard Business Review* entitled 'The Balanced Scorecard: Measures that drive performance'.[1] It is built on the belief that if you cannot measure it, you cannot improve it.

It is said that Norton proposed the title 'The Balanced Scorecard' following a game of golf with an IBM executive. The balanced scorecard for business had parallels with the scorecard used in a round of golf.

Developments of the model

Kaplan, a Harvard Business School professor, later suggested that his balanced scorecard could work effectively with the other strategy models. For example, McKinsey created the 7S tool in which it listed seven components (all beginning with 'S') that are required for a strategic plan. These components are strategy, structure, systems, staff, skills, style/culture and shared values. This begs the question of how you devise a measurement for something as vague as 'strategy' or 'shared values'. However, the point is fair – other frameworks may propose components that should be included in the balanced scorecard. A SWOT analysis could identify strengths, weaknesses, threats and opportunities of a company that will determine its future success and should be included in the scorecard.

Nowadays it has become important for a company to demonstrate its environmental, social and governance performance (ESG). These metrics can be used to build a 'sustainability scorecard' which is likely to have significance with investors, employees and customers.

The model in action

'The Self Store' is a company that offers storage units where people can keep furniture and belongings that need a temporary home. Tradespeople also hire the units because they need somewhere safe and convenient to keep their equipment and materials. The key to a company such as The Self Store is occupancy. When occupancy falls below 80 per cent it loses money. Its occupancy was slightly higher than 80 per cent and it had an objective of raising it to 95 per cent. In order to do this it used the balanced scorecard:

- **Financial:** The financial metrics to be included in the scorecard were those that are likely to be relevant to most companies. They included revenue, net profit, gross margin, fixed costs, variable costs and cash in the bank.

- **Customers:** The key performance indicators for customers were 'length of stay of customer', 'revenue per customer', 'profitability per customer', 'time required to service customer', 'number of new customers' and 'Net Promoter Score® of customer'.

- **Learning and growth:** When customers first make contact with The Self Store they have a number of obvious questions: Do you have space? How much space do I need? What will this cost? What access will I have and at what times of day? Why should I choose The Self Store? Staff at the company were assessed on their ability to answer these questions effectively and the measure was included on the scorecard.

- **Internal processes:** These were 'customer visits per day of the week', 'number of times the free van was used' and 'number of complaints per month'.

Identifying the key performance indicators focused attention on factors critical to the growth and profitability of the company. This in itself led to improvements. In addition to the KPIs in the balanced scorecard, data was available on the type of customers – domestic versus trade, length of stay (less than six months, six months to a year, and over a year), and how the customer was acquired (e.g. through recommendation, seeing an advert, or through local knowledge).

Before the balanced scorecard analysis was carried out the company believed it should seek more business from tradespeople rather than domestic customers because tradespeople kept their storage units longer. However, tradespeople proved to be harder work as they made more frequent visits to the storage units, picking up tools and delivering materials. They also demanded lower prices and so the profitability was not as high as from domestic customers.

As a result of the balanced scorecard The Self Store was able to build its occupancy rate to 95 per cent and, crucially, to significantly improve profitability by focusing on domestic users.

Some things to think about

- What is the overall objective for your company?
- What measures will determine your ability to meet the overall objective – specifically financial measures, customer measures, learning and growth measures and internal processes?
- How easy is it to measure these different attributes?
- With what frequency will the measures be made?
- How can the measures be used to track and determine trends in performance?
- How can the measures be used to analyse segments of threats and opportunities facing the company?

Note

1 Kaplan, RS and Norton, DP (1992) The Balanced Scorecard: Measures that drive performance, *Harvard Business Review*, January–February

Benchmarking 08

Setting targets for business and marketing KPIs

What the model looks like and how it works

Success in business is largely about being better than the competition. To be better than the competition it is necessary to have something to compare. These somethings are usually referred to as key performance indicators (KPIs). The KPIs could measure a host of different things but they all drive towards doing things better, faster and cheaper. These are the means by which a company achieves a competitive advantage.

The comparisons that are sought through benchmarking could be internal, within a company, comparing the performance of different aspects of the business or different business units. They could also be external comparisons. These are most useful as they give an indication of how an organization is performing against a competitor or an industry standard.

Benchmarking can also be against unrelated businesses when a company is seeking to find out what can be achieved by world-class organizations. This is particularly the case with companies benchmarking their Net Promoter Score® (NPS) (see Chapter 38). The NPS comparisons within their 'consideration set' provide benchmarks that are close to home, while those with the very best companies in different markets give a higher aspiration at which to aim.

The aim of benchmarking is to improve performance. There are four measures of importance:

1 **Measures of time:** how long it takes to produce something, how quickly the phone is answered, the speed of response to an enquiry, the time taken to deal with a complaint.

2 **Measures of quality:** the number of defects in a product, the length of life of a product, the cost of maintenance of a product, the ability of a product to withstand stress, the reliability of a product.

3 **Measures of cost and effectiveness**: the price of a product, the cost per application or use of a product, the cost of maintenance of a product, the savings that a product confers.

4 **Measures of customer satisfaction**: overall satisfaction with a product, satisfaction with different aspects of a product, the likelihood to recommend a product, the likelihood to repurchase a product.

These benchmarking measures are attempts to improve processes in some way, to see if costs can be reduced, profits can be increased and customer loyalty can be strengthened.

There is no single model for the benchmarking process but there is usually a sequence of steps such as is shown in Figure 8.1.

Step 1: what is the problem that needs benchmarking?

The starting point has to be a business problem or opportunity. Someone in an organization will point to a part of the organization that needs improving.

Figure 8.1   The benchmarking wheel

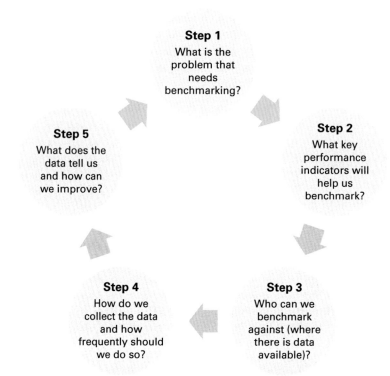

SOURCE Based on Fred Reichheld, Bain & Company, and Satmetrix Systems (2003)

For example, it may be determined that a company is suffering from a high churn – many customers are being lost. It could be that a company is facing high costs because of product failures. These problems are identified at the planning stage and, at this time, the goals and objectives of the benchmarking are set.

Step 2: what key performance indicators will help us benchmark?

Following on from the identification of the problem, it is now necessary to determine what benchmark should be chosen for the purposes of measurement. For example, in the case of a company that is suffering a high loss of customers, should the benchmark be its NPS, which is often used as a measure of the loyalty of customers? This alone may not be sufficient. It may also be necessary to determine what drives customer loyalty and to benchmark these factors as well.

In the case of a company with many product failures, a measure of the number of failures would be insufficient. It would be important to understand what is causing the failures and in what part of the manufacturing process these are occurring.

Step 3: who can we benchmark against (where there is data available)?

The benchmarking plan has to be practical. It is no good identifying measures for which data cannot be found. It may be highly desirous to compare the product failures of different manufacturing companies, but which companies would be prepared to share such sensitive data? In step 3 it is necessary to find benchmarking partners or at least to identify benchmarks that are up to date and available.

It makes sense to benchmark performance metrics amongst companies that are in the same 'consideration set'. In addition, it is helpful to benchmark beyond the immediate competition. Consumers are exposed to best-in-class performance in their daily life, even though this may be from companies in completely different businesses. If Amazon can confirm a purchase within milliseconds and deliver it within 24 hours, someone buying chemicals from a stockist may not be sympathetic to a lengthy delay in acknowledging the order or making the delivery. Benchmarking examines who is best in industry and it also compares against best practices in other industries.

Step 4: how do we collect the data and how frequently should we do so?

There is usually a cost involved in collecting data that should be taken into account. Internal data has a relatively low cost compared to external data that may need collecting through a survey. There is not normally a problem obtaining internal data. It is within the powers of any organization to set up this process and to generate data sets as frequently as necessary. In the case of quality standards such as product failures, the frequency of collecting the data could be daily. However, metrics such as the NPS change relatively slowly over time. The frequency of collecting and analysing these could be every six months or annually.

Step 5: what does the data tell us and how can we improve?

The final step is to make sense of the data and drive action. It can reasonably be assumed that many companies setting out to benchmark against the best in class will find that they fall short. The big question therefore is how to make the improvement. Hopefully, some data will point to corrective action. For example, in the case of a company with a high customer churn, it is likely that the NPS will be lower than the industry standard. This in itself does not show how the improvement can be made. It does suggest that if a deeper dive takes place into the drivers of the loyalty score, a weakness could be identified. Drivers of loyalty could be, for example:

- overall quality of the product or service;
- being treated as a valued customer;
- speed of service;
- friendliness of staff;
- handling of problems and complaints;
- handling of enquiries;
- competence of staff;
- ease of doing business;
- being kept informed;
- helpfulness of staff.

The benchmarking process is portrayed as a wheel (Figure 8.1) because it is assumed that there will be continuous adaptions such as introducing new KPIs and new benchmarking partners.

The origins of the model

The term 'benchmark' originates from the chisel marks cut into walls of buildings and used as a reference point by surveyors for measuring altitude. In business it is used as a reference point for comparing almost any performance measure with others. It is a standard that serves as a valuation against other companies or parts of a company.

The Xerox Company is often credited as the originator of benchmarking, which it pioneered in 1979.[1] Benchmarking has most of its history in quality management. The wave of interest in improving quality led to the establishment of the *Benchmarking Journal* (1994), which is focused on total quality management. The introduction of the NPS, a customer loyalty metric developed by (and a registered trademark of) Fred Reichheld, Bain & Company, and Satmetrix Systems, has given a boost to benchmarking beyond quality. It was introduced by Reichheld in his 2003 *Harvard Business Review* article 'The one number you need to grow' (see Chapter 38).[2]

Developments of the model

Benchmarking processes are constantly changing, influenced by the development of management systems and statistical methods. There is no single model for benchmarking; it is a philosophy – an approach to comparing performance levels between different companies or parts of an operation. A search of the internet suggests there are at least 60 different benchmarking models, though most can be summarized as stepwise similar to that shown in Figure 8.1. Over time, various consultants have amended the model, usually adding or removing steps but essentially moving in the same direction.

The model in action

It is reported that Southwest Airlines, in an attempt to improve the turnaround time of its aircraft, used the benchmark of the auto racing pits rather than compare itself to other airlines.[3] As a result, the benchmarking exercise helped Southwest to make much more significant improvements to gate maintenance, cleaning and customer loading operations than would have been possible with an inter-industry comparison.

It is likely that every corporate organization has benchmarked its operation at some time or another. Some companies have become known as the best-in-practice benchmarks. American Express is renowned for its billing systems, Disney World for customer experience, General Electric for its management processes, Hewlett-Packard for order fulfilment, and Ritz-Carlton for training.

Documented examples of benchmarking are manifold. Xerox faced a logistics and distribution issue in its warehousing and examined LL Bean's fulfilment methods to successfully improve warehouse productivity by 5 per cent.[4] Motorola identified a problem with the time it was taking between order receipts and product delivery. It studied Domino's Pizza order and delivery procedures to reduce its cycle time. As a great fan of benchmarking, Motorola sent a benchmarking team to Japan to study how automotive companies managed quality in their manufacturing facilities. This enabled the company to lower the defect rate and to reduce manufacturing costs.[5]

Some things to think about

- The key to benchmarking is to find data against which to benchmark. External data may be the gold standard but if it is not available then find an internal data source that is. It is better to have frequent benchmarking tracking data with imperfections than to seek perfect benchmarking data that is not readily available.

- Be realistic with your KPIs. It can take two or three years to make a significant positive difference. Be patient and do not lose sight of a long-term goal.

Notes

1 Tucker, FG, Zivan, SM and Camp, RC (1987) How to measure yourself against the best, *Harvard Business Review*, January
2 Reichheld, FF (2003) The one number you need to grow, *Harvard Business Review*, December

3 Murdoch, A (1997) [accessed 31 August 2010] USA: Lateral Benchmarking Or… What Formula One Taught An Airline, *Management Today*, www.managementtoday.co.uk/ (archived at https://perma.cc/E8PY-BCW8)

4 Dragolea, L and Cotîrlea, D (2009) Benchmarking – a valid strategy for the long term? *Annales Universitatis Apulensis Series Oeconomica*, **11** (2), pp 813–26

5 Quality Magazine (2003) Motorola: a tradition of quality, https://www.qualitymag.com/articles/84187-motorola-a-tradition-of-quality (archived at https://perma.cc/W3X6-UKNP)

Blue ocean strategy 09

Kick-starting innovation and new product development

What the model looks like and how it works

Blue ocean strategy is to guide and stimulate innovation. It is the brainchild of W Chan Kim and Renée Mauborgne, two professors from INSEAD. They observed that companies tend to engage in head-to-head competition in their search for growth and this leads to a bloodbath – a red ocean. They suggest that an alternative and more profitable strategy for growth comes from tapping new opportunities in 'the blue ocean'. They argue that a blue ocean strategy allows the simultaneous pursuit of differentiation and low cost (and not either/or). By moving into a blue ocean (a new market) a company creates new market space and in so doing makes the competition irrelevant.

The starting point for developing the model is to examine why some companies succeed while others fail. Their study of successful and less successful companies shows that some markets are overcrowded and this limits everyone's growth. Market spaces or blue oceans can be created by value innovation while at the same time driving down costs. These two strategies will beat the competition or make the competition irrelevant so it is not necessary to fight them head-on. Every market was once new and the key to success is to find a market that you can make your own.

A key aspect of the model is understanding how value is perceived and how this affects both suppliers and customers. From the supplier's point of view, Michael Porter suggested they could position themselves as having a differentiated product or a low-cost product. This is challenged by the blue ocean model. The blue ocean model says that costs are always under pressure from competitors. Over time the differentiating factors are eliminated as suppliers copy each other and seek to compete by making cost savings. The buyer is the winner as they reap the benefits of superior value. With a blue ocean strategy it is possible to pursue a strategy of both low costs and differentiation.

As part of the process for finding a blue ocean, the authors suggest asking four searching questions about customers and the marketplace. This leads to actions that could all point to a new blue ocean:

- **Reduce:** which factors that are offered to customers should be reduced well below industry standards?
- **Eliminate:** which factors offered to customers are taken for granted and should be eliminated?
- **Create:** which factors offered to customers should be created because they have never been offered and they will be valued?
- **Raise:** which factors offered to customers should be raised well above the industry standard?

The search for a blue ocean is likely to extend the market beyond those customers served at the present. Non-customers are seen in different tiers. Beyond customers a company targets at the present, there are three tiers. The first tier buys a minimal amount of product out of necessity. The second and third tiers are non-customers who choose an alternative solution or have never thought of the offering as an option. It is to all of these tiers of customers that you look for a viable blue ocean idea.

The search for the new idea is based on a sequence of four questions (Table 9.1), each designed to determine its commercial viability. Each

Table 9.1 Sequence of the blue ocean strategy (adapted from original source)

Step 1	Utility	Is the new idea really useful to people? Is there a strong reason why someone should buy the new product?	Yes/No
Step 2	Price	Is the proposed price of the product one that most potential customers will pay?	Yes/No
Step 3	Cost	At the price you want to charge and with the anticipated volumes you will sell, will you make a profit?	Yes/No
Step 4	Adoption	Will there be any major barriers that will stop you attaining your goals?	Yes/No

question requires the answer 'yes', before the idea can pass to the next step. If an idea receives the answer 'no' on any of the steps, the idea must be reconsidered or eliminated.

The origins of the model

In 2004, W Chan Kim and Renée Mauborgne outlined their theory in a book entitled *Blue Ocean Strategy: How to create uncontested market space and make the competition irrelevant*.[1] The book was based on a study of 150 different strategies carried out by companies across 30 industries.

Developments of the model

There is no doubt that the blue ocean model has been successful. The book has sold more than 4 million copies worldwide. The metaphors of the red and blue ocean are striking and memorable. As is often the case, blue ocean theory has similarities to previous business models. Gary Hamel and CK Prahalad in 1994 wrote a book entitled *Competing for the Future*,[2] in which they talked about whitespace, a place where businesses could create and dominate emerging opportunities.

The idea of searching for 'the new bottled water' has obvious appeal. In practice it is much more difficult. Most of the examples of blue oceans are business concepts developed before the model was available. They are promoted as post-rationalization models. That said, the concept has many fans and there are success stories that can be attributed directly to it. In 2006 Nintendo declared in a press conference for the launch of their highly successful Wii video game that the blue ocean strategy was used in its development. In comparison to the Microsoft Xbox or the Sony PS3, the Wii product was much cheaper and it had a motion stick, which placed it in a different space in the field of computer games. It brought into the market people who were not big computer-game players and opened up a new blue ocean.[3]

The model in action

W Chan Kim and Renée Mauborgne use numerous examples to show how companies have developed blue oceans for themselves.

Yellow Tail, an Australian brand of wine, considered the traditional wine market as one that is complicated, patronizing, heavy on terminology and as a result frightening to certain groups of consumers. Yellow Tail created an offer that comprised just one red wine (a Shiraz) and one white wine (a Chardonnay). Theirs was a simple offer with a product that was appealing because it was sweeter and easier to drink. As a result, the Yellow Tail product did not focus on traditional wine drinkers but extended into a larger group of people looking for something easy to drink as an alternative to beer, cocktails or even a soft drink.

Cirque du Soleil has been identified as a blue ocean company. Traditional circuses offer a product that is widely recognized but very similar. Clowns, jugglers and animals are the circus's formula for entertaining families. Cirque du Soleil broke this mould by creating exceptional and surprising acts of gymnastic and artistic theatre, which still had appeal to families but also attracted a wider range of adults who marvelled at the completely different circus performances.

In the airlines industry, NetJets has been identified as a blue ocean company. NetJets saw a market for point-to-point travel in which commercial airlines and corporate jets competed. However, corporate jets have a very high cost even though they offer less hassle. Commercial airlines offer a pay-as-you-use service but at the expense of high travel time and not necessarily to desired destination points. NetJets saw blue ocean space in the middle of this market and offered the ability to buy 50 hours of travel per year, providing a point-to-point service that is faster than commercial flights, less hassle and providing increased productivity to business travellers. They opened up a new market for air travel.[4]

Some things to think about

- Really understand your customers. Look at what they buy, see how they use the products, find out what frustrates them and how they overcome these frustrations.

- Look at the outliers and extremes of your customers. What do they do? It is here that you may find your blue ocean rather than in the mainstream middle ground.

- Aim for the stars and be happy if you land on the moon! Most realizable opportunities lie with tier one customers rather than in tiers two or three.

Notes

1 Chan Kim, W and Mauborgne, R (2004 [2015, expanded edn]) *Blue Ocean Strategy: How to create uncontested market space and make the competition irrelevant*, Harvard Business School Publishing Corporation, Boston

2 Hamel, G and Prahalad, CK (1994) *Competing for the Future*, Harvard Business School Press, Boston

3 O'Gormon, P (2008) Wii: Creating a blue ocean the Nintendo way, *Palermo Business Review*, 2

4 www.blueoceanstrategy.com/bos-moves/netjets/ (archived at https://perma.cc/T8T8-35FU)

Boston Consulting Group (BCG) matrix

10

Planning a product portfolio or multiple strategic business units

What the model looks like and how it works

The Boston Consulting Group (BCG) matrix is a model for strategically planning how each product or subsidiary company within a group is performing. It is a model for use by companies with a diverse product range or an organization with a number of subsidiary companies. The products or subsidiary companies can be positioned within the model to determine future strategy for the company.

The matrix has two dimensions. First it considers the attractiveness of a market judged by its growth. Second, it considers each product's market share relative to the largest competitor in the industry. This growth/share matrix is now a central part of every business school's curriculum on strategy, offering a systematic tool for portfolio management.

Creating the BCG matrix requires a good deal of market intelligence. Data is required on the market shares of competitors of each product and on the growth opportunities.

The tool is made up of four squares or quadrants with relative market share along the X axis and growth along the Y axis.

Stars

The upper-right quadrant is for products of stellar performance. Products within this quadrant have a strong position in their marketplace and enjoy high growth. Not surprisingly, such products are labelled 'stars'. A product positioned in this quadrant could enjoy a monopoly position or it could have a significant feature or benefit that gives it an advantage over the competition. The high level of growth for such products will demand an investment in cash for stock and production but this should be more than justified. Products with a high market share are nearly always price leaders and can be highly profitable. Apple would place its iPhone in this quadrant.

Dogs

The bottom-left quadrant presents the exact opposite to stars in that a product positioned here has a low market share relative to the principal competitor, and growth would similarly be low. Products in this square are labelled 'dogs'. They may be aged and waning and in need of a product refresh. However, this may not be justified if the market itself is static or declining. Within the Virgin portfolio, its cola drink ultimately became a dog. It survived for 16 years in a vain attempt to win share against Pepsi and Coke in the static market for carbonated drinks. It was difficult to make a profit in this environment and it is therefore no surprise that its manufacturer, Silver Spring, entered administration in 2009.[1]

Cash cows

The bottom-right quadrant represents products that are important within almost every portfolio. These are products with a relatively high market share though growth opportunities are low. Products in the quadrant generate cash for the business because of their strong competitive position. They are therefore 'cash cows'.

As products mature within their markets, most are likely to end up in this quadrant. These products play an important supporting role for generating cash that can be invested in other products in the portfolio. They can be the most profitable products for a company and so it is useful to have a number in a portfolio. Most established companies have a number of products that have become cash cows. For Kellogg's it is their cornflakes. I imagine that Unilever would put Marmite in this quadrant.

Question marks

The top-left quadrant contains products that need support. These products have a low relative market share and a market environment promising strong growth. A product in this quadrant may be able to increase its market share and move east and become a star. However, there is uncertainty as to whether this is possible. There may be factors that inhibit the increase in market share. For this reason, products within the top-left quadrant are labelled 'question marks'. Such products may be newly launched, enjoying rapid sales in a growing market but still with a lowly market position. Many of the electronics and software products that are launched would suit this label. A few will become stars while most will have a short, fast life before being overtaken and falling from the sky. The uncertainty associated with products in this group means that a company must think carefully about investing in them. They need to be watched vigilantly to see which direction they are taking.

BCG argues that a strong company should have a balanced portfolio. Dogs may or may not have a place in product portfolios. These apart, other products could be usefully distributed so that there are:

- A small number of stars because their high share and high growth secures a profitable future for the company. Their appetite for cash is high so they should not dominate a portfolio.

- A good number of cash cows are to be recommended if possible because they supply funds to invest in the stars and question marks that will generate growth.

- A good number of question marks are useful so that they can be cultivated (if possible) into stars.

The origins of the model

Led by Bruce Henderson, the founder of the Boston Consulting Group, a number of the company's consultants developed the matrix between 1968 and 1970. In 1970 they published the theory as 'The Product Portfolio'.[2] It aimed to help organizations to analyse their product lines and portfolios in a structured and systematic way, indicating where investment should be focused.

During the early development of the model the high and low growth positions were from top to bottom, and high and low market shares were from left to right. There was nothing critical about this layout except it was convenient at the time. This format existed for a number of years before others found it more convenient to use an X-axis scale that went low to high from left to right.

Developments of the model

The fact that the BCG matrix has stood the test of 50 years is an indication of its usefulness as a strategic planning tool. The model shows products or business units that justify (or not) the allocation of resources. Its strength is its simplicity. However, being simple means that it does not always offer clarity of direction. For example, a company with a high market share in a growing market may not necessarily be profitable if there are high costs involved in maintaining the share. Also, an attractive growth rate may not be a guarantee of profits if the growth is vulnerable, in that it could be quickly overtaken by an alternative technology. Blackberry, the cellular phone company, could testify that its rapid growth and high market share were no guarantee of future prosperity.

There is also an assumption that dogs are to be expunged from a portfolio. Yet there are many companies that can generate profits from a product with a low market share and low growth opportunities, as long as they keep costs in check.

In the period since the BCG matrix was proposed, everything has speeded up. Companies and products develop faster and they spend much less time in a quadrant than they did 40 or 50 years ago. Furthermore, market share is less of a predictor of success for a company now than it was then. This may indicate that a portfolio today should have more question marks in it than was the case a few years ago. You cannot be certain which of the question marks will get traction so you need more in play in order to increase the chance of success.

Sometimes the BCG matrix can be used in conjunction with another business strategy model to add clarity. For example, the products could be lifted from the BCG matrix and placed into a product life-cycle model to give further clarity on what the future holds for them (Figure 10.1) (See Chapter 46.)

Figure 10.1   Placing the BCG quadrants into the product life cycle

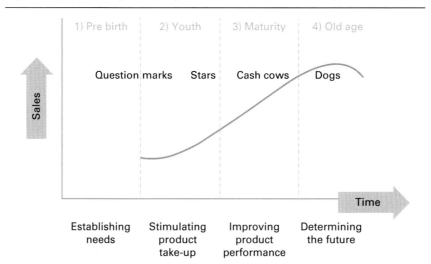

The model in action

Apple offers an excellent case study for positioning their products into the BCG matrix. As outsiders we can only do this schematically and without the privilege of the intelligence that will be available to Apple itself. However, the purpose of the exercise is to stimulate thought as to how the tool works in action rather than to pretend that each Apple product has been perfectly positioned:

- **Stars:** the iPhone has most certainly been a star for Apple. It has exhibited high growth and achieved a high market share. All products tend to mature and the iPhone is reaching that position. It is moving towards being a cash cow and most certainly it generates a huge amount of profit for the company.

- **Question marks:** the Apple Watch is relatively new to Apple's portfolio and was introduced with high expectations. The watch had a somewhat slow start but has gained much popularity (Apple does not disclose the number of watches it sells). At one stage it may have been a 'question mark' but there is no doubt now that it is moving into the 'star' box. As it adds new features such as those related to health it will find new customers beyond those early adopters who bought it because it was cool.

- **Dogs:** it seems unfair to classify the amazing Mac PC as a dog. However, its share of the PC market is low and growth is similarly low. This is an example of how the BCG model does not necessarily point to a solution. The implication of the model is that dogs are to be eliminated from the portfolio. However, in the case of Apple, why would they do this when it is generating acceptable profits? Apple products that are more identifiable as dogs are the iPod and the iPad. Since its peak in 2008, iPod sales saw a steady decline so that it has finally been discontinued. It is possible that iPads will go the same way. They have maintained a significant share in the tablet market but tablets appear to be losing popularity. iPad sales are falling and it seems that this could be a future 'dog'.

  And what happened to iTunes? This wasn't so much a 'dog' as a reinvention. It has been moved into the Apple Music app from where it can be managed and synced to the iPhone.

- **Cash cows:** as has been pointed out in this chapter, most successful products mature and become cash cows. The iPhone is entering this phase and iTunes is already there. These are products that will fund the heavy investment Apple has in question marks, which it hopes will become the new stars (Figure 10.2).

Figure 10.2   Apple's portfolio in the BCG matrix (With apologies to Apple as the products are positioned by the judgement of the author for illustration only)

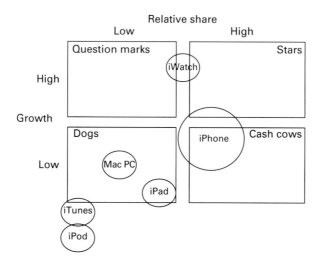

Some things to think about

- Bear in mind the importance of a balanced portfolio for your products and brands. A good number of 'question marks' are needed in the hope that one or more will become 'stars'. However, they are a drain on finances and are the reason why cash cows are so important to provide the necessary funding for future growth.

- If it is difficult to place products/SBUs in the BCG matrix, consider using the directional policy matrix (see Chapter 22).

Notes

1 Virgin Cola, https://en.wikipedia.org/wiki/Virgin_Cola (archived at https://perma.cc/8FK2-672T)

2 Henderson, B (1970) *The Product Portfolio*, Boston Consulting Group, Boston

Brand audit   11
Improving the strength of a brand

What the model looks like and how it works

For most companies and organizations a brand is recognized as one of its most important assets. A strong brand is often the reason companies are acquired at a huge premium over and above the value of their bricks, mortar and machinery. Yet, assessing the strength of a brand and placing a monetary value on it is not easy. For this reason international accounting standards do not allow companies to place a value of their brands on their balance sheets unless this is a figure that can be demonstrated by a financial transaction (i.e. the company or brand can be demonstrated to have a value because it was acquired at a premium). This does not stop companies wanting to get an indication of the value of their brands to see if their investment in these intangible assets is paying off.

There are numerous models for carrying out a brand audit. Some require inputs from proprietary databases and to that extent they are 'black boxes' in that they cannot be applied by just anyone.

A well-recognized model for valuing brands is from Interbrand, a branding agency that is part of Omnicom. Its brand valuation model is used to publish an annual report on the world's 100 most valuable brands.

Interbrand's economic value-added model assesses the value and ranking of the world's top brands, and is based on five steps:

1 **Segmentation:** brands operate in defined segments. The starting point for the model is to determine which segments are appropriate for the measurements.

2 **Financial analysis:** within the brand segment(s) that is being assessed, the income for the brand is measured according to its ability to generate returns that exceed the cost of capital employed. A five-year forecast of revenues is generated.

3 **Demand analysis:** the drivers of demand that lead to the purchase of the brand are assessed. These could include quality, innovation, design, value for money, etc.

4 **Brand strength analysis**: now the strength of the brand is assessed relative to competing brands on factors such as customer satisfaction and loyalty, market share, levels of awareness and market growth expectations. This leads to a brand strength score.

5 **Calculation of the net present value of brand earnings**: the final part of the assessment determines the future brand revenue and profitability, which is then discounted according to a rate that is deemed appropriate for the industry in which the brand competes.

The Interbrand model has stood the test of time. It was developed by Interbrand and the London Business School in 1988. However, it is a model that most business people would be unable to apply themselves and to that extent it must be regarded as proprietary.

A number of models, similar to that from Interbrand, are used for measuring brand equity. Brand Finance of London uses a 'Royalty Relief' method. This was developed in 1996 by David Haigh who, prior to founding Brand Finance, worked at Interbrand. Not surprisingly, there are some similarities between the two models. There are four steps in the Brand Finance model:

1 A brand strength index is calculated based on various inputs such as the investment that has been put into the brand, the performance of the brand in terms of satisfaction and loyalty, etc.

2 The brand strength index is then applied to a 'royalty rate', which is a specific indicator of the strength of the brand for a company in an industry sector.

3 The royalty rate is then applied to future forecast revenues for the brand.

4 Finally, the future brand revenues are discounted to a net present value, which is deemed to be the brand value.

There is another way of thinking about brand values and that is to check the health of key elements of the brand rather than put a monetary figure on them.

For those who want a simple model they can apply themselves, B2B International developed a brand health model based on three or four inputs:

1 **Awareness and usage**: a strong brand achieves high scores on the components of the AIDA model – awareness, interest, desire and action. These measures would be assessed by market research for brands in the competing sector.

2 **Brand position**: a strong brand stands for something. It has values that make it distinct from other brands. The strength of a brand position can be assessed by testing word associations with the brand and assessing to what extent it is differentiated from other brands in the market.

3 **Brand delivery**: a definition of a brand is 'a promise delivered'. The brand delivery strength is measured by asking customers who use the brand, their satisfaction with it on various dimensions and also their likelihood of recommending the brand (a measure of advocacy leading to the Net Promoter Score®).

If required, a fourth element could be added to assess the degree of alignment people inside the company have with the external views. The various scores in the components of the brand health wheel (Figure 11.1) can be summed to produce an overall brand score.

David Aaker in 1996 made a strong contribution to the brand audit model in an article published in *California Management Review*.[1] In the

Figure 11.1   The brand health wheel

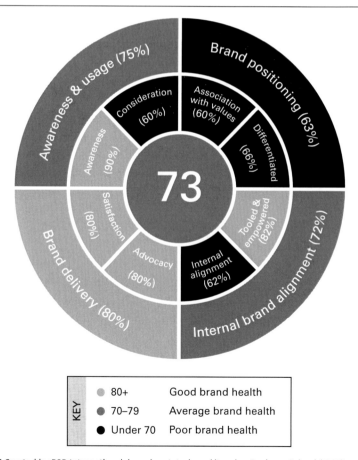

KEY		
●	80+	Good brand health
●	70–79	Average brand health
●	Under 70	Poor brand health

SOURCE Created by B2B International, based on Interbrand/London Business School (1988)

article he identified 10 measures for a brand that he called 'The Brand Equity 10'. These 10 measures he grouped into five categories. He argued that any or all of the measures may be relevant depending on the brand and its context (Table 11.1). For example, a company in the food and drink industry may put more weight on certain factors than one in the IT industry.

Table 11.1 David Aaker's brand equity 10 (1996)

Group 1: Loyalty measures		
1	Price premium	The percentage price premium that people will pay for a similar product
2	Satisfaction/loyalty	Satisfaction with the product and likelihood to recommend it
Group 2: Perceived quality/ leadership measures		
3	Perceived quality	The quality of the product versus that of competitors
4	Leadership	The perception of the brand as a market leader and one that is innovative
Group 3: Associations/ differentiation measures		
5	Perceived value	The degree to which the brand is seen to provide good value for money
6	Brand personality	The associations with the brand and the degree to which it is differentiated
7	Organizational associations	The degree to which people associate a brand with a company that they trust and admire
Group 4: Awareness measures		
8	Brand awareness	The percentage of people who are aware or have heard of the product (which could be front of mind or prompted)
Group 5: Market behaviour measures		
9	Market share	The market share of the brand in its competitive set
10	Price and distribution indices	The percentage of outlets carrying the brand or the percentage of people who have access to it

SOURCE Adapted from Aaker (1996)

The origins of the model

In the 1950s consumer goods companies such as Unilever, General Foods and Procter & Gamble developed the discipline of brand management. During this period the various components of brands came into focus. Companies recognized the importance of top-of-mind awareness as a measure of brand strength. They learned the importance of developing insights into the values associated with the brand and making them distinctive.

It was in the business-school boom of the 1990s that brand valuation models were developed by Interbrand and then by Brand Finance. Today almost every major market research company has a tool kit for measuring brands. Kantar has its BrandZ, TNS its NeedScope, Ipsos its Brand Value Creator, GfK its Brand Vivo. There are dozens more brand models offered by other market research companies, all aimed in some way at tracking the key components of awareness, use, satisfaction, recommendation and value. Significantly they are all heavily branded themselves in an attempt to appear special and different.

Developments of the model

There have probably been more developments in the brand audit model than any other business framework. This reflects the massive differences between, for example, toothpaste and microchips. Toothpaste brands will be strongly driven by awareness, values and emotion whereas microchips (think Intel inside) may be driven by technology, patents and commercial deals. The model for assessing the brand of breakfast cereal, for example, is likely to be quite different to that which is used to measure the brand name of a corporate enterprise. Brand models need to be flexible to accommodate these different requirements.

The model in action

RSM International is a global audit, tax and consulting network that had its origins in 1963. It has grown organically and through acquisition over the years so that it collected a plethora of different operating brand names. The member firms of RSM are independent accounting and advisory firms, each of which practises in its own right and is unified as part of the network.

Some used the RSM moniker together with the name of the local partner in a country. In the United States it was known as McGladrey, using one of the names of the three companies that made up the RSM initials – Robson Rhodes (UK), Salustro Reydel (France) and McGladrey (United States). Baker Tilly joined the group in the UK in 2014.

A strong brand by definition is one that is consistent and uniform wherever it operates. As is often the case, acquisitions lead to a confusion of this principle. It is also the case that branding carries with it strong emotions so that understandably there was a lot of local support for the local brands that had developed over the years. RSM recognized that it needed to unify the brand if it was to become a strong contender in the global competitive field of mid-tier accounting firms.

In 2015 the company carried out a market research programme of 2,000 firms around the world in the mid-tier sector where RSM competes. The survey measured the prompted and unprompted awareness of the different mid-tier accounting-firm brands, the values attached to them and their performance amongst people that use them. These three components of the brand led to the rebranding of the company across all its geographies as simply RSM. The research was also important in being able to objectively show the strengths and weaknesses of all the brands within the portfolio of RSM so that an objective decision could be made on how it could be unified.[2]

Brands have always been important, though more so since their careful management and direction in the last 20 years. Measuring the value and performance of the brand has therefore become important and is not taken lightly. Whenever a change is made, there is usually some sort of reaction from customers since, as consumers, they 'own' the brand. Their reaction to a name change is 'What are you doing with my brand?' This did not stop Mars changing the name of the Marathon chocolate bar to Snickers. A brand audit may well have suggested this was unwise but, within the global strategy of Mars, where Snickers was the brand used everywhere except in the UK, they felt it made sense to unify the brand – a decision not unlike RSM changing the McGladrey brand in the United States.

Some things to think about

- All the components of the brand audit are important. However, if you have to choose the most important metrics they are:

- unprompted awareness;

- the position/associations of the brand;

- its loyalty score.

These three measures are critical to a brand's success. How does your company perform on these measures relative to your direct competitors?

- Is your brand big enough and strong enough to be measured in financial terms?

Notes

1 Aaker, DA (1996) Measuring brand equity across products and markets, *California Management Review*, **38** (3), pp 102–20

2 Baker Tilly renamed RSM as firms adopt global brand, www.accountancyage. com/2015/06/10/baker-tilly-renamed-rsm-as-firms-adopt-global-brand/ (archived at https://perma.cc/H5ZP-CL8N)

Bullseye for brand positioning

12

Finding the core values of a brand

What the model looks like and how it works

A brand is something that is recognizable to a customer both in their head and their heart. It is a combination of a name, logo, images, facts and emotions that are associated with the brand. These combine to make a bond with a brand and hopefully create a level of loyalty to the point where they will choose it to the exclusion of all others.

In a world that is crowded with brands it is important that a brand stands out – in a good way. Cutting through the fog created by other brands and offerings isn't easy. A good brand occupies a clear and simple position in the minds of customers. And of course, the brand must deliver against its promise or people will go elsewhere.

The bullseye brand positioning framework brings together many elements of a brand to distil them into just a word or two that describes its essence – what it stands for. It is a framework to determine and develop a brand position. This brand position can be used to communicate it to everyone in the organization so they know where it stands and its purpose. Importantly it is also used to position the brand in the shelf space of customers' (and potential customers') minds. The whole purpose of having a strong brand position is to ensure that the brand is distinctive, differentiated and desirable and so has a competitive advantage.

Building a brand position requires a structured approach. The bullseye framework collects and analyses how customers feel about a brand, determines what makes it special, shows how the position can be substantiated, and distils it into just a couple of words – the brand essence or the brand mantra.

The starting point is to collect data on the competitive environment and the customer. What are the competitive brands, where do they compete, and how strong or weak are they? What are the points of difference between the brand and competitors' brands? What are the points of parity (where are they the same)? These questions are asked in order to find the 3Ds – why the brand is *desirable*, where it is *distinctive*, and how its position can be *defended*.

It is now possible to develop the bullseye framework. As the name suggests this looks like a target with concentric circles that work towards the centre and the eye itself. Around the outside of the framework are listed all the feelings that the brand engenders.

This analysis of the brand in terms of how it relates to customers gets to the emotions of the brand and from this a brand proposition can be developed – a statement of what the brand stands for. It is important that a brand delivers against its promise and so it is necessary to see how this can be substantiated. Working towards the inner circle of the bullseye it is worth listing points of evidence that confirm that the brand is living up to its promise. The best brands develop a personality. These are traits that give a brand a distinctive character so that customers get attached to it, just as they would if the brand was a person. The bullseye is a flexible tool and the substantiators, the brand proposition, and the brand personality can be built in. Finally, in the centre, in the bullseye, is the brand essence – a short distillation of what two or three words describe the brand.

The origins of the model

The term 'brand' originates from the hot iron with its distinctive mark that was seared onto the rumps of cattle so that a farmer could distinguish his animals from others on the range. These symbols or brands had great value in determining the ownership of the cattle. The term is widely used in business in a very similar way. A logo or distinctive mark of a company allows customers and potential customers to easily recognize what it is and what it stands for.

Of course, a brand is much more than a symbol or logo. It is all the associations that are attributed to something. It could be argued that as people we are each a brand in the sense that we have a unique identity and position that is different to anybody else. Product brands are seen in a similar way.

Figure 12.1 Example of a brand bullseye

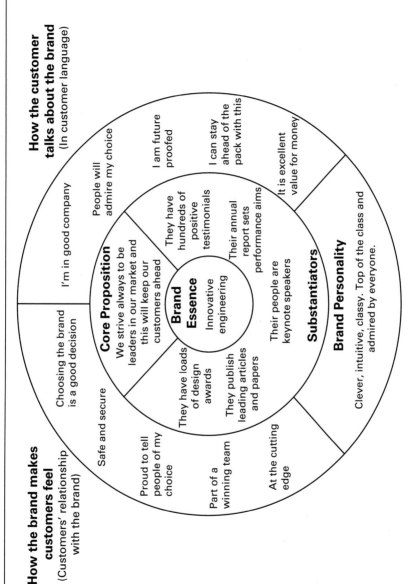

How the customer talks about the brand
(In customer language)

How the brand makes customers feel
(Customers' relationship with the brand)

Core Proposition
We strive always to be leaders in our market and this will keep our customers ahead

Brand Essence
Innovative engineering

Substantiators

Brand Personality

People will admire my choice

I am future proofed

I can stay ahead of the pack with this

I'm in good company

It is excellent value for money

Choosing the brand is a good decision

They have hundreds of positive testimonials

Their annual report sets performance aims

Safe and secure

Their people are keynote speakers

Proud to tell people of my choice

They have loads of design awards

They publish leading articles and papers

Part of a winning team

At the cutting edge

Clever, intuitive, classy. Top of the class and admired by everyone.

How the brand comes across to customers
(Attributes of the brand's personality)

Advertising executives have long recognized the significance of brand positioning. Jack Trout, an American advertising man, started talking about brand positioning in the 1960s. He joined forces with Al Ries and they wrote an article on brand positioning in 1969. These thoughts were developed and in 1981 they published a book called *Positioning: The battle for your mind*.[1] They didn't use the term 'bullseye' in the book but they did recognize that in an over-communicated society it is important to simplify a message. A brand does just that. Other advertising gurus such as David Ogilvy picked up the story of brand positioning and brand essence. Ogilvy described a brand as 'the intangible sum of a product's attributes'.[2] These intangibles add up to make a brand attractive to the point where consumers insist on it rather than any alternative.

Developments of the model

Various consultants and advertising agencies use concentric circles to arrive at a brand essence. Some use three concentric circles before arriving at the bullseye in the centre. Others may break the circles into segments with explanations of the core proposition or the brand personality. All the frameworks start with feelings and attributes of the brand and drive towards the bullseye in the centre which is distilled to the brand essence.

The model in action

Market research or an internal brainstorming is needed to establish how the brand makes people feel. These are its current brand values and any relationship it has with the marketplace. In the example in Figure 12.1 it is suggested that the company is at the cutting edge with its products and services. This makes people feel that they can be proud of their choice and that it will help them stay ahead of the competition. The brand is one that appears to be winning because it is ahead of the pack and often leading the way.

How the brand makes customers feel isn't necessarily how they articulate the brand. It is therefore worthwhile thinking about what people associate with the brand. For example, they may believe that the brand makes them look interesting or it may be about value for money.

From these customer feelings and articulations it should be possible to determine a personality for the brand. If the brand was a person or an animal what would it be and what would be its defining characteristic?

With the outer circle completed it is possible to move on and define a proposition for the brand. This may be a couple of sentences or a paragraph that states what the brand is and how it achieves this position. It is important that these attributes and personification of the brand can be substantiated and so it is worthwhile listing evidence that can be used to defend the brand position. This could be things such as awards, numbers of patents filed, articles published, Net Promoter Scores® etc. The idea is to have a factual base to defend the brand as defined.

Working from the outside to the centre ensures the different aspects of the brand are covered before arriving at just two or three words that summarize what the brand stands for. This is the brand essence or the brand mantra. In Figure 12.1 this essence is 'Innovative engineering'. This isn't a tagline or something that is shouted out in every promotion, but it is a guiding principle for the brand. It is now up to the promotional team to develop this brand essence into a powerful campaign. We don't have the inside track on how Coca-Cola used a bullseye framework to determine its brand position. What we do know is that they built their creative strategy around a brand that positioned itself as 'the only one' – 'the real thing'. The essence of the brand was that it was the first cola and therefore the authentic one. Pepsi had to develop a different brand position. It focused on taste, with promotions that said Pepsi was *lipsmacking, thirst quenching, ace tasting, motivating, cool buzzing, high talking, fast living, ever giving, cool fizzing,* and ultimately the Pepsi challenge. Fairly banal-sounding brand positions can be turned into very distinctive promotional messages.

Once complete a bullseye framework may seem obvious and simple. Managers can use it to achieve an internal consensus of what the brand stands for and the communications specialists can ensure that all messages are in line. Arriving at the brand position isn't usually achieved in one work session; it is likely to take days if not weeks of discussion. During this process it will be constantly reshaped until everyone is happy with the positioning.

Some things to think about

- Do you have a position for your brand at the present? Is this position the best one for the brand?
- Why do you think people buy your product?
- Having bought your product, how do you think they feel about it?

- In what way do you think your product is seen to be different from the competition? In what way is it better? In any way is it thought to be worse?
- If your brand was an animal, what animal would it be?
- If it was a person, how would you describe that person (gender, age, jobs, marital status etc)?
- How would you describe the personality of your brand?
- What single word or short sentence describes the essence of your brand?
- What evidence do you have to substantiate that the brand perceptions are valid?

Notes

1 Ries, A and Trout, J (1981) *Positioning: The battle for your mind*, Warner, New York

2 Ogilvy, D (1983) *Ogilvy on Advertising*, Prion, London

Business model canvas   13

Looking at key building blocks to see where improvements can be made

What the model looks like and how it works

Business Model Generation: A handbook for visionaries, game changers, and challengers, by Alexander Osterwalder and Yves Pigneur, is a bestseller.[1] It has achieved this distinction because it shows how a business proposition fits together using engaging graphics. The authors suggest nine blocks that look at the infrastructure of a business including the offering, customers, finances and revenue streams.

A business model is a framework that is all-embracing, describing how a company creates, delivers and captures value. This is in contrast to some of the frameworks in this book which focus just on elements of the business such as promotions, pricing, new product development, innovation and the like.

The nine building blocks of an organization do not work independently; rather they integrate with each other in different ways to create, deliver and capture value. In no particular order, they are as follows:

- **Value proposition:** The company or organization exists to supply customers with something they need. Customers have a job to do and what they buy from the organization helps them do it. It is important for a company to fully understand which of the customers' needs are being satisfied and to what extent. Questions asked within this block are 'What is our value proposition to our customers?', 'What job are we performing for our customers?', 'How can we reduce pain for our customers?', 'Which of our customers' needs are we satisfying?'.

- **Key activities:** The company makes or supplies things. It performs a number of different activities which in some cases could be manufacturing and in other cases could be buying, selling or adding value in a particular way. The question to be asked is 'What key activities do we need to perform in order to deliver our value proposition and satisfaction to our customers?'.

- **Key resources:** In order to perform the key activities, resources are required that are likely to include people, buildings, equipment, distribution channels, patents, relationships with suppliers etc. The questions here is 'What resources are required in order to perform our key activities and deliver satisfaction to our customers?'.

- **Key partners:** No company exists in isolation. It has suppliers of various kinds ranging from those that provide services through to those that offer products. The quality of these partners and their relationship with the company has a significant bearing on its success. Here we want to know answers to 'Who are our key partners and suppliers?' and 'What key activities do our partners perform for our company?'.

- **Customer segments:** A company should recognize that not all its customers are the same and some will have a greater predilection for its products than others. Recognizing the needs of these different segments and being able to satisfy them is crucial to the success of a business. Ask 'Who are the different groups of people we serve and what within our offer do they really value?'.

- **Customer relationships:** A strong company will have a good mix of customers and good relationships with them. It will have good customer satisfaction scores and customers with high levels of loyalty. Questions are 'What type of relationships do we have with our customers?', 'How do these relationships vary between customer segments?', 'Which segments are key to our company's success and how can we build upon these?'.

- **Channels:** A company has to move its offer through to customers and it will do so directly and through distributors and marketing channels. Many companies have online offers as well as using bricks and mortar distribution. The means by which these products get to market is another vital component of a business's strength. Here we want to know 'Which channels are used to buy our products?', 'Which channels are our strengths and which could we use to better effect?'.

- **Revenue streams:** Money comes into the company from sales and creates a revenue stream. It is the lifeblood of the company and a measure of success is the degree to which this works efficiently with a minimum number of bad debts and a good number of fast payments. Questions here are 'What is it in our offer that customers value and are willing to pay for?' and 'For each of our offers could we achieve greater revenue and margin by raising or lowering our prices?'.

- **Cost structure:** Whatever the company makes will have a cost made up of variable and fixed costs. The efficient management of these costs is crucial to the competitiveness and profitability of the company. Questions are 'What are the costs associated with our business model?' and 'How can we change our cost structure to the benefit of customers and our profitability?'.

These building blocks are worthy subjects. The model covers all the key parts of a business and so makes it possible to identify strengths and weaknesses. In this way the focus can be brought onto parts of the business that need attention. Also, working through each of the nine building blocks, the final result would produce a very useful marketing plan.

Undoubtedly one of the strengths of the model is that it brings together all the key activities of an organization in a form that will readily lead to a business strategy.

The origins of the model

The Business Model Canvas was proposed by Alex Osterwalder as part of his PhD research in 2005. It was turned into a book (*Business Model Generation*) where he joined forces with Yves Pigneur, his graduate supervisor and a computer scientist. The nine components of the business model can easily be drawn on a whiteboard or using software tools such as Strategyzer. Strategyzer is a consultancy firm that was co-founded by Osterwalder. It provides software tools and templates for applying the frameworks.

Developments of the model

The Business Model Canvas can be used with other frameworks. For example, the Business Model Canvas does not include blocks that look at external forces such as competition or external threats and opportunities. The Business Model Canvas can be used with a SWOT analysis or a brand positioning framework.

It has been suggested that one of the most difficult parts to get right on the Business Model Canvas is the value proposition. The value proposition is the product or service that is on offer and is valued by the customer. Working out this link between the offer and what is valued has resulted in another tool from Alex Osterwalder – the Value Proposition Canvas.[2]

The Value Proposition Canvas looks at the offer made by a supplier and how it relates to the customer. It starts with the product as it is sold by the supplier by considering three things: the attributes of the product and service on offer, what these attributes provide that enable the customer to build value, and how the attributes relieve pain for the customer.

It then relates the offer to the customer who buys the product. This is the customer profile. The customer profile is made up of the jobs the customer does with the product, how the product provides positive value, and thirdly how it reduces pain for the customer.

The model in action

Fulco (the name is made up to protect the identity of the company) began life providing simple warehouse facilities. In the early days of Fulco's business it had customers who received orders online. These customers asked Fulco to provide fulfilment services: holding stock, packing and despatching the orders. This side of the business grew rapidly until Fulco dropped warehousing and concentrated on fulfilment. The owner of the business used the Business Model Canvas as a health check and to ensure it was as efficient as possible in the rapidly growing fulfilment market:

- **Value proposition:** Fulco provides fulfilment services for businesses with online customers. It maintains stock, receives orders, packs and dispatches them and deals with any returns. This is a competitive market in which Amazon is a major player. There are many other smaller fulfilment companies, some of them working independently and others working together with Amazon. Fulco is based in a part of the UK where there is a plentiful supply of labour, relatively low-cost warehousing and good access to the motorway system. It therefore has a cost advantage over other competitors. It gave itself a score of 9 out of 10 on this building block.

- **Key activities:** In order to accommodate a rapidly growing number of customers Fulco invested in new software and systems. It used Mintsoft cloud-based fulfilment software, Xero accounting software and Capsule

CRM software. These simplified the earlier Excel system and improved efficiency. The Mintsoft software is a leader in fulfilment and easily meshed with all customers. Having the software run from the cloud meant it was easy to operate from different geographical locations. A major success factor leading to the growth of Fulco has been its IT systems which have enabled it to scale up. This building block was considered a strength of Fulco and it awarded itself another high score of 9 out of 10.

- **Key resources:** In the first instance the key resource of Fulco was its warehouse space. As the business grew rapidly this proved inadequate and a challenge has been to acquire more suitable space. This was difficult as warehousing space was at a premium following the pandemic. With the help of the local authority additional premises were located and converted for fulfilment. Another key resource was staff. In a matter of just two years the company grew from five employees to 100. Obtaining the right warehouse space and recruiting staff is a difficulty for Fulco and on this building block it awarded itself a score of 6 out of 10.

- **Key partners:** The company has a number of key partners including couriers, recruitment consultants and marketing specialists. Other key partners have helped it grow, including the local authority that was eager to support a growing business and investors who were happy to provide the finance. It received a score of 9 out of 10 on this building block.

- **Customer segments:** Fulco has around 50 customers, the largest of which are Amazon aggregators. These are companies that have acquired organizations selling through Amazon marketplace. The aggregators themselves were growing rapidly and so Fulco could ride on their coat tails. This building block is both a strength and weakness. It is a strength because the Amazon aggregators have helped it grow rapidly but it is a potential weakness because they provide significant revenue which could, at short notice, be taken elsewhere. It awarded itself a score of 7 out of 10 on this building block.

- **Customer relationships:** Fulco employs a customer relationship manager to look after its large customers. In applying the Business Model Canvas it concluded that it should carry out regular surveys of the people to whom it delivers so that it can feed back to its customers independent data showing that it is doing a good job. Fulco gave itself a score of 7 out of 10 on this building block.

- **Channels:** Fulco's business is delivering direct to customers who have ordered online. Fulco doesn't have any delivery vehicles of its own and uses specialist delivery companies such as DPD and The Royal Mail. Fulco works well with its couriers and does a good job servicing the online customers. For this it received a score of 8 out of 10.

- **Revenue streams:** Fulco has excellent relationships with its customers and they all pay by direct debit. Invoicing is highly efficient and there is a positive cash flow whereby Fulco receives money before it has to pay couriers and suppliers of packaging. This is a strong building block and achieved a score of 10 out of 10.

- **Cost structure:** The location of Fulco outside the south-east of England means that it has a cost advantage on both labour and warehousing over a number of competitors. For every £1 cost of storage the company receives £4 in revenue, a figure that it believes it can increase still further. This makes it one of the most profitable fulfilment companies in the UK. Again, this is a key strength of Fulco and received a score of 9 out of 10.

The Business Model Canvas proved useful as a health check and pointed to areas that needed some attention – managing the key resources, customer relationships and customer segments.

Some things to think about

- Look at the questions posed in the nine blocks that make up the Business Model Canvas. How would you rate your company's success in each of these blocks? Where is your company strong and where are you weak?

- Having completed all the blocks on the canvas, what strategy do you propose for the business?

- What are the key indicators in each building block that should be measured as you pursue your strategy?

- Consider creating a Business Model Canvas for key competitors. What does this tell you about their strategy and their strengths and weaknesses?

- How could you use the Business Model Canvas for testing the viability of new ideas?

- How could the Business Model Canvas be used for sharing the strategy through different departments within the business?

Notes

1 Osterwalder, A and Pigneur, Y (2010) *Business Model Generation: A handbook for visionaries, game changers, and challengers*, John Wiley & Sons
2 Mansfield, T (2019) Value Proposition Canvas explained: How to match your services to customer needs, Inter Action Consortium

Competitive advantage matrix

14

Working out requirements to obtain a
competitive advantage

What the model looks like and how it works

The Competitive Advantage Matrix, created by Boston Consulting Group,
assumes stable industry conditions. It is based on the premise that a competitive advantage can be achieved by differentiation and/or economies of
scale. As with any matrix it has two axes. The horizontal axis measures
economies of scale (i.e. the size of business). The vertical axis measures the
number of different opportunities there are for achieving differentiation (i.e.
the ability of the company to differentiate from its competitors). This results
in four quadrants:

- **Fragmented businesses** (in the northwest of the matrix, small businesses
  who have a variety of different ways in which they can achieve a
  competitive advantage). Typical of such companies are small retailers
  who can compete in different ways. Some could have a specialist product,
  others low prices, or a site on a busy thoroughfare. These companies
  don't have size on their side but they are able to differentiate and win a
  competitive advantage through playing in a niche. Think of restaurants,
  printers, engineering jobbing shops and the like, all of them with loyal
  customer bases.

Figure 14.1   The Competitive Advantage Matrix

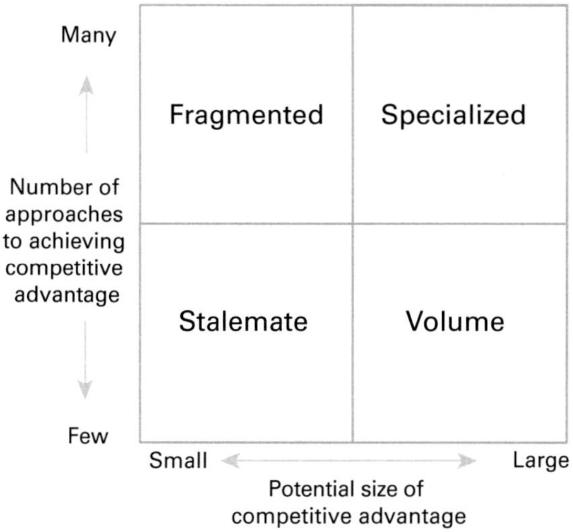

SOURCE Boston Consulting Group's Advantage matrix from Strategy in the 1980s by
Richard Lochridge

- **Stalemated businesses** (these are companies in the southwest of the matrix. They are small businesses that have few options for competing – hence their stalemate position). Examples of companies in this part of the matrix are those specialized manufacturers of metal components that are found in the Midlands of the UK or the Great Lakes area of the US. Stalemated companies produce commodities that have little to differentiate them from the competition and their survival depends on them managing their costs as much as possible. These companies have much less opportunity for achieving a competitive advantage than others in the matrix.

- **Specialized businesses** (here in the northeast of the matrix a company has a big competitive advantage and there are many approaches to achieving that competitive advantage). Examples here are the strongly branded food companies. A company such as Kellogg's has massive scale as well as a strong brand. Other companies could compete with Kellogg's by having large scale but making own-brand cereals for supermarkets. In this corner of the matrix companies with scale have different ways of achieving a competitive advantage.

- **Volume businesses** (in the southeast of the matrix companies have a big competitive advantage and very few ways in which that competitive advantage can be achieved). A typical example would be the car industry where vehicle manufacturers need scale to be competitive and the only way they can achieve this is in large assembly sites.

The framework helps understand where a competitive advantage comes from and so can be useful in guiding future strategy. For example, if you know that you are a stalemated business, there is no point in attempting to compete by increasing the volume of your output or trying to differentiate, but you may be able to gain some advantage by finding a location for your business where there is low-cost labour. Or it may be possible to build a reputation for the company in terms of reliability and so move into the fragmented quadrant with a 'trusted' brand.

The origins of the model

In 1981, Richard Lochridge, a Boston Consulting Group consultant, developed a two-axis matrix to show how companies can develop a growth strategy.[1] The Competitive Advantage Matrix sits in parallel with what is frequently referred to as the BCG Matrix, or the Growth Share Matrix (that of cash cows, dogs, question marks and stars). It hasn't achieved the recognition and use of the BCG Matrix (growth/share matrix) but it is (as are all frameworks) useful for building a big picture of how a company can grow.

Developments of the model

The Competitive Advantage Matrix follows the Growth Share Matrix. The Growth Share Matrix posits that a product line or business that enjoys high market share and a rapid growth rate is a 'star'. When a company has different business units and product lines, the stars play an important role in financing long-term growth. Equally, business units or product lines with a low market share and low growth rate are classed as dogs and need fixing or removing from the portfolio. Cash cows have a high market share and low growth and are useful for financing investment. Products with a low market share but a high growth rate are deemed question marks because their future is uncertain. They may grow share in the future and become stars but equally they may not maintain a high growth rate in which case they will fall and become dogs.

Business success is about achieving competitive advantage and to this extent BCG's Competitive Advantage Matrix is helpful. As with all frameworks it doesn't stand on its own. It implies that a profitable strategy can be achieved by either scale or creating a distinctive offer, but it doesn't necessarily predict future success. Toyota may be a successful car manufacturer through its huge market share and volume production, but it may be overtaken by electric vehicles in the future. A restaurant may have a distinctive offer which gives it a strong position in its locality until an entrepreneurial restaurateur opens a new place on the other side of the street.

The model in action

This is a classical strategy framework as it posits that a competitive advantage can be obtained by positioning the company optimally in an attractive market.

A company that produces a product with little or no differentiation from competitive products and which is produced in low volumes, would need to think carefully about its future. This product may be going nowhere.

Nowadays, many car designs look the same. Also, most cars are reliable. This means there is little opportunity for differentiation and the strategy has to be efficient production. It is why there has been a good deal of rationalization in the automotive market with companies such as Saab going out of business while Toyota and Volkswagen have endured through their high market shares and volume business.

A business in the fragmented segment is one that stands out as different (for example a local restaurant) but it may have a limited opportunity for building scale.

Specialized companies have the advantage of producing products that are very different to those of the competition. If there are also volume opportunities, such a company could do very well. Pfizer reaped hundreds of millions in profits from Covid vaccines through both differentiation and scale.

Some things to think about

- Where is your competitive advantage? Is it a differentiated offer or is it an efficient level of production that competition can't easily match?

- How could you improve your competitive advantage? What are the opportunities for building volume and/or differentiation?
- Where are the threats to your competitive advantage? Which competitors could usurp your position? How could they do so?
- How profitable is your competitive advantage? To what extent are you using your competitive advantage to generate cash flow and higher earnings?

Note

1 Lochridge, R (1981) Strategy in the 1980s, published in *Perspectives on Strategy* from The Boston Consulting Group, pp 56–7, https://www.bcg.com/about/ overview/our-history/growth-share-matrix (archived at https://perma.cc/ GVJ4-UPCD)

Competitive intelligence

15

Assessing market strengths and weaknesses

What the model looks like and how it works

Competitive intelligence (CI) is, as the term suggests, market intelligence that is focused on finding out as much as is possible about business competitors. All companies face some level of competition. Understanding the strengths and weaknesses of competitors is critical in determining a business strategy. A profile of competitors is required for product planning, pricing, strategy and acquisition policy.

Given time, a considerable amount of intelligence can be obtained on competitors. Researchers seldom have unlimited time and so must set out to collect as much information as possible within confines. In some companies CI is a continuous process. Topics that are usually featured in a competitor intelligence-gathering exercise are:

- Financial data on the competitor:
    - company revenue, number of employees, number of plants;
    - exports (including geographical breakdown);
    - net profit and gross profit;
    - current assets and fixed assets;
    - return on assets;
    - trend of financial data over time;
    - ratio analysis (of revenue to employees, debtor days, etc).
- Customers of the competitor:
    - target customers;

- key customers;
- share of wallet of the competitor at customers;
- loyalty of customers to the competitor.

- Products and turnover of the competitor:
  - the range of products sold by the competitor, their performance, specifications and prices;
  - the revenue and market share for major product lines;
  - the importance of spares within the competitor's product portfolio;
  - the importance of service within the competitor's revenue.

- Prices of the competitor:
  - the pricing policy of the competitors, including known discounts;
  - the timing of price increases and whether they are instigated independently or follow a lead.

- Distribution:
  - route to market used by the competitor;
  - key distributors.

- Deliveries:
  - the speed with which the competitor can fulfil an order;
  - the reliability of deliveries on time and in full.

- Promotions:
  - the size of the competitor's promotional budget;
  - approximate breakdown of the promotional mix;
  - the attendance of the competitor at exhibitions.

- Selling methods:
  - the size and organization of the competitor's sales force;
  - the geographical coverage of the sales territory;
  - quality of the competitor's sales force.

- Production facilities/capacity:
  - the production capacity of the competitor;
  - current production levels;
  - the capacity level at which the competitor breaks even.

- Company organization and philosophy:
    - the management structure of the competitor and its relationships with parent bodies or subsidiaries;
    - associations with distributors and other partners;
    - any patents held by the competitor and when they expire.

Any collusion between competitors could be seen as against the public interest. This covers behaviours such as price fixing, carving up geographical regions and customers within them, restricting the supply of products, etc. This does not preclude a company from learning as much as it can about the competitor from as many sources as possible. Intelligence on the subjects listed above is available on most companies though it may need to be pieced together from different sources.

Sources of competitor intelligence

The usual sources for competitor intelligence are:

- **Financial data:** publicly quoted companies have to produce detailed accounts that are made available within months of the end of their financial year. Considerable detail is available in the 10-K reports on US public companies and these are available either on the company websites or on the Edgar database of the US Securities and Exchange Commission (SEC). Financial information on companies is available in the UK from Companies House, even though the detail of it is limited for small and medium enterprises. Hoovers is a good source of data for companies throughout the world. For most companies it is possible to get a close fix on the number of employees in a company and this can be easily converted to a proxy for annual revenue through applying an estimation of the revenue per employee.

- **Websites:** we live in an age of self-promotion where companies post a considerable amount of data about themselves on their websites. Alerts can be set up so that any change to a website sends a notification to the researcher. Competitor intelligence can be found on websites beyond those of the competitors themselves. Industry journals and newspapers run stories about company activity and often mention the activities of competitors. There are websites such as www.glassdoor.com that report on the culture of an organization from people who have worked there.

- **Google maps:** Google Maps and Google Street View allow us to have a good look at the fabric and the premises of companies without leaving our desk.

- **Market research reports:** market research reports are available at modest costs that cover almost every industry, including specialized niches. The market research reports provide intelligence on the structure of markets and market-share data on suppliers.

In addition to the publicly available data on the internet and in journals, other sources of CI are:

- **Customers:** shared customers can be a source of intelligence on competitors. Customers can report competitors' product performance, deliveries, sales service, prices, etc. This can provide useful benchmarking metrics such as customer satisfaction and NPS.

- **Suppliers:** companies that supply materials and information may well supply competitors and be prepared to share views on them.

- **Distributors:** these companies deal with a wide range of different suppliers and customers, some of which may be competitors.

- **Industry experts, journalists and observers:** there are always people in an industry who acquire knowledge on companies from attending seminars, conferences and exhibitions.

- **Past employees:** if they are not bound by confidentiality agreements, past employees may be prepared to share intelligence on where they previously worked.

The origins of the model

CI took off in the United States in the 1970s. In 1980, Michael Porter published his book, *Competitive Strategy: Techniques for analysing industries and competitors*.[1]

In 1986 the Society of Competitive Intelligence Professionals (SCIP) was founded, offering insights and training on competitor intelligence and setting standards for the work. Since then it has morphed into Strategic and Competitive Intelligence Professionals (SCIP) (with its own journal, *Competitive Intelligence Magazine*).[2]

Developments of the model

CI has become an important tool for multinational corporations. They use CI to benchmark, scenario plan, and identify risks and opportunities.

CI is a form of market intelligence although it is focused on risks and opportunities. All professional CI practitioners adhere to ethical standards and these are addressed through the Strategic and Competitive Intelligence Professionals organization. Observing ethical standards in data gathering is not only important to the practitioners of the intelligence gathering, it is also important to their employers who would otherwise risk breaking the law if data was collected by subterfuge or illegal means.

The model in action

A major supplier of maintenance and repair products wanted to expand into technical component distribution. It was interested in acquiring high-volume resellers of semiconductors, PCBs and specialized electronic lines. The geographical area of interest covered the whole of western Europe.

The project began with a listing of companies that were known and thought to be suitable acquisitions. This was supplemented by desk research. Parameters were set so that only companies with revenues of more than €10 million per annum were targeted.

An internet search identified published reports on the electronic components market in Europe and these showed the market size and trends for electronic components over the last decade. The reports identified countries with a sizeable demand for electronic components and therefore countries where the research should focus.

Within the countries that were selected for research, a listing was made of the key distributors of electronic components and top-line information was collected on revenue and the number of employees. The number of employees was always available for each company that was profiled. Where there were gaps in company revenue, estimates were made by applying a reasonable estimate of revenue per employee. Following an examination of distributors' websites, a traffic-light system was devised to show the degree of fit with the acquiring company.

For companies that were a good fit, detailed company profiles were constructed. These examined the different routes to market used by the target companies (online, catalogue, field sales, shops) and whether they supplied

Figure 15.1   Assessing the appeal of acquisitions from competitor intelligence

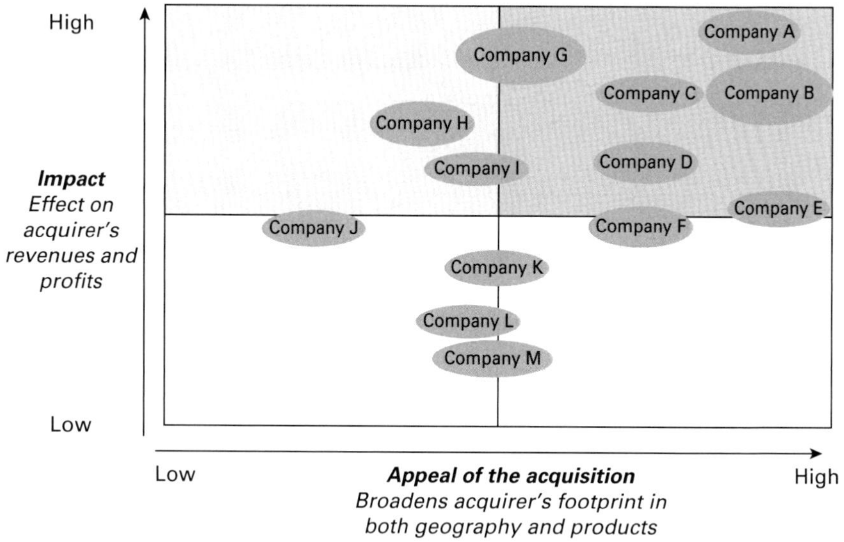

SOURCE Figure created for illustration only

business to business (B2B) customers or business to consumer (B2C). A Dun & Bradstreet rating was obtained on each company to indicate the maximum credit and the companies' 'failure scores' and 'delinquency scores' (respectively an estimate of each company's risk of failure and risk of late payment).

Companies were plotted on a matrix to indicate the impact they would have on the acquiring company's revenues and profits and the degree to which they would broaden the acquirer's footprint across different geographies and products (Figure 15.1).

Due diligence was carried out on a number of companies and successful acquisitions were made. As a result, the acquiring company is now one of the largest distributors of electronic components in Europe.

Some things to think about

- Consider setting up a continuous programme of gathering competitor intelligence. Use your sales force and Google alerts to keep up to date with changes. Create an easily accessible repository where customer intelligence can be filed and shared (perhaps on the company's intranet).

- Keep encouraging the people who are your eyes and ears for intelligence. They need to know that what they are collecting and sharing is valued.

- An ad hoc competitor intelligence survey should begin with the questions 'What do we want to find out about this competitor and what will we use the intelligence for?' Remember to 'join the dots' between pieces of market intelligence. For example, adverts for a new product development manager could indicate that the competitor is bound on an innovation strategy.

Notes

1 Porter, ME (1980) *Competitive Strategy: Techniques for analysing industries and competitors*, Free Press, New York
2 www.scip.org/ (archived at https://perma.cc/W4BX-HPWW)

Conjoint analysis 16

Assessing optimum pricing and the value of component parts

What the model looks like and how it works

Conjoint analysis is a tool used to determine the value people place on different offers. Marketers have always been suspicious of asking customers simple questions about how much they would pay for a product. Simple questions do not drill down into what people really value. Marketers want to know what people value as this influences the messages they communicate in trying to create customer interest. Those attributes of the offer that are of greatest value can be singled out to create a communication that is distinctive, desirable and defensible. Marketers also want to know the optimum price for a product. On the one hand, they do not want to leave money on the table and, equally, they do not want to overprice their product such that it is not purchased.

All choices involve compromises and trade-offs. We may want a high-quality product with lots of bells and whistles but, if we cannot afford it, we will have to settle for something less. As the ideal is rarely attainable, we need an approach that allows us to simulate this decision making in the questions we ask. Conjoint analysis provides the framework for asking people what they value in different offers. In order that we can develop appropriate questions, we need to break down the products and services into their features and benefits, which we call attributes. These attributes can be offered at different levels – high quality/low quality; delivered in an hour/delivered in a week, and so on. It is these attributes and the levels of the attributes that make up the conjoint offers that are shown to respondents and who are asked to say which they would choose.

The principle of conjoint analysis starts with a listing of the key attributes of an offer. To take a simple example, let us imagine that a manufacturer of envelopes wants to know the value attached to the colour of the envelope, the sealing method and whether it has a window or not. In the example in Table 16.1 there are two concepts with three attributes and a price at two levels. Which would you choose?

Table 16.1 Attributes table (1)

Attribute	Envelope A	Envelope B
Colour	White	Brown
Sealing	Glue	Self-seal
Window	No window	Window
Price	50 cents	40 cents

The example in Table 16.1 has been limited to two concepts made up of different levels of the attributes. More concepts could be added. For example, concept C could be added, which is the same as concept A except it is brown. Concept D could be added, which is the same as A except it would be self-seal, and so on. Each would have a different price. The design of the concepts is a crucial step in a conjoint project, and time is required to narrow these down to those that affect buying decisions. In the example of the envelopes, there are only two concepts with three attributes and two levels of variation of each attribute. In many conjoint studies there can be up to seven attributes and four or five different levels of each. This means that there can be hundreds if not thousands of permutations of the different attributes and levels. The conjoint researchers use software to distil these many permutations to around 30 or so bundled offers that are shown to people. Each offer has a different price. Respondents are shown four or five of these offers at a time and asked to choose which they would buy and which they would reject. In a typical survey this means a respondent looks at five or six different screens with four or five choices per screen – a total of 30 or so different offers, all with different prices. The choices that are made by respondents are analysed in special software, which ultimately calculates the utility value for each of the levels of the attribute. In this way, it is possible to see which of the combinations is most favourable and how much people value the different attributes and their levels.

Returning to the envelope example, which had only two concepts to choose from, we can see that a total utility figure can be calculated for envelopes A and B (Table 16.2). Out of the two choices, envelope B is preferred and has a utility value of 85 (note the utility value is not out of 100, it is just a relative value calculated from the data responses). When we examine the detail, we see that a white envelope is valued more than a brown envelope. This causes us to think that if we had included a third concept, envelope C, which was white, self-seal and with a window, it would have been the preferred option (depending on the price).

Table 16.2   Attributes table (2)

Attribute	Envelope A	Envelope B
Colour	White (25)	Brown (15)
Sealing	Glue (5)	Self-seal (10)
Window	No window (10)	Window (15)
Price	50 cents (30)	40 cents (45)
Overall	(70)	(85)

The origins of the model

Conjoint analysis is a statistical tool and is based on work by the French economist Gérard Debreu in 1960,[1] and followed by further work by US mathematical psychologist R Duncan Luce and statistician John Tukey in 1964.[2] The original conjoint theory was based on just two attributes and it was not long before other statisticians constructed conjoint measurements with more attributes. For the marketer who is a non-statistician, the application of conjoint modelling can be daunting. It is helped by excellent software, the most famous of which is from Sawtooth. However, even this needs a practitioner who is used to applying it. It is therefore a tool for the statistician rather than the marketer.

Developments of the model

In the early days of conjoint, respondents were shown printed cards that described the concepts. Respondents shuffled the cards and placed them in preferred and rejected piles. From the 1980s onwards conjoint analysis was carried out on computers and today it is virtually all online. There have been many updates to the way the conjoint questions are asked and analysed. In modern conjoint, respondents are asked to reveal more about their preferences before they review the concepts. This allows the concepts to be adapted to the different needs of respondents. For example, a buyer at a large company may be just one of a group of decision makers and might be shown only attributes that are appropriate. This could be in contrast to someone who makes a purchasing decision at a small company and who is concerned with all the attributes in the buying decision. This is adaptive choice-based conjoint.

The great attraction of conjoint analysis is the ability to arrive at a scientific assessment of what people value. However, there are limitations to conjoint that need to be borne in mind:

- **Sample size:** in order to obtain reliable results it is usually necessary to interview at least 100 target respondents and preferably 200. In some B2B markets it is not possible to achieve these sample sizes.

- **Number of attributes:** the design of the conjoint concept is critical. Conjoint analysis becomes unreliable if there are a large number of different attributes, including price. Similarly, the number of variables for each attribute needs to be limited to between three and five levels, otherwise the potential combinations of concepts becomes too large to manage.

- **Respondent fatigue:** respondents who take part in a conjoint survey are asked to look at a number of different screens, each with different offers (with different prices). It is easy for them to become 'punch drunk' with so many offers to view. Unless the attributes and the variables are quite distinctive, the offers can blur and seem very similar. When this happens, respondents get confused and tired and do not give their full consideration to the choices, choosing any at random to complete the tedious interview.

The model in action

A manufacturer of carpet tiles for use in offices wanted to test its existing designs against some new designs. A decision was made to focus the survey on key decision makers. These were fit-out contractors who design and install new office environments: 100 respondents took part in the online survey and were screened to ensure that they specified a significant amount of carpet flooring per annum.

Testing carpet tiles online has its limitations. Respondents are not able to touch or feel the products. It was necessary therefore to accept this limitation and focus on two aspects of the design – the colour and the visual texture. Both were shown in photographs. Other attributes that were tested were the length of the guarantee, the environmental friendliness of the carpet tiles and the requirement for a stain guard. It was decided not to include the brand as an attribute or variable.

An analysis of the results showed that the attitudes to the different carpet tiles varied depending on the projects carried out by the companies. Those fitting out offices in major cities had different choices to those working with government offices. The fit-out contractors had customers with different budgets and this influenced their choices of carpet tiles.

Colour turned out to be the prime feature for most of the specifiers. This was followed some way behind by texture and the wear guarantee. The environmentally friendly attribute proved to be more important to contractors serving the public sector.

As a result of the conjoint analysis, the company was able to select new designs that could be targeted at different audiences. They were able to establish prices that resulted in the new designs fitting comfortably alongside those already in the portfolio. The research enabled the company to develop a carpet tile range for commercial offices and another range for public offices.

Some things to think about

- Conjoint is appropriate if you are trying to work out the importance of the different mix of attributes in a product. However, if all the attributes are fixed and locked in, and you just want to test prices, it might be better to use van Westendorp or Gabor–Granger (see Chapter 39).

- When designing your conjoint survey, limit yourself to five or six different attributes plus price. If you have too many attributes, you need a large sample size and it can be confusing to respondents if they are shown too many variations of the offers.

- If you can only find a maximum of 100 respondents to take part in the survey, consider using a different tool such as SIMALTO (see Chapter 51).

Notes

1 Debreu, G (1960) Topological methods in cardinal utility theory, in K Arrow, S Karlin and P Suppes (eds), *Mathematical Methods in the Social Sciences*, Stanford University Press, Stanford, pp 16–26
2 Luce, RD and Tukey, JW (1964) Simultaneous conjoint measurement: a new scale type of fundamental measurement, *Journal of Mathematical Psychology*, **1** (1) pp 1–27

Customer activity cycle

Determining opportunities to lock in customers and give them more value

What the model looks like and how it works

Many business frameworks argue that there is an evolutionary cycle. We recognize the evolutionary cycle in human life. There is an obvious sequence from youth to maturity and old age. The customer activity cycle identifies phases during which customers think and behave differently about the products they buy. Recognizing these differences over time can be helpful in identifying how customers perceive value in the products they buy.

The customer activity cycle originated with Sandra Vandermerwe, a professor of international marketing and services at the University of London's Imperial College. In 1993 she wrote an article in *The Columbia Journal of World Business* that introduced the concept of the customer activity cycle.[1] By identifying points in the customer activity cycle it is possible for a company to provide customers with more value.

The starting point of the customer activity cycle is to identify key moments of truth at different stages of interaction with the customer. A moment of truth is that point when a customer engages with the brand and when the interaction causes the customer to form an opinion about it. A moment of truth can occur at any time, for example when a customer sees an advert, when the product is purchased, and when it is used or consumed.

Sandra Vandermerwe pushed the view that suppliers should keep an eye on the final consumer of the product, not necessarily the intermediary that buys it. The key is getting to know how these final customers use the product and therefore how they value it. Such insights might show that users have a need for services or intangibles that weren't otherwise recognized. For example, a supplier of building products to merchants may deliver wooden pallets. These wooden pallets then pile up at the merchants' outlet and become a nuisance. The supplier of building products could see this as a problem and set up a service to deal with the redundant pallets.

The framework suggests that an end user of a product works through three stages: the PRE stage is all about recognition and choice; the DURING stage is when things happen and purchases take place; and the POST stage is when the supplier stays with the customer, understanding their needs and developing solutions to satisfy them:

- **The PRE stage:** this stage is full of decisions. Here the customer is working out what the problem is and deciding what to do. There may be a number of choices to make as to which solution is best. Not only are there likely to be different solutions, there will certainly be a range of products that can be purchased. A supplier that understands the consternation of end users will be in a good position to guide their decision so that it closely matches the final customers' needs.

- **The DURING stage:** now the end user is doing things. In this stage it is important that the supplier has processes in place that can deal with problem solving. In using the product the final customer may need helplines that show what to do and how to do it. The delivery and storage of the product is likely to be important to the customer.

- **The POST stage:** winning the customer is only half the battle. It is important that the customer stays loyal and it is in this POST stage that loyalty is created. Staying in touch with the end user and fully understanding how they are moving forward will help. In this way the customer will feel they are valued and the supplier may be able to adjust the offer to accommodate any changes that are taking place.

The origins of the model

The customer activity cycle is a sequential framework. Just as the evolutionary cycle moves from youth to maturity and old age, the customer activity cycle moves from PRE, to DURING, to POST.

In the early 1900s, Elias St Elmo Lewis, an advertising man operating out of Philadelphia in the United States, picked up the ideas of Frank Dukesmith (see Chapter 5) and introduced the concept of a customer life cycle which became known as the AIDA model. In the acronym AIDA, 'A' stands for awareness, which is the first stage in the customer cycle when the customer learns of a product. This is followed by 'I', which stands for interest. Whatever the customer learns about the product generates some interest which may lead on to 'D', desire and a wish to acquire it. The final 'A' in the acronym stands for action when a purchase is made.

There are similarities between the AIDA framework and the customer activity cycle. Both are sequential and both deal with the process of winning customers. The AIDA framework is a descriptor of behaviour to the point where a product is purchased whereas the customer activity cycle focuses on an understanding of the needs of the end user and how these can lead to greater loyalty.

Developments of the model

The concept of a life cycle has been with us forever and the customer activity cycle does not appear to have remained the exclusive property of Sandra Vandermerwe. Authors have picked up the subject and added more stages, renamed them and shown how they can be used in specific applications. There has been much interest in showing how it has an application in e-commerce. A focus on each stage of the customer activity cycle enables companies to improve their website design, their search engine optimization and e-marketing. Feedback at each stage shows what is working and what needs improving. This is a very strong link to those who see the customer activity cycle as a key element of building customer loyalty.

The model in action

In October 2000 Vandermerwe wrote an article showing how the customer activity cycle was used to advantage by Baxter, a healthcare company that made disposable bags for kidney dialysis in the home.[2] The company's products were considered relatively expensive and as a result were losing market share. Baxter took a deep dive and looked at each point in the customer activity cycle, seeking to find opportunities for adding value. They did this by going beyond selling the bags and looked at the patients who used the bags. They learned how patients managed their lives around the treatment, how they updated prescriptions and how they disposed of the bags. Baxter stopped thinking of itself as a dialysis bag manufacturer and added value by thinking more like a dialysis patient caregiver. These added-value components within the Baxter offer enabled patients to stay at home longer rather than having to go into hospital for treatment. Baxter also decided to market drugs to the renal sufferers as these were complimentary products that improved the patients' customer experience. This understanding of customers' needs at different points enabled Baxter to defend and strengthen its position.

Some things to think about

- Who are the end users of your products or services?
- What do you know about the engagement of your offer with end users in the PRE stage (when they are deciding what to buy), the DURING stage (when they are making the purchase), and the POST stage (when they are using the product)?
- In each of these stages, what attributes of your offer are used and valued by end users?
- What attributes of your offer are not used and are therefore junk to end users?
- How can you change or add to your offer to make it more appealing to end users at different stages of the activity cycle?

Notes

1 Vandermerwe, S (1993) Jumping into the customer's activity cycle: a new role for customer services in the 1990s, *Columbia Journal of World Business*, **28** (2)
2 Vandermerwe, S (2000) How increasing value to customers improves business results, *MIT Sloan Management Review*

Customer journey maps 18

Assessing the current performance of marketing and sales processes

What the model looks like and how it works

Customers do not arrive out of nowhere. They begin, not as customers, but as prospects, in the first instance becoming aware of a supplier, acquiring knowledge, becoming interested, making comparisons with other suppliers and eventually placing orders. In other words, it is a journey of exploration with different requirements from the supplier at each stage. It does not end when the orders are placed; in fact it could be the start of another lengthy part of the journey as the customer repeats orders, buys other products within the portfolio, possibly becoming more intertwined with the supplier. Of course, something could go wrong or the customer may no longer require the product and the journey could end. This is a journey that may continue if the supplier/customer relationship is rekindled at some stage in the future.

The concept of the customer journey is simple. Its usefulness is understanding the many touch points or moments of truth (MOT) that are met on each stage of the journey. Each of these touch points has an influence on the customer that could enhance or detract from the relationship. These MOTs are potential pain or pleasure points.

The moments of truth do not all occur with sales and marketing staff. Receptionists, delivery people, technicians, finance departments and production departments at a supplier could all interact with the customer at some stage on the journey. The customer journey is therefore a reminder of the life cycle of a customer, how they are treated in this life cycle and where there are weak points that need rectifying.

The customer journey can be mapped. The customer journey map (CJM) provides a blueprint for action:

- It brings the whole company together as the map will show the strengths and weaknesses of interrelationships between internal departments and how they affect the customer.

- It shows weaknesses in the company and how they can be rectified. It is an important tool in improving the customer experience.

- It indicates where changes are required, for example in introducing new touch points to handle the customer on their journey.

- It identifies points of strength of the company that can be highlighted in the customer value proposition.

- It shows competitive strengths and weaknesses and so points to strategies for using these to gain a competitive advantage.

- It identifies the emotions of customers on their journey. These emotions are cues for how best to communicate with the target audience.

A customer journey map is made up of a spine (the major stages that the customer goes through in the life cycle with the supplier) and all the moments of truth during each of these stages. At the point of developing the spine, there are some questions that should be asked:

- What are customers doing at this stage?

- What would motivate a customer to move to the next stage?

- What are customers' concerns and uncertainties at this stage? What barriers might prevent them moving to the next stage?

- What would alleviate these barriers, concerns and uncertainties?

- What effort is required by the customer or potential customer in moving to the next stage?

A moment of truth or touch point is an intervention between the customer or potential customer and the company. This could be a visit to a website, an advert in a journal, an anecdote told by another customer, the way the phone is answered at reception – indeed there could be hundreds of moments of truth that influence customers and potential customers. The skill of customer journey mapping is to identify the most important ones that influence people on the journey.

An example of a spine and the touch points are shown in Figure 18.1.

Figure 18.1 An example of a customer journey map showing spine and touch points (moments of truth) (2016)

AWARENESS	INTEREST	DECISION	SERVICE SET-UP	SERVICE DELIVERY	RELATIONSHIP STRENGTHENING	CONCERN	LEAVE	RETURN
How customers become aware of Company X	How customers become interested in doing business with Company X	The things that help customers make the decision to do business with Company X	What Company X does when setting up a new customer account	The day-to-day elements involved in the delivery of the agreed service	What Company X does to develop ongoing relationships and delight its customers	How Company X deals with concerns and complaints	What Company X does when a customer wants to leave	How we win back previous lost customers
Trucks/Livery	Prospect material	Proposal/ presentation	Customer site visit	Phone/fax/email for order	Additional product installs	Receiving complaints	Leaving phone call	Prospects lists
Brands – portfolio	Promotional offers	Face-to-face visits	Customer site assessment	Customer places order	Customer training	Following up complaints	Stop ordering altogether	am contact plan
Brand – umbrella/ corporate	One-stop-shop offer	Agreement	Welcome call	Customer places order – phone call	Business Dev. Manager	Price rise letter	Visit	Lapsed customer call
CSR	Existing product lines	Can't service/ notify of rejection	Account creation	Product delivery	Free service extras	Standard am calls	Last chance visit	
Word of mouth	Lending		Face-to-face rep visits	Customer service calls	Loans/commercial manager			
Site/plant visibility	Brand's literature				Promotional support			
Prospecting					am phone call			
Charity involvement					Customer audit			
Social media					Face-to-face visit			
					Favourable credit/ increase limit			

Moments of truth

- Critically important
- Extremely important
- Very important
- Important

SOURCE B2B International (2016)

In the example in Figure 18.1, the moments of truth that are important have been identified by light and dark shading. The company is a supplier of construction materials. It wouldn't matter whether the company was an airline, a manufacturer of metal parts, a retailer or a professional service company, the spine of the CJM (that goes from left to right at the head of the map) is likely to have similar headings. There is always a stage of awareness leading to interest, and a build-up of knowledge before due consideration is given to making a purchase from the company.

Once the outline map of the spine and the moments of truth have been laid out, it is then necessary to revisit the map, identifying moments of truth that are weaknesses/pain points and those that are strengths/delights. In this way, the CJM will point to moments of truth that need improving and so lead to actions.

A company developing a customer journey map could carry out customer research to identify the stages and the moments of truth. While useful, this is not always essential. A cross-functional team representing different parts of the company, perhaps weighted towards sales and marketing, could produce an excellent CJM without any customer interviews. In workshop fashion the team would debate and agree on all the points of the journey and where the company is strong and weak. Members of a company know very well their weak points, in fact they tend to overstate them.

The steps that could be involved in producing a customer journey map are shown in Table 18.1.

The origins of the model

Jan Carlzon, the CEO of Scandinavian Airlines, wrote a book called *Moments of Truth*.[1] The year was 1987 and the book told the story of how Carlzon turned around the ailing airline SAS into a profitable company and airline of the year. He did this by focusing on all the small interventions (and big ones) that affected customer views of the airline and addressing these to make sure that the moments of truth never let down the company.

Over the next 10 years, various marketers picked up the concept of moments of truth and linked them into stages of the sales process, so developing the customer journey. Articles using the term customer journey mapping began appearing around 2010. Since then there has been an explosion in the use of the tool and it would be very hard to say who was the original inventor.

Table 18.1 Steps in producing a customer journey map

	Description of step	Action
Step 1	Agree on segment	Choose a target segment for the CJM
Step 2	Invite to workshop	Recruit 10 to 20 people to the workshop from different disciplines
Step 3	Run workshop	Run the workshop. Begin with an explanation of the CJ concept, the spine and the moments of truth
Step 4	Setting the spine	In the workshop agree on the stages of the spine
Step 5	Determining moments of truth	In the workshop have groups list all the moments of truth at each stage of the spine
Step 6	Establishing importance of MOT	In the workshop groups review each other's work to agree on the moments of truth and their level of importance
Step 7	Determining pain and pleasure points	In the workshop groups determine which of the moments of truth are pain points and which are delight points

Developments of the model

The original customer journey maps were a simple horizontal spine below which hung the moments of truth for each stage of the journey. Today the model has been refined with many additions. At each of the stages there may be the addition of any number of things that could add to an understanding of what is happening. For example:

- the needs of the customer during each stage (which could be separated into product needs and service needs);
- negative and positive feelings during each stage such as enjoyment, interest, excitement, relief, informed – as well as boredom, annoyance, anxiety, stress and confusion;
- perception of risk held by the customer or potential customer within the stage (high, medium or low risk).

In fact, the journey allows for almost any mapping of what is going on in the different stages – what different people want, what is important, what is done well, how different people feel. As with all such tools, it is better to start simple and map the key moments of truth and where the company is strong and weak. Refinements and validation can take place over time.

The model in action

Customer journey mapping is sometimes carried out as a one-off exercise or as a precursor to a market study. In the case of the building materials company for which the example is shown in Figure 18.1, a customer journey map was prepared in a workshop before the research began. It fulfilled three functions:

1 It brought together a cross-section of senior managers to think about their customers, their potential customers and how they are served by the company. In doing this it identified, before the research began, a number of actions and improvements.

2 For the researchers it highlighted the touch points that needed to be built into the survey. It helped the design of the questionnaire.

3 It linked the research project to the customer journey map so that managers in the business could see a course of action. The involvement of the managers in the mapping process meant that they took ownership of the research and it resulted in lots of successful initiatives and actions.

The workshop required a day of everyone's time and a few hours were spent afterwards turning the flip charts and Post-it notes into a schematic flow diagram that contained all the stages and moments of truth. This looked very much like Figure 18.1.

The customer journey was subsequently validated in the interviews that followed. The customer interviews resulted in a few amends to the map, after which it was turned into an infographic of poster size that was placed on walls around the building materials company. These posters provided visual reminders of the importance of delivering excellent experiences for customers throughout their journey with the company.

Besides acting as a synopsis of how the customer engages with the company, the posters were a catalyst in making everyone at the company more customer orientated. They formed a centrepiece as people stood around them and talked of yet more ideas as to how the experience for customers could be improved.

Some things to think about

- Define the spine of the customer journey. The starting point is nearly always AWARENESS, and the last point could be RETURN (i.e. indicating a lost customer returning to the fold).
- For each stage on the spine of the journey list all the interactions (touch points) between the customer and the company.
- Go through every touch point and mark it according to:
  - which are essential;
  - which are performed really well from the customers' points of view;
  - which are pain points for the customer;
  - which touch points customers would be prepared to pay for.
- Once the journey map is validated, turn it into an infographic and consider posting copies around the company to raise awareness of the importance of delivering excellent customer experiences.

Note

1 Carlzon, J (1987) *Moments of Truth*, Ballinger Publishing Company, Cambridge MA

Customer lifetime value   19

Estimating customer spend over their lifetime with the company

What the model looks like and how it works

The concept of customer lifetime value (CLV) acknowledges the importance of keeping a customer over a long period of time. The model is philosophically linked to customer experience, as keeping a customer for a long time means there is an implicit requirement for the customer to be continuously cared for. A company that seeks a lifetime value from its customers is not looking for a one-off sale. The model also plays to the fact that it is less costly to maintain a customer than to acquire one. So, once found, a company should do its best to keep the customer active for as long as possible.

The cost of acquisition of a customer will vary considerably from business to business. To make an obvious and dramatic point, Boeing and Airbus face an enormous cost in winning a customer compared to a baker's shop on the high street. The customer lifetime value model presupposes that the cost of acquiring a new customer by an aircraft manufacturer, a baker or any other company is known. This cost is not just the cost of the salesperson calling on a customer; it is all the costs associated with acquisition. This could include all types of advertising, both traditional and digital. Working out the average cost of acquiring a customer means assessing the total marketing expenditure and dividing it by the numbers of new customers acquired each year. This in itself is not a precise figure as some of the marketing budget will be aimed at maintaining existing customers.

The CLV model is especially useful to companies that have an extended relationship with customers – i.e. customers who continue to buy over a number of years. Some businesses are not like this. Although in theory the builder of homes could sell two or three homes to a customer in their life-

Figure 19.1 Profit/loss and sales during the customer life cycle

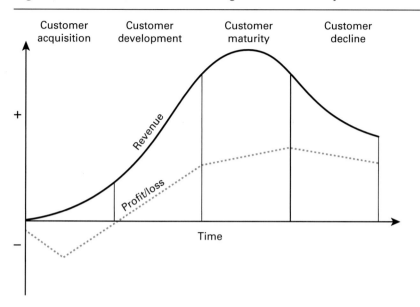

time, the chances are that the deal with most house buyers will be a one-off purchase. In this situation there needs to be sufficient profit in the one-off deal to cover all the acquisition costs. Our focus in this chapter is on companies that carry on serving customers over a number of years. It is worth pointing out that a person moving into a new house, while maybe not rushing out to buy more houses from the developer, offers a great opening for becoming a surrogate salesperson. If they have had a good experience in buying their property they may well recommend the housebuilder to visitors. This is a different model and is described in Chapter 38 – the Net Promoter Score®.

During the life cycle of a customer with a company it can be expected that sales will be slow during the initial period of doing business. Growth in sales to the customer will speed up until it flattens off and eventually stops or declines. Customers seldom last forever and on average they have a life cycle – a number of years during which they are active. When customers start buying from the company they may do so with trial orders. Once satisfied that the products meet their requirements, sales will likely increase. During the early stage of the life cycle, the newly acquired customer may not be profitable. This is illustrated in Figure 19.1.

A simple formula is used to calculate the customer lifetime value:

Annual profit per customer × number of years they remain a customer – the acquisition cost = customer lifetime value

This formula can be refined by taking into account the fact that a dollar earned in five years' time is worth less than a dollar in the hand today. Setting aside for the moment the complication of adjusting for the net present value, the simple formula for calculating customer lifetime value has three components:

1 The cost of customer acquisition.

2 The annual profit per customer.

3 The average customer retention rate.

The customer retention rate is calculated by knowing, on average, how many customers are lost each year. Assuming that a company loses 20 per cent of its customers a year (this is known as its churn rate) and it retains 80 per cent, we can determine that the average lifetime of a customer is five years.

We can now calculate the customer lifetime value. Table 19.1 shows how it would work with some made-up numbers.

This simplified model could be refined by applying a discounting rate to the cash flow during the forecast years. It also assumes that the customer does not have any support costs once they have been acquired. If these are relevant, they can easily be built into the formula as a cost to be subtracted over the lifetime of the customer.

The CLV model can drive business strategy:

- The CLV can help segment customers. Analysing customers by their lifetime value may indicate that there are some groups of customers that are highly profitable over their lifetime and some that are not. A profile of profitable segments could indicate what types of customers should be acquired in the future.

- Linking the CLV with share of wallet could identify customers with a high lifetime value and a low share of wallet. These would be obvious targets as the low share of wallet suggests an opportunity to win more sales.

Table 19.1   A simple calculation of customer lifetime value

Cost of acquiring the customer	$200
Net profit per customer per annum	$600
Average lifetime in years	5 years
Customer lifetime value	$2,800

- The CLV analysis may show that customers that arrive by different channels have different lifetime values and this could be another pointer as to where to focus for improved profitability.

- The CLV could identify a segment of customers that have been loyal over a number of years. This could lead to the development of a special loyalty scheme to reward them and to ensure that they do not go elsewhere.

- The CLV may indicate that it is worth spending more on acquiring a customer even though this would result in higher upfront costs. The extra acquisition cost will be justified if it can be shown that the customer will carry on buying products well into the future. The analysis could point to the justification for more marketing activities in order to improve the CLV.

- The CLV could be useful in improving customer relationship management and customer experience. If it can be shown that additional communications during the lifetime of a customer generate more sales, the customer lifetime value will increase and the customer experience will be enhanced.

The challenge in calculating the customer lifetime value is obtaining realistic data on the profit generated by a customer in his or her lifetime. This requires suppositions to be made on the future behaviour of the customer. Will they continue to buy the same amount of product? Will they buy through the same channel and, if not, how will this change the costs of maintaining the customer?

The origins of the model

CLV first emerged in 1988 in a book entitled *Database Marketing*, by R Shaw and M Stone.[1] The model has been quickly and widely adopted by many consultants. Calculating CLV analysis is now standard procedure amongst most large retailers, though it is still to be widely adopted in B2B markets.

Developments of the model

The simple CLV model described in this chapter is the one that is most frequently used. As has been pointed out, it does not take account of the fact that money in the future will be worth less than it is today and requires adjusting to net present value using a discount rate. Accountants are very familiar with these types of adjustments whereas marketers are not.

The biggest problem with the CLV model is the assumption that customers will carry on buying as they always have done. For example, a baker may acquire a customer who visits the shop once a week and at first just buys a loaf of bread. But what if this customer can be persuaded to call in three or four times a week to buy confectionery products? This build-up of business may not happen for a number of weeks or months and so there needs to be some additional sophistication to show how, on average, a customer's spend changes during their lifetime.

The model in action

CLV metrics have an important part to play in businesses that are relationship focused. They are also appropriate where a business has a high churn rate as it could indicate the importance of spending more money on customers to reduce the churn and improve their lifetime profitably. Such businesses include fitness gyms, telecommunications, airlines, banking and insurance services, and many companies in the B2B sector. Through a CLV analysis it will become clear that products and services with apparently low values mount up over time and may well justify a significant promotional spend to persuade customers to start transacting and become a lifetime customer.

Consider a company that runs a gym. A typical gym member spends $20 per month for three years before they cancel their membership. This means they will have generated $720 in total revenue over the lifetime of this membership. Knowing the lifetime value of an average customer, the gym owner can take a view that it could be worth spending $200 per customer to draw them in as a member. Free starter membership and promotions could be offered for this purpose. If in 18 months' time the gym installs a buffet bar that sells snacks and drinks, this would almost certainly be used by the gym member and make additions to the lifetime value of the customer. When an offer changes in this way, the model should be adjusted to account for the extra revenue.

Some things to think about

Calculate three important metrics:

- **Profit per customer:** work out the average revenue per customer and, crucially, the net profit per customer.

- **Average lifetime:** work out how long a customer stays a customer.
- **Acquisition cost:** work out how much it costs to win a customer by adding up all your annual marketing costs and dividing it by the number of new customers you acquire in a year.

Work out the lifetime value of your customer based on:

Customer lifetime value = (Profit per customer × Average lifetime of customer) – Acquisition cost per customer

Now figure out which metric(s) you can change to improve the customer lifetime value.

Note

1 Shaw, R and Stone, M (1988) *Database Marketing*, John Wiley & Sons, New York

Customer value proposition 20
Creating a compelling purchase motive

What the model looks like and how it works

Every company has an offer. The offer is in the form of products or services or a mixture of both. It is what a company sells. Almost always this offer is sold into a competitive environment. Successful companies are good at selling their products or services against the competition. They do this with strong sales arguments advancing the reasons why their product is the best and why it should be purchased. This has always been the case in commercial environments.

What is relatively new is the way we think about an offer. Sales-orientated companies see their products and services as stock, something that needs to be sold in order to make a profit. They focus on the here and now. They watch their sales on a daily or weekly basis, all the time checking to see whether they are hitting budget. There is nothing wrong with this, it is fundamental to most businesses. However, it has its dangers. The pressure to achieve immediate sales may lead to high levels of persuasion, so much so that customers are induced to buy something that they don't really need. The sales teams, faced with aggressive budgets, may exaggerate the benefits of the product to meet their weekly targets.

Price is an important driver in a sales-orientated company and the sales teams will always be looking to do a deal. The focus on pushing products at any price may force prices down and squeeze profits. Sales-orientated companies put themselves in danger of becoming more interested in getting rid of their products rather than meeting the needs of their customers.

Marketing-orientated companies take a longer view. They seek to understand the needs of the market and to develop products and services that satisfy those needs. They want their customers to come back for more. Marketing companies sell the sizzle rather than the steak. They push the benefits of their products and services and not just the features. Crucially, they aim to sell value. They want their customers to feel that the products and services they have bought are good value so that they become long and loyal advocates.

It is the philosophy of marketing that has led to the term customer value proposition (CVP). This rather pretentious term refers to the offer with the emphasis on the words 'value' and 'proposition'. There is recognition that products and services present a proposal to a customer – possibly a solution to a problem; certainly something to meet a need. Very often the CVP is a promise of a reward if the purchase is made. These components of the CVP are all the things that are valued by customers and for which they will pay a premium.

Communicating products and services as value propositions gives the customer a reason to buy and justifies the price. A good CVP will differentiate a product and give it a competitive edge. There are a number of steps in developing a CVP and these are shown in Figure 20.1.

Below are some templates that can be used to complete each step:

Step 1: agree the segments to be targeted with the CVP

Use a directional policy matrix that considers the attractiveness of your CVPs against each segment you serve. In the example in Figure 20.2, segment 4 looks as if it should be deselected on the grounds that it is not attractive and your position is very weak. This may be the case but before such drastic action with a large group of customers (indicated by the size of the circle) consideration should be given to see if there is any means by which the CVP for the segment could be changed to improve its position. So too, the directional policy matrix draws attention to segments 2 and 3 where changes to the CVPs for the segments could either make them more profitable or move them into the north-east corner. Segment 1 is most certainly a target even though the revenue from these customers is smaller than the other segments.

Step 2: consider personas to be targeted

List all the people in the decision-making unit responsible for choosing a supplier (Table 20.1). Indicate the influence they have on choosing a supplier so that it becomes apparent who are the key decision makers.

Figure 20.1   Steps in designing a customer value proposition

Step 1	Agree the target audience	Establish the segments for which CVPs are required. The aim will be to develop a separate CVP for each segment.
Step 2	Agree the personas who will be targeted within the segments	Each segment will address a decision-making unit (DMU) made up of different personas. Who is the main decision maker in each DMU for each segment?
Step 3	Determine the demographic characteristics of the principal persona in the segment	Establish the title, seniority, age, gender, lifestyle, personal interests, etc of the principal persona in the segment. Give this person a name. Make them real!
Step 4	Establish the behaviour of the principal persona in the segment	Establish the key behavioural characteristics of the principal persona in the segment. Do they stay loyal to their suppliers or switch? Do they use a number of different suppliers? How frequently do they have contact with their suppliers? Etc.
Step 5	Establish the needs of the principal persona in the segment	Establish the key needs of the principal persona in the segment. Give separate consideration to their functional needs from the product, their service needs that support the product, and their intangible needs (e.g. brand, reputation, corporate image). What is the ranking of importance of these different needs in driving the choice of supplier? Which of these needs are basic (hygiene) and which are 'defining needs' – those that are special and different for this persona in the segment?
Step 6	Compare the performance of key suppliers on the needs	List all the key suppliers including your own company and rate each on a score out of 10 for their performance on the various important needs.
Step 7	Plot the needs of customers against your comparative advantage	On an XY graph, plot the needs of customers against your comparative strengths. Those factors that are important needs and where you have a strength should be the backbone of your CVP. What can you offer the customer that they value and what can you offer them that is better than the competition?
Step 8	Create a banner headline	What would you say to a customer if confronted by the elevator test?
Step 9	Pass the CVP through the 3D test	Rate your CVP in terms of it being desirable (i.e. it gives people what they want), distinctive (i.e. it looks special and gives someone a reason to buy), and defensible (i.e. you have proof points to justify your claims).

Figure 20.2 Directional policy matrix used to select a target segment

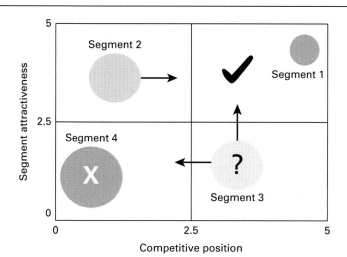

Step 3: build a portrait of the key decision maker

It is important to understand what makes the key decision maker tick. Give this person a name and suggest their demographics. It is important to aim the CVP at somebody rather than just anybody (Figure 20.3).

Step 4: establish the behaviours of the key decision maker

Now look at how the key decision maker behaves in their job. Questions to ask are (the list is not exhaustive):

- How many suppliers do customers use for the product in question?

- How loyal are customers to suppliers? What is their switching behaviour?

- What frequency of contact do customers want from suppliers? What type of contact are they looking for?

- To what extent are customers controlling of suppliers?

- How accessible are customers when an attempt is made to set up a meeting?

Table 20.1   Titles of people in the DMU and their influence: example

Titles of people in the DMU	Percentage of influence on the choice of supplier
Technical Manager	60%
Procurement Manager	30%
Production Manager	10%
Total	**100%**

Figure 20.3   Create a persona as a target

My name: ....

I work at .... where my job is .... I am .... years old and have been at the company .... years. I have a wife, three kids and a dog. What keeps me awake at night is ....

In five years time I hope to have achieved .... at my company.

The company where I work values .... above all else. When I look for a supplier, I look for one that is ....

I guess what my colleagues say about me when I am not in the room is ....

Step 5: establish the needs of the key decision maker

Following on from the behaviours, now answer the following questions on the needs of the key decision maker:

- What are the primary needs of this person?
- What are the unmet needs of this person or those needs that are not totally fulfilled?
- What would be the 'nice to haves' that would make this person feel better?

Figure 20.4 Comparison of CVP with the competition

Questions that need answering	Our performance in meeting needs (score out of 10)	Competitor 1 (score out of 10)	Competitor 2 (score out of 10)	Competitor 3 (score out of 10)
Primary needs:				
1._____	_____	_____	_____	_____
2._____	_____	_____	_____	_____
3._____	_____	_____	_____	_____
4._____	_____	_____	_____	_____
5._____	_____	_____	_____	_____
Unmet needs:				
1._____	_____	_____	_____	_____
2._____	_____	_____	_____	_____
3._____	_____	_____	_____	_____
4._____	_____	_____	_____	_____
5._____	_____	_____	_____	_____
'Nice-to-have' needs:				
1._____	_____	_____	_____	_____
2._____	_____	_____	_____	_____
3._____	_____	_____	_____	_____
4._____	_____	_____	_____	_____
5._____	_____	_____	_____	_____

Figure 20.5 Grid to work out which features/benefits should be included in the CVP

Think twice before including any needs that fall in these squares in our CVP. If they are to work in our CVP we need to improve our competitive advantage on these needs.

Competitive advantage (5 is best)

Important need (5 is most important)

Whatever is in the squares in this shaded area is a candidate for our CVP

Figure 20.6 Building the elevator pitch for the CVP

Headline	The elevator pitch
Target audience	For you dear customer...
Value	... we know you value xxx...
Superior	... and our product is the best on the market because xxx...
Profit	... which means you will benefit by xxx...
Call to action	... let me suggest the next step is xxx.

Figure 20.7   Checking the CVP against the 3Ds

To what extent is the CVP	Score out of 10	In what way is it... ?
Desirable (does it meet what people want?)		
Distinctive (in what way does it stand out from other companies' CVPs?)		
Defensible (what 'proof points' have we got that it will do what we say?)		

Step 6: compare your company against the competition

A CVP should present the offer as distinct from the competition. In this step the needs and unmet needs of customers are listed and the performance of a company's offer in meeting these is measured against the competition (Figure 20.4).

Step 7: needs that resonate and are differentiated

The top five needs required by customers are now plotted against how the company performs against the competition in meeting those needs (Figure 20.5).

Step 8: build a banner headline

A CVP should resonate with customers and be short and snappy. The CVP must cut through the noise that is made by other companies that are talking to customers at the same time. To arrive at this pithy description of the CVP, build an elevator pitch by completing the blanks in Figure 20.6.

Step 9: pass the CVP through the 3D test

The CVP needs to be challenged to ensure that it delivers against its promise. If it receives a score of less than 8 out of 10 on any of the 3Ds – desirable, distinctive, defensible – it will be necessary to rework and improve them (Figure 20.7).

Step 10: launch, monitor and adjust the CVP

The CVP will need to be communicated internally so that everyone within the company uses it in the same way. Consideration needs to be given as to how it will be presented to customers on the website and in marketing materials. Responsibility needs to be given to people for each implementation task together with deadlines. As always, there is the need to measure, monitor and adjust the CVP to make sure that it stays aligned with customers' needs.

The origins of the model

In the early 1940s Rosser Reeves of the advertising agency Ted Bates & Company coined the concept of a unique selling proposition (USP). This referred to the unique benefit that a product or service offered to its customers. The USP provided a focus to advertising campaigns throughout the 1950s and 1960s. It was not until 1961 that Reeves formally presented his theory of the USP in his book *Reality in Advertising*.[1] Marketers were encouraged to think carefully about the needs of their customers and how their products could be differentiated from the competition.

The concept of customer value propositions had its genesis in the 1980s under Ray Kordupleski who later published *Mastering Customer Value Management*.[2] The emphasis changed from picking out points of differentiation to determining what customers value. This has been explored by many subsequent authors, including Al Ries and Jack Trout in *Positioning: The battle for your mind*.[3]

Developments of the model

In the early days of developing CVPs, managers, in their eagerness, listed the many benefits that they believed their offering delivered to customers. Inevitably this weakened the CVP as there was no indication as to the key differentiating features, the ones that really mattered. In many respects this was a step backwards from the unique selling proposition.

This led to the development of value propositions that featured favourable points of difference of the product or service relative to the competition. However, this was not perfect as a product or service may have several points of difference from the competition and yet it may not be clear which differentiating feature the customer really values. The final step has been to build CVPs that resonate and focus in that they pick out points of differentiation for those features and benefits that are valued by the customer.

The model in action

James Anderson, James Narus and Wouter van Rossum wrote an article 'Customer value propositions in business markets' in the *Harvard Business Review* in 2006.[4] They told the story of a manufacturer of speciality resins that are used in architectural paints (i.e. those used on buildings). The manufacturer of resins produced a high-performance product that would better meet the strict environmental standards that were being introduced.

As is often the case, this new product had a higher cost of production and would need to be sold at a higher price. The sales teams at the resin company did not believe that the CVP of a more environmentally friendly product would carry a premium price. In order to validate the CVP, market research was carried out.

The sales teams' concerns proved to be correct. Painting contractors said that their prime requirement from paint is that it should cover an area quickly, the paint should dry quickly and it should be durable. Environmental improvements were 'nice to have' but not a key driver of decisions.

The resin manufacturer went back to the drawing board and developed a product with a faster drying time that allowed two coats to be applied during a single eight-hour shift. This improved productivity on the part of the painting contractors and meant that a price premium was justified. The new resin was launched with the CVP communicating the high level of productivity and with a secondary mention that it would be environmentally compliant. The new product was enthusiastically accepted with a 40 per cent price premium over traditional resin products.

Some things to think about

- Have in mind a very clear persona of the target for your customer value proposition.
- When developing your customer value proposition, focus on just one or two of the most important benefits or features of your product. Don't present the customer with a laundry list that will dilute the importance of all the attributes.

Notes

1 Reeves, R (1961) *Reality in Advertising*, Alfred A Knopf, New York
2 Kordupleski, R (2003) *Mastering Customer Value Management: The art and science of creating competitive advantage*, Pinnaflex Educational Resources, New Jersey
3 Ries, A and Trout, J (1982) *Positioning: The battle for your mind*, Warner Books, New York
4 Anderson, JC, Narus, JA and van Rossum, W (2006) Customer value propositions in business markets, *Harvard Business Review*, March

Diffusion of innovation

Launching new products and services

What the model looks like and how it works

We all love something new. New is one of the most powerful words in the marketing vocabulary. It promises improvements. It suggests excitement. Yet we all react to 'new' in different ways. Some of us cannot wait to get our hands on a new product. We love 'new' for the benefits it gives us and the status it conveys. Equally, some of us are fearful of 'new'. Experience has told us that it often does not deliver what we hoped and wanted and for this reason we prefer sticking to what we know.

It follows, therefore, that new products and services are not embraced by everyone in the same way. An innovation that is launched into a market is diffused rapidly to some people and slowly to others. In order to explain the process by which a new idea or product is accepted, several theories have been proposed, as set out below.

The two-step process

This theory argues that new products and ideas are accepted first by a small group of the population – opinion leaders.[1] These people are key to the diffusion of the new product – because if they like it, they will promote it and the general population will accept it. We can see this happening in certain markets where the voice of the opinion leader really does count. New cars are reviewed by journalists and their comments can have an enormous effect on the success of the launch. Theatre critics can make or break a new musical or play. Within companies there are gurus whose views on new products will influence people who work with them.

The trickle-down effect

Many new products are expensive in the first instance. Only the wealthy or the privileged few can afford them. This may give the product status in the eyes of the masses, who wait for the time when the price of the product falls and becomes more affordable.[2] The first mobile phones cost a relative fortune and were the size of a brick, but they were only available to those with a high income or a high position in politics or business. As the prices tumbled they became available to us all, including kids at school.

The diffusion of innovations

This theory was promoted by Everett Rogers,[3] who argued that any new product would be received in a different way by five groups of people:

- **Innovators (accounting for 2.5 per cent of the population):** a group of people who are always eager to be first to own a new product. These people are risk takers and want to be seen as leaders.

- **Early adopters (accounting for 13.5 per cent of the population):** this is an educated group of people, often young rather than old. They are leaders in their social environment.

- **Early majority (accounting for 34 per cent of the population):** as the name of this group suggests, it addresses a mass market where informed people begin to adopt the product.

- **Late majority (accounting for 34 per cent of the population):** eventually the product is accepted by a large but sceptical and traditional group of people, often made up of the lower socio-economic classes.

- **Laggards (accounting for 16 per cent of the population):** when everyone else has accepted the new product, those who have resisted it to the end finally give in.

Crossing the chasm

This theory assumes a gap or chasm between the different groups recognized by Rogers. The chasm theory was promoted by Geoffrey Moore,[4] who began life as an academic, moved into corporate management and eventually became a consultant. He argues that in the earliest stages of a product launch there is a significant gap between the innovators and the early adopters and the early adopters and the early majority. He sees the very first buyers within a market as technology enthusiasts who will buy anything new just to see what the products are like. These geek-like people may not have any or much buying influence within an organization and so it is important to engage beyond them and move the products into the early adopters. This may be easier said than done because of the chasm that separates the groups.

Technology acceptance model

This theory is particularly associated with new technologies in which the adopter would need to believe that it would enhance their job performance without a huge degree of effort.[5] For example, when computers were first launched, many people were fearful of the technology, believing that it would be a big effort to learn how to use these new tools and, to what effect, as they could do the job just as quickly in the traditional manner. The same could be said about software products, including dictation software, which, by the way, is being used to write this book.

It goes without saying that in order for someone to buy an innovative product they have to have knowledge of it. This means that the AIDA model (see Chapter 5) plays an important role in building awareness, interest, desire and action. The decision to buy the product is based on someone's belief that there will be a relative advantage compared to the product it supersedes. However, this is uncertain and many people are risk averse and so will postpone the decision until they have more evidence of its utility.

The diffusion of innovations

Rogers' model of diffusion has become the most accepted of the theories. In his work, he determined proportions of any population that are likely to fall into the different groups – innovators, early adopters, early majority, late majority and laggards. He proposed that the distribution of these groups closely follows that which we would expect in a normal bell curve. He split the five groups so that half the population is to the left of the curve (people who are early to embrace innovation) and half is to the right-hand side of the curve (people who embrace innovation at a later stage). However, the classification of the adopters is not symmetrical and there are three categories adopting early and only two adopting late. This is because research shows that innovators and early adopters can be recognized as exclusive groups whereas the laggards are homogeneous.

There are many innovations that simply never get off the ground. In order that an innovation can get traction amongst a large group of people, there needs to be a 'tipping point' – a proportion of people who find the new product attractive and in sufficient numbers to spread the word to the next group.[6] It is widely held that the tipping point exists between the early adopters and the early majority; that is, at the point where 16 per cent of the population have accepted the innovation. It is at this point that there is a chasm, which if not jumped, will mean that the innovation is in danger of atrophying.

The diffusion of ideas spreads quickly in some markets. This is the case in toys and electronic products, which quickly catch the imagination of people in sufficient numbers to pass the chasm and spread quickly through the wider population. There are many examples of electronic and digital products that have made multimillionaires out of their inventors in just a handful of years.

Many other products can take years to develop to commercial fruition. Carbon fibre was invented in the 1950s but its use was restricted to sports goods and limited applications for nearly 30 years until accepted in aerospace engineering. Even now, it will be many more years before it moves beyond the early adopter stage. In 2008, graphene was invented; a new material that is ultra-lightweight yet stronger than steel. A product such as this needs time to prove itself as suitable in different applications and also as a material that can be easily and cheaply mass-produced. It is likely to be many years before this passes through the whole diffusion curve.

The origins of the model

Diffusion was studied in the late 19th century, principally by anthropologists, geographers and sociologists. Marketers had for many years been interested in innovation but mainly for the purpose of promoting new products. They understood the importance of building knowledge, awareness and interest in innovations in order to create a curiosity that leads to a purchase. These models focused on the launching of innovations rather than exploring the beliefs and attitudes of a general population to innovation.

In 1957 Rogers completed a doctoral dissertation based on the usage of a new weed spray by Iowan farmers. This led him to propose the concept of different groups with different adoption rates. He later looked at innovations in a variety of other industry verticals and found a considerable commonality in his original theoretical framework. In 1962, while an assistant professor of rural sociology at Ohio State University, Rogers published the first edition of *Diffusion of Innovations*. It is now in its fifth edition (2003) in which he relates it to the spread of the internet and how this has affected the communication and adoption of new ideas.[7]

Developments of the model

The diffusion of innovations is now widely accepted as a viable business model. From its origins showing the diffusion of a new pesticide, it has been adapted to the fast pace of technology innovations in electronics and software. The focus of interest in diffusion has helped other researchers to understand the subject better. Researchers have pointed out that the diffusion of an idea does not necessarily mean that it is used continuously by the audience. Innovators and early adopters may be the first to try it and they may also be the first to abandon it and move on to something else that is new.

The model only explains the behaviours of a population with regard to a new product. It does not explain how to motivate that population to buy the new product. There have been many new keyboards developed that are quicker and arguably better than the old QWERTY keyboard, but none have yet gained traction with a wide population. Similarly the idea of speaking a common language around the world, such as Esperanto, might make a lot of sense but persuading large groups of people to use it has proved impossible.

The model in action

Many innovations are the repackaging of old wine in new bottles. These are not true innovations in the sense that they are discussed in this chapter, they are a presentation of the same product in a different form. Small tweaks and improvements that are made to products are not innovations in the way that they were described by Rogers.

Knowing that a population is made up of the five different groups of people from innovators to laggards is useful to marketers who want to develop new products or new value propositions. This opportunity was recognized by a large paper merchant that delivered to printers throughout Europe. The company carried out research to gauge the interest of printers in a range of new value propositions. These included different delivery options such as super-rapid delivery, night-time deliveries and deliveries at specified hours of the day. In the survey, printers were asked how likely they would be to buy additional services such as consignment stock, additional products not currently in the portfolio, and a variety of consultancy and advice services. In the same survey, respondents were asked to what extent they identified their company on the innovation spectrum suggested by Rogers. The questions were phrased so as not to bias the response:

Which statement best aligns with your company's views on new technologies?

- New technology is important to us and we would be one of the first to use a new product or service (classified as innovators).

- We are perhaps not the first users, but use new technology before most others (classified as early adopters).

- We prefer to wait until the early problems are worked out (classified as early majority).

- Our organization is not in a hurry to buy or deploy the latest technologies (classified as late majority).

- We would always wait as long as possible and only deploy new technologies when our existing infrastructure is redundant and there is no alternative (classified as laggards).

The distribution of printers in the survey mirrored closely the distribution suggested by Rogers in his 1962 thesis. Crucially, it was determined that a certain type and size of printing company was more interested in the new value propositions than others and this enabled the paper merchant to segment its customer base to offer service innovations where it knew they would be well received.

Some things to think about

- A useful segmentation of your customers is to understand where they sit in terms of the diffusion of innovation. This will enable you to promote new products and services where they will be more readily received.

- In B2B markets, radical innovations can take a number of years to gain traction.

- Aim to get your new products accepted by opinion leaders who will influence the rest of the market.

Notes

1 Katz, E and Lazarsfeld, PF (1955) *Personal Influence: The part played by people in the flow of mass communications*, Free Press, New York
2 OECD (2015) *Innovation Policies for Inclusive Growth*, OECD Publishing, Paris
3 Rogers, EM (1962) *Diffusion of Innovations*, 1st edn, Free Press of Glencoe, New York
4 Moore, G (2014) *Crossing the Chasm*, 3rd edn, Harper Collins, New York
5 Davis, F, Bagozzi, R and Warshaw, R (1989) User acceptance of computer technology: a comparison of two theoretical models, *Management Science*, 35 (8), pp 982–1003
6 Gladwell, M (2000) *The Tipping Point: How little things can make a big difference*, Little Brown, London
7 Rogers, E (2003) *Diffusion of Innovations*, 5th edn, Free Press, New York

Directional policy matrix   22

How to prioritize segments or new ideas

What the model looks like and how it works

The directional policy matrix (DPM) is a tool for guiding strategic policy. A company with a number of business units may want to know which deserves investment and which should be divested. Product managers may have a portfolio of products with different levels of performance and opportunities. Which of these products will be strongest in the future and are there any that should be dropped? The Boston matrix (see Chapter 10) is a useful tool for this analysis and the DPM is a variation of it.

Marketers find the DPM an essential business model for guiding their segmentation strategy. Not all customers are the same, but some do have similarities. The way that customers are classified according to their differences and similarities is 'segmentation'. A segment is a group of customers with common characteristics that are relevant to the product or service they are buying.

Segmentation is at the heart of any marketing strategy as it enables a company to more successfully meet the needs of customers and so satisfy them. Also, it is of great benefit to the company supplying the products and services as it is able to group customers together to meet their needs rather than treat them as individuals. As a result, the supplier benefits from greater efficiencies as well as gaining a competitive advantage by supplying groups of customers in a way that could give it a competitive advantage.

There are many different ways in which customers can be segmented. Common themes are as follows:

- Physical characteristics:
  - demographics: gender, age, geographical domicile, social class, income group, family size, etc;

- firmographics: (for B2B companies) the size of the company in number of employees and revenue, the industry classification of the company, the age of the company, its geographical location, etc.
- Behavioural characteristics:
  - customer or potential customer: or indeed if it is a lapsed customer or a returning customer;
  - buying patterns: frequency of purchase, amount purchased, bundles of products purchased, etc;
  - usage behaviour: amount of product consumed, how it is consumed, where it is consumed, etc;
  - supplier behaviour: single sourcing, dual sourcing, loyalty to a supplier, regular switching, etc;
  - decision-making behaviour: number of people in the decision-making unit, status of these people, key decision makers, influencers.
- Needs:
  - key requirements in terms of the offer: such as quality, durability, ease of use, availability, price, technical service, etc;
  - emotional needs from the supplier and brand: status, reassurance, excitement, safety.
- Psychographics:
  - lifestyle, values, opinions, attitudes and interests of the customers.

The aim of a successful segmentation is to discover groups of customers with common characteristics that are likely to be the most profitable or that have the highest growth potential.

The DPM is a tool to determine how to invest in different opportunities. It is very often used to show the strategic attractiveness of different segments but it could be used also for directing policy on brands, business units, new product opportunities – indeed almost any group of options that a business might need to consider. It is based on two factors – the position of the segment in terms of its prospects for profitability and the position of the segment in terms of its competitive position, as explained below.

Attractiveness of the market

The prospective profitability for a segment (or business unit, or product) is a major consideration when considering any future investment. Quite clearly, a low-profit opportunity would suggest no investment. There may well be some uncertainty about this prediction. If a competitor withdraws from the market it could change the situation. New or pending legislation that favours a segment or product could put a different light on things. These factors should be built into the assessment.

Other factors to bear in mind when assessing the attractiveness of the market would be the growth prospects for the segment, the number of competitors within the industry and their strengths and weaknesses.

Competitive capability

The competitive capability examines the company relative to other suppliers to the segment. Competitiveness will be determined by the strength of the customer value proposition of the company within the segment relative to competitors. The strength of the brand and the loyalty of customers could also be taken into consideration, as could its manufacturing units, their age and productivity, patent ownership, ability to innovate, etc.

When plotting market attractiveness and the company's competitive capability, it is worthwhile using a measure based on market intelligence. The use of a weight or rating will sharpen the positioning and become a metric that can be adjusted as things change. So for example, when working out the attractiveness of the market, a list is made of all the factors that make it attractive – growth rates, segment size, profitability, price elasticity, legislation, etc. Each of these is weighted in terms of importance. The segments are then rated (say using a scale from 1 to 5 where 5 is strong and 1 is weak) and a weighted score is devised. In a similar way, weightings can be developed for the competitive position. See Tables 22.1 and 22.2.

The DPM is a prioritization tool. The two dimensions of industry attractiveness and business strength help managers to focus on the key issues. It points to a strategic direction and therefore it is action orientated, hopefully leading to a more profitable company.

If the weighted scores are plotted on a grid where the market attractiveness is the Y axis and the business unit strength is the X axis, possible strategic directions are suggested. In the example taken from Tables 22.1 and 22.2, Segment 1 has a medium to high market attractiveness and a medium to high competitive position. This indicates an opportunity for investing and building the brand. Segment 2 on the other hand is positioned with a significantly lower score in terms of market attractiveness even though its competitive position is reasonably strong. This suggests a future strategy of harvesting the brand.

Table 22.1   Using weights and ratings to determine attractiveness of the market

Factor	Weight	SEGMENT 1		SEGMENT 2	
		Rating	Weighted score	Rating	Weighted score
Segment growth rate	0.45	5	2.25	4	1.8
Segment size	0.3	3	0.9	2	0.6
Segment profitability	0.25	1	0.25	1	0.25
Total score	1		3.4		2.65

Table 22.2   Using weights and ratings to determine the competitive position

Factor	Weight	SEGMENT 1		SEGMENT 2	
		Rating	Weighted score	Rating	Weighted score
Market share	0.35	4	1.4	5	1.75
Company profitability	0.2	2	0.4	2	0.4
Brand value	0.3	3	0.9	1	0.3
Dominance in market	0.15	2	0.3	3	0.45
Total score	1		3		2.9

Brands scoring low on competitive position but nevertheless situated in an attractive market could find it worth trying to find a niche in which they can focus. A brand that scores high on its competitive position but faces a market that is low in attractiveness could be worth defending and refocusing. As might be imagined, a brand facing a low competitive position and low market attractiveness should be withdrawn from the portfolio.

The origins of the model

In the 1970s General Electric (GE) together with McKinsey are credited with developing the first directional policy matrix.[1] The DPM proposed by GE and McKinsey is very similar to the Boston matrix based on the two axes of market growth and market share, except it is more nuanced in proposing different strategies. Namely:

- **High market attractiveness/strong competitive strength** – invest to protect the brand.
- **High market attractiveness/medium competitive strength** – invest to develop the brand.
- **High market attractiveness/weak competitive strength** – focus the brand on certain segments.
- **Medium market attractiveness/strong competitive strength** – build the brand selectively.
- **Medium market attractiveness/medium competitive strength** – harvest the brand.
- **Medium market attractiveness/weak competitive strength** – selectively focus the brand or harvest it.
- **Low market attractiveness/strong competitive strength** – defend or refocus the brand.
- **Low market attractiveness/medium competitive strength** – harvest the brand.
- **Low market attractiveness/weak competitive strength** – consider withdrawing the brand.

Developments of the model

The DPM has been widely used by consultants throughout the world and has been modified by many of them. Shell refined the GE–McKinsey model by using similar axes and modifying the recommended actions in the grid.

The model in action

A supplier of ready-mix concrete supplied 15,000 different customers per year. These customers ranged from large civil engineering companies building multistorey buildings, bridges, airports and the like through to very small builders who needed some ready mix for the base of a garage or the foundations of a house. The company commissioned research to find out the different needs and behaviours of its customers.

The findings from the research showed a number of different ways that customers could be grouped. The segmentation that was chosen was based on a mixture of needs and company size.

A segment that was considered highly attractive and where the company had a strong competitive position was where customers required a technical product. The building of a skyscraper or a railway viaduct needs concrete that is to a high specification. A good deal of technical advice goes into the offer and such customers are almost always large civil engineering companies. In fact, the ready-mix supplier had a high share of this business – and winning more would be difficult. It was a segment where it needed to maintain its leadership.

Although the 'techie' segment was a profitable sweet spot for the company, it was not the largest outlet for its products. Two other segments were served. One was made up of companies that buy a significant amount of ready mix throughout the year. These general construction companies used the ready mix for a variety of purposes and were demanding in their requirements. Delivery at an appointed hour was important, for otherwise the labour gangs that worked the ready mix were hanging around and wasting time and money. This 'value' segment was highly competitive. The ready-mix supplier could see from the research that there was an opportunity to differentiate itself from the other suppliers by offering a wider range of services to the segment. It added timed deliveries, special mixes and technical advice that could be bought by the hour. This improved the profitability of the segment and gave a competitive edge.

The third and largest group of customers by number were labelled 'small fry'. These were customers who had an occasional need for ready mix, usually for small construction jobs in residential properties. The segment was unattractive as the cost to serve was high, the growth prospects were limited, and the profitability was low. This looked like a segment to divest. However, after consideration and some experimentation, the company found that it could significantly increase its prices to the small-fry customers without losing much business. This made the segment more attractive and worthy of special focus (see Figure 22.1).

Figure 22.1 Using the directional policy matrix to guide segmentation strategy

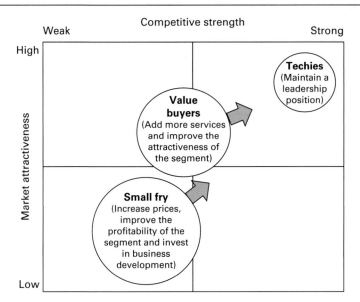

SOURCE After GE/McKinsey (early 1970s)

Some things to think about

- Use the directional policy matrix to focus your strategy.
- The biggest opportunity is usually associated with improving your competitive strength (as was the case with the 'small fry' and the 'value buyers' in Figure 22.1). This requires you to know your strengths and weaknesses.
- Use a SWOT in conjunction with the DPM.

Note

1 Coyne, K (2008) Enduring Ideas: The GE–McKinsey nine-box matrix, *McKinsey Quarterly*, September, http://www.mckinsey.com/business-functions/strategy-and-corporate-finance/our-insights/enduring-ideas-the-ge-and-mckinsey-nine-box-matrix (archived at https://perma.cc/ST34-D2X4)

Disruptive innovation model

23

Identifying unique ways of beating the competition

What the model looks like and how it works

Mature markets often have a small number of suppliers. These oligopolies become fat and lazy and may stop caring about their customers. Most of the care and attention is focused on large customers and it is not unusual that smaller customers are ignored. Such environments are fertile ground for disrupters.

A disrupter is a new entrant to a market who sees a gap left by the large incumbent suppliers. Usually the disrupter is small and eager to win business from anywhere. The smaller customers that are eschewed by the oligopolists are easy pickings for the disrupter. Indeed, the oligopolists do not notice or do not care when, in the first instance, small crumbs are taken from underneath their table.

The disrupter does things differently. They find ways of meeting the needs of the mass market, usually by producing a product or service in a more cost-effective way. The first motor cars did not disrupt the market for horse-drawn buggies. They were expensive and available only to a privileged few. Horse-drawn buggies were disrupted only when Henry Ford launched his Model T, which was highly competitive because it was mass produced to the simplest of designs.

Over time most customers expect the performance of products to improve and generally they do.

When incumbent suppliers in a market seek growth through innovation, they tend to focus on the middle to higher end of the market. These are customers with money. However, with these innovations the incumbents are in danger of producing products that are overspecified for the low end of the market and eventually for the mainstream market.

It is into this environment that a new entrant can be disruptive. The lack of interest that the incumbent supplier has at the bottom end of the market means that the new entrant's disruption will hardly be noticed and it will be tolerated in the first instance. The product offered by the new entrant might be of lower performance than existing products, which may themselves be overspecified for the needs of this bottom-end segment. The disrupter's products win sales because they are good enough and significantly cheaper. This allows the new entrant to gain traction and rapidly build up sales because it is addressing a significant part of the market. In a short space of time the disrupter can move from the low end of the market into the mainstream, by which time it is too late and too difficult for the incumbent to take retaliatory action.

Low-cost airlines disrupted the market, not only by taking business from the legacy airlines, but also by opening up air travel to people who previously could not afford it.

The dilemma for the incumbent is holding on to their profitable business. They are driven by the need to maintain profit margins and find easy pickings at the high end of the market rather than competing in the mainstream or the aggressive low end. It is for this reason that large companies set up separate business units to attack and disrupt the market. It would be hard for them to do so within the traditional set-up, which hates to rock the profitable boat.

There is a distinction between the disruption that takes place at the low end of the market by a more efficient supplier and one that better meets the needs than the products served by incumbents. A new importer offering cars with a better build quality or superior fittings is not a disruptor, it is simply a better supplier.

The origins of the model

The concept of the disrupter was introduced in 1995 by Joseph Bower and Clayton Christensen in an article in *Harvard Business Review* entitled 'Disruptive technologies: catching the wave'.[1] The model was originally described as disruptive technology but it was recognized that disruption may also take place in forms other than technologies such as a new entrant offering lower prices, a new channel to market, or a more efficient method of production of the product. Following the seminal article in *Harvard Business Review* in 1995, Christensen expounded his theory in what has become a bestselling book, *The Innovator's Dilemma* (1997).[2]

Developments of the model

The theory of disruptive innovation is easily understood and best described by case studies. Christensen, the academic father of the model, produced many subsequent articles and papers providing additional explanations. Those additional explanations were required because it is easy to become confused. Is a market that becomes disrupted by an entrant offering a new high-end, premium-priced product, one that is truly disrupted? Is Tesla disrupting the automotive market? There is no doubt that Tesla and electric vehicles have already disrupted the traditional automotive market. We can expect more of this with further new entrants as they have less to lose than long-established vehicle manufacturers. The theory of disruptive innovation argues that disruption begins with the low-end mass market though, as we are witnessing in electric vehicles, it can also trickle down from the high end.

Most of us would think that Uber and the effect that it has had on the taxi industry makes it a classic example of disruptive innovation. Christensen argues that Uber is not a disruptive innovator. He believes it is a company offering innovation in the sense that it represents incremental improvements to the existing taxi industry.

It seems to the author of this book that the precise definition of disruptive innovation detracts from the usefulness of the concept to marketers. It does not really matter whether the disruption begins at the low end of the market and moves upwards or starts at the high end of the market and moves down. Either way, the innovation is disruptive of the traditional market. 3D printing has not yet disrupted the market but it may well do so in years to come as it becomes a much more cost-effective method of producing components.

The model in action

There are many examples of disruption:

- Traditional encyclopaedias have been disrupted by Wikipedia.
- Traditional telephone companies have been disrupted by Skype, WhatsApp and 'free phone' apps.
- Personal computers are being disrupted by smartphones.
- Lightbulbs have been disrupted by light-emitting diodes (LEDs).
- Metal, wood and glass have been disrupted by plastic.
- CDs have been disrupted by digital media.

- Traditional film has been disrupted by digital photography.
- Typewriters have been disrupted by computers.
- Short-distance flights have been disrupted by high-speed rail.

Disruptive innovation can in theory be the brainchild of any company. However, the drive to disrupt a market is much greater by someone who is not an incumbent. It is understandable that an incumbent will fear disruption because it threatens its position in the profitable market. An entrepreneur, a small company and a new entrant have less to lose. Their ability to invest in order to exploit their innovation may be limited but this need not matter. They are looking for a small number of people who will embrace the innovation – these are the innovators and early adopters in the diffusion of innovation model described by Rogers (see Chapter 21). The diffusion of innovation identifies hurdles that have to be overcome early in the life cycle of the product launch. These 'chasms' that need to be jumped between the innovators and early adopters and the early adopters and the early majority can be sticking points for a disrupter.

For many years, steel was produced in large integrated steelworks using the Bessemer process. These huge mills had a high energy cost associated with heating the blast furnace. Blast furnaces need to operate continuously and this can be a problem during periods of low steel demand because the furnace must be kept hot. At times of full production these steelworks are highly efficient. However, demand is seldom steady as it pulses around the world. This opened an opportunity for a new form of steel production – the minimill. Minimills use scrap steel as their raw material. The electric arc furnace used in a minimill is much more flexible and can easily be started and stopped on a regular basis. They do not need to produce the massive volumes of the integrated mill. Minimills can be located close to a point where there is a high demand for steel. Integrated steel mills are under pressure to locate close to supplies of energy and raw materials.

The minimill disrupted the traditional market for steel production. It began producing simple products such as reinforcing bar and, since the late 1980s, has produced steel strip. This enabled companies such as Nucor in the United States to rise quickly from nowhere in 1968 to become one of the world's largest steel producers.[3]

Large corporations know the threat of disruptive innovation. They nearly all have research and development programmes that are aimed at discovering a profitable disruption. We can imagine the difficulty that a large manufacturer of lightbulbs would face if its research and development department invented the everlasting bulb. Would it hide the technology or would it launch it and disrupt its own profitable business?

Companies such as Google have business units aimed at launching disruptive technologies. They are big enough and rich enough to do so and they still maintain an entrepreneurial spirit. More traditional companies find it difficult and may deal with the disruptive innovation threat by making acquisitions of small companies that offer promising innovations that could gain traction in the market.

Some things to think about

- To be a successful disrupter you usually need to have a low-cost solution that can attack the bottom end of the market. Disruptors offer cheaper products and they also offer innovative products. The Dollar Shave Club is not only cheaper, it is delivered by mail.

- An incumbent company can best protect itself by setting up a stand-alone separate unit. Dow Corning protected itself in the silicone market by launching an online source of silicones called Xiameter (see Chapter 45).

Notes

1 Bower, JL and Christensen, CM (1995) Disruptive technologies: catching the wave, *Harvard Business Review*, January–February
2 Christensen, CM (1997) *The Innovator's Dilemma: When new technologies cause great firms to fail*, Harvard Business Review Press, Boston
3 Chavez, L (1981) The rise of mini-steel mills, *New York Times*, 23 September

Edward de Bono's six thinking hats

24

Brainstorming problems and generating new ideas

What the model looks like and how it works

The six thinking hats framework is employed to make meetings more efficient and more valuable. The model was devised by Edward de Bono.[1] He argues that the thinking that takes place in meetings is often confused. There is too much information, too many emotions, and people try to do too much at once. He proposes separating out these confused thoughts by applying the concept of six thinking hats. The metaphor of putting on a hat that is associated with a certain thought process focuses thinking in a defined direction. Each hat has a colour and the colour maximizes the sensitivity of thought in a specific direction.

The six thinking hats are used for idea generation (such as new product development) and problem solving (such as how to improve customer loyalty). The hats are a device that channels thoughts in a particular direction and so discovers ideas that may not otherwise arise. By limiting the amount of time spent on each hat, the meeting is much more effective.

De Bono's hats are symbols that indicate a particular way of thinking. When a colour of hat is donned, it channels thinking in a specific direction. In this way, the wearing of a hat simplifies the thought process and it also allows a switch in thoughts. If someone has negative thoughts or a block in their thinking, it can be changed with the colour of the hat.

The six thinking hats framework works best when the people in the meeting understand the rules of the game and the meaning of the different hats.

People do not have to physically wear a coloured hat – although they could do. The idea is that they own the concept of the coloured hat and what it stands for. Team members wearing these coloured hats are now able to think clearly and objectively and look at problems from new and different angles. Most discussions are adversarial, with people arguing their different points of view. The Six Thinking Hats tool gets everyone thinking in the same direction as they don each coloured hat. In so doing, more and better ideas are generated. It is therefore a tool for creative and lateral thinking. The tool can be used for problem solving and also for new product development, building new value propositions, arriving at different segments, scenario planning, war games, etc.

The thought processes that someone would be responsible for if they are allocated a certain colour of hat are as follows:

- White hat: this is the hat of facts and figures. Whoever wears the white hat must consider the validity of the facts. What do we have? What don't we have? What do we need? How can we get it? Whose fact is it? Is it one that can be believed?

- Red hat: this is the hat of hunches, emotions and feelings. The people wearing the red hat must consider the place of emotions in the thinking process. With this hat they can share fears, likes, dislikes, loves and hates, and do not need to justify their thoughts. Feelings can be based on lots of experience and this could produce a very strong intuition.

- Black hat: this is the hat that prompts people to be careful and cautious. It points out difficulties, dangers and potential problems and as a result it prevents mistakes. The people who wear the black hat must play devil's advocate and suggest why something may not work. It points out why something might not fit the concept. It is not a negative hat but one that brings people to reality. De Bono considers it to be one of the most powerful of the hats as long as it is not used to kill ideas. The black hat can be brought out early on to see if there are any problems that need to be overcome and it can be used at the end to check that there are no insuperable barriers.

- Yellow hat: this hat is about logical thinking. Someone wearing the yellow hat would look at the feasibility and the benefits of an idea. It is associated with positive thoughts and optimism.

- Green hat: this is the hat of creative and lateral thinking. The people wearing the green hat need to be provocative, suggesting new concepts and alternative ideas. The green hat can be used at any stage in the process to get some new ideas. It is an antidote to the black hat, which says why things cannot be done.

- Blue hat: this is the hat of control and monitoring. The wearer ensures that the ideas remain focused and ensures that the guidelines in the model are observed. They drive the team towards the goal.

The hats represent a specific direction of thinking. This is the strength of the argument for the model because it focuses thoughts of a particular kind. Each hat may be used for a limited time before a new one is donned. Equally, a group broken into teams may pass a coloured hat from one group to another so that everyone has a chance of exploring the thoughts that are generated by that hat.

The hats can be used in different ways. The team could be broken into groups that are assigned different colours of hats so they work on the problem and put forward their thoughts in line with their assigned guidelines. Alternatively, if it is a small group, everyone could wear the same hat for a period of time and then move on to another colour. Someone working on their own could use the six thinking hats model to help their thinking.

The origins of the model

Edward de Bono was a physician, psychologist and consultant specializing in lateral thinking. He published the *Six Thinking Hats* as a book in 1985.[2] This followed a prolific career of authorship during which de Bono wrote papers and books on different ways of thinking and problem solving. He is known as 'the father of lateral thinking', a concept that he introduced in 1967.

Developments of the model

De Bono proposes that his six thinking hats model is flexible. Normally a session begins with the blue hat, which sets the goals for the exercise. It also ends with the blue hat, at which time the team can assess whether the goal has been achieved and agree on the next steps. The sequence of the other colours of hats is up to the team. Often the white hat follows the blue one, so that at an early stage ready knowledge can be shared on the subject. This could be followed by the green hat to generate new ideas. The red hat allows people to express their feelings about these ideas. The yellow hat raises discussion on all the benefits of the ideas before the black hat is introduced to warn of dangers and difficulties. At any stage in the process, one of the colours could be reintroduced. For example, feelings might change as the ideas are developed and the red hat could be donned two or three times to collect the new feelings.

It is advised that people do not spend too long wearing each of the hats. Quick thinking is encouraged and somewhere between two and four minutes per hat appears to be a recommended time for discussion. That said, it is not intended that the time period should be limited. If there is a good deal of background data on the subject, it may be that the white hat needs a much longer time allocation.

The model in action

Six thinking hats have been credited with successfully improving the efficiency of all types of meetings. A famous example is the use that Motorola made of the tool to develop a new high-tech hand-held device in the early days of computing.[3] The company carried out exhaustive research on consumers and, for a day, the team had white hat time as facts and figures on the market were discussed. The group then moved into a green hat session to generate new product ideas. These were evaluated using yellow and black hat thinking. Red hats then prioritized the best ideas. A successful product was developed and launched under the brand name Accompli. It was a mobile virtual office, something that has been replaced now by the iPhone and the Amazon Echo but which was highly successful at the time.

A major benefit of the Six Thinking Hats approach is the speed with which ideas can be generated and approved within teams. Compaq Computer used the tool on many occasions when considering new ideas.[4] Teams were given an outline of the overall goal and asked to prepare and present their ideas showing neutral details, facts, information, facts that are still needed, and the overall plan. The presentations by the teams took around 25 minutes and participants were surprised that the usual frustrating debates and arguments were significantly reduced. The success of the tool resulted in it being used across numerous divisions in the new Hewlett-Packard/Compaq conglomerate.

Some things to think about

- The six thinking hats tool needs a moderator. This person should be able to explain what is required, keep an eye on time spent wearing each hat to ensure that things move quickly, and make sure that the ideas are captured and recorded. This person would usually wear a blue hat.

- The team should return to a particular colour of hat if it is thought that more ideas can be generated.

- The six thinking hats activity can be made more fun if people wear appropriately coloured hats, or move to a place in the room that is a designated hat colour.

Notes

1 www.debono.com/ (archived at https://perma.cc/2EJC-8QPQ)

2 de Bono, E (1985) Six Thinking Hats, Little Brown and Co, Boston

3 https://angelmind.pl/wp-content/uploads/2016/06/Motorola-Lateral-Thinking-Six-Hats-Case-Study.pdf (archived at https://perma.cc/9JB3-QSRU)

4 http://leewardteam.com/wp-content/uploads/2017/09/case-study-hp.pdf (archived at https://perma.cc/636M-GF98)

EFQM excellence 25 model

Improving an organization's quality and performance

What the model looks like and how it works

The European Foundation for Quality Management (EFQM), based in Brussels, is a not-for-profit organization established with the purpose of increasing the competitiveness of companies. Central to this objective the organization promotes a model of excellence, which it believes drives competitiveness and quality.

The EFQM model takes a holistic view of an organization, which means that other models, more specific in their aims, can fit within it. The model accepts that organizations must sustain a healthy financial growth and that satisfied customers are essential to build a strong brand and loyalty. Customer satisfaction surveys, employee satisfaction surveys and financial results (for example) fit within the EFQM model.

Products and services need to be constantly developed and must deliver value to customers. They must be supported by excellent service. All this is achieved by the people within the organization and so attracting and training people is an integral part of the model.

The EFQM excellence model looks at the cause and effect between what an organization does and what it achieves – the premise being that if an organization wants to achieve a different result, it has to change something within the organization.

There are three integrated components of the model:

- **The fundamental concepts:** these are the pillars of a company that are required if excellence is to be achieved.
- **The criteria:** the ingredients of the excellence recipe and the results they deliver.

- **RADAR**: the control and monitoring process for ensuring excellence.

These three components of the model can be described in more detail.

The fundamental concepts of excellence

The fundamental concepts of excellence are the things that any company has to do to deliver superb quality and performance. They are the hygiene factors of excellence. They include:

- ensuring that the organization offers added value to customers;
- ensuring that the organization is environmentally friendly, sustainable and fits into the world around it;
- ensuring that the organization has the capability to respond to change;
- ensuring that the organization is innovative so it can continually improve;
- ensuring that the organization has the right ethics within its vision;
- ensuring that the organization is agile and quick in the things it does;
- ensuring that the organization has a culture of empowerment and nurturing talented people.

The criteria

The model shows how certain components of a company affect its results. The way an organization operates is through five 'enablers' and four 'results'. The enablers group and the results group each have an importance 'weight' of 500.

The enablers group

- Leadership (weight of 100) – it all begins here. These are the people who shape the organization, set its values and inspire people to perform.
- Strategy (weight of 80) – this is the way that an organization achieves its goals.
- People (weight of 90) – excellence in any company must have people who can deliver it. They must have the capabilities and inspiration to perform.
- Partnership and resources (weight of 90) – excellence requires an organization to have the right factories, offices or physical assets and the right suppliers and partners who can support the operation.
- Process, products and services (weight of 140) – a smooth manufacturing or production process is essential in any excellent organization.

The results group

- Customer results (weight of 200) – these are based on the satisfaction and loyalty scores that arise from customer surveys.

- People results (weight of 90) – these are based on the scores from employee perception surveys.

- Society results (weight of 60) – these are the scores that a company achieves from its sustainability programmes.

- Key performance results (weight of 150) – these are the financial results on sales and profitability achieved by the organization.

RADAR

The RADAR is the final part of the model and it monitors progress. It is an acronym of:

- Results: is the strategy delivering the right results?

- Approaches: does the organization have the right plan to deliver the results?

- Deploy: is everything being deployed in a systematic way to ensure the achievement of results?

- Assess and refine: is there a learning environment that adjusts activities should this be necessary?

The EFQM model is dependent on an organization being data driven with a business plan, regular reports aligned to the strategic plan, a feedback survey from customers, an employee perception survey and sustainability policies.

The model is promoted via EFQM, a not-for-profit organization based in Belgium, and which offers members' training, visits to companies operating the model and benchmarks for good practice.[1]

The origins of the model

In 1988, 14 European business leaders met with the intention of forming a European foundation dedicated to increasing the competitiveness of European businesses. The leaders represented (mainly) manufacturing companies such as Fiat, Volkswagen, Electrolux, Ciba-Geigy, Bosch, Renault,

British Telecom, Sulzer and Nestlé. They established the European Foundation for Quality Management in October 1989 and set up a team of industrial and academic experts to develop the EFQM model. The holistic model was designed to be applied to any organization regardless of size or sector.

Developments of the model

The EFQM model has been around for 30 years and is particularly strong in Europe where it originated. It claims to have more than 30,000 organizations using it.

The model is regularly reviewed to incorporate new ideas, concepts and learning. At the time of writing, the last revision was published in 2019. The aim has been to improve the agility of corporate structures so that they move quickly to adapt to the changing global economic environment. The latest adaption to the model encourages organizations to develop an entrepreneurial culture and provides a roadmap of questions and ideas to prompt improvements and change.

The model in action

The EFQM organization publishes many examples. The model appears to have found significant use in service organizations such as health care, public administration and education. However, it is also widely used in corporate organizations. An example is given on the EFQM website of Ricoh Deutschland,[2] a subsidiary of Ricoh Company Ltd of Japan. The company is a market leader in multifunctional printers and has a 20 per cent share of this sector in Germany. It has used the EFQM model to ensure high levels of customer satisfaction and loyalty. The company carried out customer satisfaction surveys and employee perception surveys to measure its performance. The customer satisfaction survey, for example, showed that an impressive 90 per cent of Ricoh Deutschland's customers would recommend the company – a significant result and one that is much higher than those achieved by other B2B companies. The high levels of customer loyalty mean that Ricoh has improved the renewal rate of contracts and, as a result, trading profits and sales have increased, making the company the most successful one within the group. It is a demonstration of the cause and effect of the model – improve the enablers and the results will follow suit.

Some things to think about

- Consider joining EFQM. It offers training in the tool and shares experiences amongst members.

- Central to the EFQM model are people. People play a key role as enablers. People are also an important part of the results (e.g. customer satisfaction, employee satisfaction). This has similarities to the service profit chain (see Chapter 49), which posits that profits start with an engaged workforce.

Notes

1 www.efqm.org/ (archived at https://perma.cc/5M3A-UA26)
2 https://centreforcompetitiveness.files.wordpress.com/2011/11/efqmexcellencein-action_awardsspecial.pdf (archived at https://perma.cc/Q972-KR2V)

Four corners 26

Analysing competitor strategies

What the model looks like and how it works

No company operates in a vacuum. Its success or otherwise is determined by its competitors. Understanding the competition is a fundamental requirement of any business as it develops its strategy. The four corners model, proposed by Michael Porter (see 'The origins of the model' later in this chapter), is a framework for analysing competitors and how they will react to losing or winning customers, price rises or cuts, industry shifts and environmental changes. It is a model that alerts management to competitors' actions.

The model identifies four elements that give insights into what motivates competitors to take certain actions. In the north-west corner sit the 'drivers'. These are the things that motivate a competitor to act in a certain way. In the south-west corner are the 'management assumptions' of a competitor. In the north-east corner are the 'strategies' of the competitor. In the south-east corner are the 'capabilities' of the competitor, including all its resources. These four corners come together to result in predicted actions that competitors will take given certain pressures:

- **Drivers**

  All companies are driven by something. Competitors have goals and it is important to know what they are. These goals will differ depending on the ownership of the business and its management structure. A privately owned company, run by a hungry and ambitious entrepreneur, may have very different goals to one that is a subsidiary of a global corporate organization.

  All companies have financial goals and these can vary. Some financial goals chase revenue and market share while others may seek the highest possible profit.

  Analyse all the drivers that motivate the competitor such as:

  - financial goals;
  - corporate culture;

- organizational structure;
- leadership team;
- business philosophy.

- **Management assumptions**

The way a company acts is very much driven by its management. The small cohort of managers will have a culture that influences their motivations and actions. This cultural positioning affects whether a competitor reacts defensively or aggressively to a shift in the market.

The leaders of the competitors will have different levels of knowledge about their markets. They will have their own biases and blind spots. These must be assessed in the model. For example, if a company believes it is a market leader and in a strong position it will most likely take price initiatives and expect other companies to follow.

Analyse all the management assumptions that motivate the company such as:

- companies' perceived strengths and weaknesses;
- company culture;
- attitude to competitive reactions.

- **Strategy**

Competitors will have strategies that can be recognized by their actions. Some will seek to differentiate their products and capture value, others may occupy a niche position, and yet others may choose to sell at the lowest possible price and exploit a cost advantage.

The way a competitor invests will provide an important clue as to its strategy. Investments will be made to varying degrees in production facilities, marketing or people.

Competitors will also have a way of working with suppliers, distributors and customers that will be important clues as to their strategy.

Analyse the following to see how the company acts in terms of its strategy:

- the business's differential position;
- where it offers value;
- where it is investing;
- relationship with the value chain.

- **Capabilities**

  The actions of competitors will in part be determined by their strengths and weaknesses. A company's financial resources, its marketing strengths and weaknesses, and its production capabilities will all influence how it acts.

  A company with patented products will be in a position of strength and act in a different way to one with no product advantage. The workforce skills and those of its leaders will determine how the company acts.

  Analyse the following to see how the company acts in terms of its capabilities:

  - financial strength;
  - marketing strength;
  - production strength;
  - patents and copyrights;
  - workforce strengths.

These four characteristics of a competitor combine to determine how it will react to changes in the marketplace. The model is therefore predictive, aimed at showing how a competitor will react in a given situation.

Prior to carrying out the four corners analysis it will be necessary to collect a good deal of intelligence on the competitors. Answers to the following questions are required in order to construct the model:

- What is the history of the competitor? Where has it come from and how has it arrived at its position today?

- What is the competitor's strategy in terms of its stated goals?

- How have the actions of the competitor changed over time? To what extent have they been variable or consistent?

- Who comprise the senior leadership team at the competitor, what are their ages and their roles? What are their backgrounds and what drives them? How risk averse are they?

- What is the financial strength of the competitor in terms of its revenue, costs and profitability? How has this changed over the years?

- What is the competitor's market share in the segment where your company operates?

- What are the resources of the competitor in terms of its facilities and fixed assets and their modernity?

- What is the size and structure of its labour force?
- What is the company's channel to market and how does this give it a competitive advantage, if any?
- What is the competitor's geographical footprint? In which countries is it strongest and weakest?
- What are the competitor's products and services? How big is its portfolio? How are the products differentiated and positioned within the marketplace?
- What is the competitor's brand strategy? What is the positioning of the brand and its strengths and weaknesses?
- What is the competitor's promotional strategy? How big is it? How is it broken down across the different media? Who are they targeting and with what messages?
- What is the competitor's pricing strategy and how does the company react to changes in other competitors' prices?

Answers to these questions will be necessary in completing the four corners of the model.

The origins of the model

Michael Porter, a professor at Harvard Business School, published his theories on how competitive forces shape strategy in the *Harvard Business Review* in 1979,[1] and subsequently in his book *Competitive Strategy* (1980),[2] in which he describes the four corners model.

Developments of the model

Companies have always used competitive intelligence (CI) to analyse their position in the marketplace. What sets apart Porter's four corners model is that it includes motivational factors that are likely to drive the actions of competitors.

Surprisingly, Porter's four corners model is not as widely used as his other frameworks. This could be because of the difficulty of working out the motivations of competitors. These are not always obvious and have to be pieced together from clues over a period of time.

The four corners model is often used together with a SWOT. A SWOT could be prepared on each competitor to show their strengths and weaknesses together with the opportunities and threats within the marketplace.

The model in action

In the late 1970s Rank Xerox monopolized the market for business copiers in the UK. The Japanese copier company Canon could see great potential in the UK, though they knew they would have to beat the mighty Xerox company. It would be difficult to do so if they faced the company head-on.[3]

Xerox had a global corporate culture. It was financially very strong. Its headquarters were in the United States from where it set out its strategy for dominating the copier market. It was driven to build and maintain a high market share in the UK.

The management of Xerox could rightly assume that they had significant strengths. They had the broadest product portfolio of photocopiers, the strongest brand name, and a salesforce and technical support that covered most of the UK.

It was difficult for Canon to understand Xerox's strategy in detail but the behaviour of the company suggested that it was committed very strongly to the largest economic region in the UK, which was the south-east of England.

Against this understanding of the four competitive corners of Xerox, Canon believed it had little chance of beating the company in London and the south-east of England. It therefore established itself in Scotland, a relatively small market compared to that in England but nevertheless one where it could build a position without a strong competitive reaction.

Focusing all its resources on Scotland, Canon was able to capture 40 per cent of business copiers in that market. This provided a springboard for launching into the UK. It attacked selected and tightly defined regions in England, gaining strength and a strong foothold. From these bases it was able to make a determined and successful push into London with the now established sales force and a mix of copier products at attractive prices.

This approach adopted by Canon is referred to as the 'Lanchester strategy'. It is named after Frederick Lanchester, a British engineer, and originated as a war strategy in which an easy prey is targeted to create a foothold from which a strong push can be made. It is increasingly used and referred to in business as a means of entering new markets.[4]

Some things to think about

- There are many visible clues in the marketplace as to what motivates the competition. The behaviour of a company is a good indication of its motivations.
- Competitive intelligence is vital when carrying out a four corners analysis. See Chapter 15 for a list of sources of competitive intelligence.

Notes

1 Porter, ME (1979) How competitive forces shape strategy, *Harvard Business Review* (March)
2 Porter, ME (1980) *Competitive Strategy: Techniques for analyzing industries and competitors*, Free Press, New York
3 Kapoor, V (2017) *What You Can Learn From Military Principles*, Bloomsbury India, eBook
4 www.investopedia.com/terms/l/lanchester-strategy.asp (archived at https://perma.cc/VNQ3-P6VY)

Gap analysis   27
Improving areas of weakness in a company

What the model looks like and how it works

The concept of gap analysis is simple enough. It is the identification of the difference between the current level of performance of a company and where it would like to be. The gap could be in a number of areas of a business:

- Performance gaps with customers: satisfaction and loyalty scores, delivery times, delivery in part and in full, share of wallet.
- Product gaps: gaps in the product portfolio.
- Segment gaps: groups of customers who are currently not served.
- Geographical gaps: regions or territories that could be supplied but are not at the present.

There may be many other gaps in a business such as resource gaps (shortage of certain personnel to do a job), technology gaps (absence of a technology or process that is limiting efficiencies) and intelligence gaps (lack of knowledge about the market), etc.

Performance gaps

A company can suffer a performance gap in its products. Competitors' products may last longer, work quicker and perform better. The performance gap that usually matters is that which is perceived by the customer. A good deal of business strategy is centred on understanding customer needs and making sure that they are met. Determining the gap between the customer needs and unmet needs is therefore crucial. Market research can provide this understanding by asking questions that determine the importance that customers attach to different attributes of an offer and the satisfaction that they have with the offer. High levels of importance and low levels of satisfaction on a particular attribute indicate a gap that needs to be filled.

Product gaps

A business may be limited in its growth because it has a product gap. For example, some people buy a brand of toothpaste for its taste, others look for teeth-whitening properties, some may want a product for sensitive gums. Toothpaste manufacturers have products to meet these various needs. A manufacturer may find itself in a position where it lacks a certain product in its portfolio. In the case of the toothpaste manufacturer, it may not have a product for people with sensitive gums. The manufacturer would embark on a programme to identify the size of the opportunity for the new product, the competitive environment and its ability to win market share. If all looks attractive, it would plug the gap with an appropriate offering.

Segment gaps

The example of the toothpaste for sensitive gums is both a product gap and a segment gap. There may be gaps that can be filled with an existing product. Manufacturers of disposable razors historically focused on men – an obvious market. However, women also have a need for disposable razors. Manufacturers found that the same products, possibly with handles that are pink instead of blue, can be sold to a new segment, significantly boosting revenue opportunities.

Cornflakes are traditionally eaten at breakfast time. However, a new segment could be developed by persuading kids and parents that it is an easy snack to serve at supper time, so expanding the overall market.

Territorial gaps

Businesses need growth to survive. Some growth is organic, driven by an increase in population size, greater wealth of a customer base and a healthy appetite for a product. Growth can also come through acquisition. However, there are many opportunities for growing into new markets. Gap analysis is frequently used to determine the potential market for a product. Take Coca-Cola, for example. In the United States an average of around 400 cans/ bottles of Coke are consumed per person per year. In China the average consumption per head is just 56 cans/bottles per year.[1] The consumption gap is more than 340 cans/bottles. There may be a number of reasons for this. It could be that alternative beverages are preferred, there could be deficiencies in the channels to market, there could be lower incomes that do not allow a high consumption, and there could be ignorance and lack of awareness of the product. That said, China, with a population of 1.4 billion compared to the 330 million in the United States, offers a huge potential.

At its simplest, the gap analysis model is about answering three questions:

- **Where are we now?** This is an understanding of the current state, which could be based on quantitative data such as customer satisfaction measurements, or qualitative data such as a feeling that there is underperformance in a certain area.

- **Where do we want to be?** This is a description of the future state in terms of what a company wants to achieve.

- **How do we get there?** These are the steps that will have to be fulfilled to fill the gap.

Answering the questions 'Where are we now?' and 'Where do we want to be?' can be assisted by other models described in this book. A SWOT analysis can indicate the opportunities that exist where the strengths, weaknesses, opportunities and threats intersect (see Chapter 54). The Boston matrix and the directional policy matrix could also be used to identify gaps and areas of opportunity (see Chapters 10 and 22).

Marketers have for many years used the importance/satisfaction model (ImpSat) that compares the importance attributed to aspects of an offer and satisfaction with those aspects. When the two sets of data are plotted, it indicates gaps and where attention is required (Figure 27.1).

Steps in gap analysis are as follows:

- **Step 1: identify where the problem lies**. This could be obvious and could have been identified by feedback from the sales team, customers themselves or from internal analysis.

- **Step 2: obtain a measure of current performance**. This could be from a customer survey, internal metrics, etc.

- **Step 3: determine what the performance should be**. This should be a target that will meet customers' expectations or possibly exceed them. However, the target must be realistic and achievable. It should also be a specific measure so it is possible to track and see if the actions are having an effect.

- **Step 4: determine a plan for how the gap is going to be filled**. Who is going to take action, what resources are needed and over what time period?

Figure 27.1 ImpSat chart showing where improvements are required

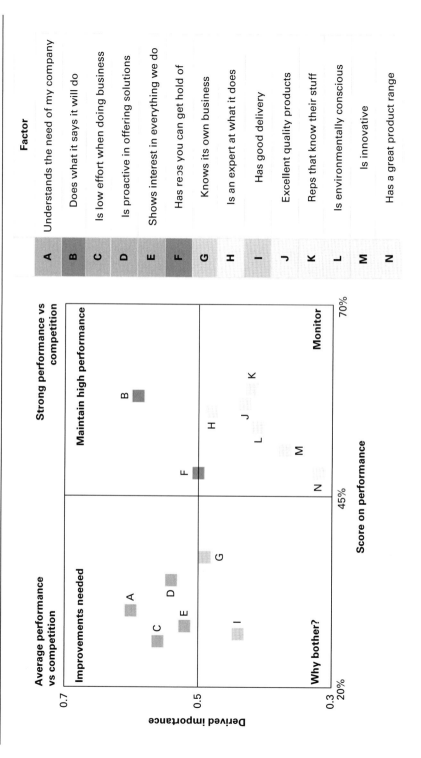

	Factor
A	Understands the need of my company
B	Does what it says it will do
C	Is low effort when doing business
D	Is proactive in offering solutions
E	Shows interest in everything we do
F	Has reps you can get hold of
G	Knows its own business
H	Is an expert at what it does
I	Has good delivery
J	Excellent quality products
K	Reps that know their stuff
L	Is environmentally conscious
M	Is innovative
N	Has a great product range

The origins of the model

Gap analysis is as old as the hills. People have always been concerned about improvements by assessing where they stand today against a target of what they would like to achieve. However, the term gap analysis is relatively new and was conceived in the 1980s by researchers at the University of Idaho, who were concerned about endangered birds in Hawaii. They took measurements of the numbers of birds and in 1989 set up a gap analysis programme (GAP)[2] aimed at dealing with the widespread habitat loss so that the bird population would begin to grow. It was the first time that the term was used in published form.

The ImpSat tool referred to in this chapter was developed in the early 1980s by market researchers who saw the power of linking data from surveys that determined the importance of certain attributes against satisfaction with those attributes. This led to the commercial application for gap analysis.

Developments of the model

Most of the tools and templates for gap analysis are in the form of spread-sheets that have various column headings – listing the problem, identifying the current state and a metric by which it can be measured both now and in the future. The tool is flexible and can be modified by the user who may want more or less detail, particularly about the action plan designed to fill the gap. For example, in Table 27.1 an extra column could be inserted to indicate the date by which the target metric will be achieved.

Table 27.1   Template for gap analysis

Problem	Current state	Current state score	Future state	Target future state score	Action
Price perception	Considered poor value for money	6 out of 10 in customer sat	Improved customer value proposition	7.5 out of 10 in customer sat	Training for the sales force on the new CVP
Delivery	Too many partial deliveries	80% on time and in full	Improved on time and in full deliveries	98% on time and in full	Invest in more stock
Etc					

The model in action

A manufacturer of specialist stainless-steel tube was concerned about losing market share. It recognized that it had problems with the availability of its product and it wanted to know to what extent this was responsible for the loss in market share. It commissioned a market research survey to establish the gap between its current performance and the ideal performance.

A survey was carried out on 200 customers who were asked a host of questions. The questions related to delivery are shown in Figure 27.2. In surveys of this kind, most ratings on importance and satisfaction fall within a 'corridor' of between 7 and 9 out of 10. The research findings showed that documentation is important but, on this factor, high levels of satisfaction were achieved. So too there was no problem with the efficiency of the order-taking staff. The main problems were the availability of the product, the flexibility in changing orders, deliveries on time and advance notice of any delays in delivery.

Figure 27.2   Gap analysis based on ImpSat findings

Sorting out the product availability issue required a substantial investment in new plant and could not be achieved overnight. However, providing a notice of delay in delivery had very little cost and could easily be implemented by the efficient order-taking staff. The company immediately trained the order-taking staff in providing explanations to customers of the delays and the reasons for them. Customers displayed a high level of loyalty to the company and appreciated the improved communication, which helped their own planning. The decline in market share was reversed.

Some things to think about

- The key to gap analysis is finding out what is important to customers and where your performance is relatively poor.

- Once the gaps have been identified, they should be sorted into quick wins (things that are easy to correct and improve) and those that need substantial resource and will take a long time. This will create a plan of action for improvements.

Notes

1 www.universitymagazine.ca/countries-that-drink-the-most-coca-cola/ (archived at https://perma.cc/2WAD-QY8E)

2 www.usgs.gov/programs/gap-analysis-project/history#:~:text= The%20gap%20analysis%20process%20itself,distribution%20of%20each% 20species%20individually (archived at https://perma.cc/6EHD-PJ34)

Greiner's growth model

28

Recognition and transition through different phases of company growth

What the model looks like and how it works

Companies want to grow. Employees expect and want salary increases and this requires growth. They want to work in an exciting and dynamic environment and this cannot happen if the company is static or declining. Furthermore, all environments change over time, which means that the option is either growth or decline. Very few companies stay static for long. Growth, therefore, is almost essential but it brings with it growing pains.

Growing pains can be financial. Rapid growth requires a good deal of working capital and it is possible for a company to run out of cash and go bankrupt even though it is growing quickly.

Growing pains can also be felt by employees. Employees say they want their company to grow but may be disturbed when the implications hit them. In a growing company, workloads increase and are stretching. Work practices change and need adjustments. New people come into organizations and this can disturb the status quo.

Greiner recognized these growing pains and developed a model that helps companies anticipate the problems so they can prepare accordingly. His model assumes phases of growth that are relatively stable. This stability does not last forever and towards the end of each phase the organization begins to sow the seeds of its own decay, which leads to another period of revolution.

Greiner identified six phases of growth that most companies are likely to face. Each of these phases has a dominant management approach that eventually becomes ineffective, leading the company into a period of crisis. The faster a company grows, the shorter the phase of growth. As the company deals with its crisis, it moves into a new phase and carries on growing. The six phases identified by Greiner are:

Phase 1: growth through creativity (crisis of leadership)

The founders of a company start small and are involved in everything. At this stage the company is young and small and communication is easy – one person to another. The organization is flat and everyone has access to the boss. As the company grows, it needs more people and more structure. Informal processes need to be formalized. The cavalier and maverick approaches of the entrepreneurs that started the company have to be replaced by professional managers. This change in style can create a leadership crisis. There is a need for an improved structure.

Phase 2: growth through direction (crisis of autonomy)

Formal procedures are installed in this second phase. There are budgets and targets to be met. The company expands its offer and people are overloaded with work. Delegation becomes a necessity but it has not yet become automatic. The founder of the business is still active and is a puppet master pulling all the strings, even though middle managers have been appointed. This phase ends with an autonomy crisis. There is a need for more controls.

Phase 3: growth through delegation (crisis of control)

In this third phase the company has recruited middle managers and the founder is able to delegate. Sometimes there is too much delegation to the divisional managers. The top levels of the company have a strategic view of where the company is going but they are not always strong in ensuring that subsidiaries and divisions are in line. New opportunities for growth may arise such as mergers and acquisitions. There is a danger that the managers of the separate business units head off in directions of their own, threatening a break-up of the company. It is a crisis of control.

Phase 4: growth through coordination (crisis of red tape)

The subsidiaries and business units have by now developed into profit centres and are becoming standardized. Their financial performance is tightly controlled and each can be judged in terms of its return on investment. The company may have a strong human resources department that has introduced profit-sharing schemes aligned to corporate goals. Controls have become tight. It is during this stage of growth that the company might find itself in a red-tape crisis.

Phase 5: growth through collaboration and cooperation (crisis of identity)

As growth continues in phase 5, new structures are introduced to manage the much larger size of the organization. The hierarchical structure of control is replaced by a matrix. Managers are involved in meeting after meeting. Enterprise software knits together the different parts of the company. There is a danger that this phase could see the end of growth for the company unless it can develop external alliances. The phase ends with a crisis of identity.

Phase 6: growth through alliances (crisis of growth)

Growth is still possible though now more likely through partnerships with other companies. Mergers, acquisitions and outsourcing take place. There is a danger that the business has become so large it is more focused on alliances than its core business and its customers. The old and the regional businesses are lost as a result of the obsession with outsourcing and acquisitions.

The origins of the model

Larry Greiner developed his organizational growth model and published an article entitled 'Evolution and revolution as organizations grow' in the *Harvard Business Review* in 1972.[1] His theory is based on the belief that organizations go through a sequence of stages at the end of which there is a crisis.

The Greiner growth model makes the assumption that organizations continue to grow throughout the years. It is not always easy to recognize in what phase of growth a company is located. Phase 1 is easy to identify but, as the company matures, the distinctions between phases 4, 5 and 6 become more difficult to recognize.

Greiner drew upon psychology and the behaviour of individuals in formulating his theory of evolution and revolution. He recognized that each phase began with a period of evolution after which steady growth and stability followed. He concluded that this stability could not and does not go on forever and each phase ends with a revolutionary period, often of turmoil and change.

In his seminal paper on the subject Greiner listed five phases of growth, with different organizational practices:

- **Phase 1: Growth through creativity**
  Informal structure with an individualistic, entrepreneurial style. The management is focused on producing and selling products. Moving products and making profits is key.

- **Phase 2: Growth through direction**
  More centralized and functional organization aimed at driving efficiencies. The management has become directive and started to set standards. Cost centres are established. Management is now rewarded with salaries and merit increases.

- **Phase 3: Growth through delegation**
  The organization is now decentralized as it expands geographically. Managers have to get used to delegating. Head office receives regular reports on performance and profits at its subsidiaries. Managers receive bonuses depending on their performance.

- **Phase 4: Growth through coordination**
  The organization starts to consolidate. It has a number of strategic business units all with their own line staff. Head office is occupied signing off investment plans. Managers are rewarded by profit-sharing and stock options.

- **Phase 5: Growth through collaboration**
  The organization is now complex and there is a matrix of reporting systems. This means that the organization needs to be participative and agree on the goals of its subsidiaries. Problem solving and innovation have now become important. Bonuses are paid to teams.

Developments of the model

Larry Greiner's original model had five phases. He added the sixth phase in 1998. This sixth phase reflected the importance of growth through acquisitions and mergers in the globalized marketplace.

Time is one of the greatest influences on an organization. Time sets managers' attitudes so that they become rigid and outdated, and makes future change more difficult.

Size is the other major influence on the organization. As a company grows, inevitably it faces different problems. Large companies have massive communication problems compared to small companies. Large companies need hierarchies and different levels of management.

So, both time and size are drivers of change and revolution.

Greiner's tool is useful if it is possible to recognize where the company is at the present. Recognizing the looming crisis will mean that people can plan for it. People also know what to expect, and so shock and surprise is not a problem.

The speed of change is likely to vary across different industry verticals. The phases move quickly in fast-growing industries compared to those that are mature.

The model in action

Understanding where a company stands at any point of time within these different stages of development is important. If leaders of companies are aware of which stage they are in, they will know the right way to act. There are numerous case studies identifying Greiner's phases with different organizations. However, they all look through the rear-view mirror, fitting Greiner's phases to what actually happened rather than showing how an organization used Greiner's model to adapt to future growth.

The model is one that should be used by leaders, as it is they who have to deal with the crisis at the end of each phase. Many small companies do not get beyond phase 1, because the entrepreneur who set up the company is not prepared to formalize anything or bring in professional managers. For this reason most companies remain small and hit a self-imposed ceiling of growth.

The entrepreneur is still on board in phase 2 but has not yet learned to loosen control. They are involved in everything and find delegation hard. Most probably the entrepreneur is a control freak and staff are frightened to take action without her/his approval. It is likely that a company in this phase is still classified as a small to medium enterprise, with up to 250 employees. The company could hit a barrier to growth if the founder does not release the reins. During this phase there is a strong danger that the overworked owner will suffer stress problems.

In phase 3 the founder has learned the art of delegation, probably too much because the managers of the business units now see themselves as the owners of the business. With this new power the trusted lieutenants – who have been with the company from the start and who are now senior managers – are pulling in different directions. They resent interference from the centre, and growth will stop or the company will fall apart if they are not controlled.

In phase 4 the pendulum swings in another direction, with tighter controls that demand all the business units stay in line. Now, as the company reaches a significant size, with many subsidiaries and acquired businesses, its mojo is lost and it has an identity crisis. It would not be unusual at this stage for the founder to leave. The bureaucracy and red tape that is necessary to coordinate the different businesses is too much and, in any case, after 20 or 30 years of running the company it is of a size when the founder can exit with a healthy payoff.

In phase 5 the company has turned corporate. It has begun to stifle staff with endless meetings as everyone tries to collaborate and coordinate. It eventually loses its identity and will stop growing unless it can find some means of entering phase 6 and become a global organization through suitable acquisitions and mergers.

Some things to think about

- The model recognizes that growth involves pain. If managers can spot the pain, they can prepare for the next phase of growth. Pain becomes something that they should embrace because it is an indicator of a growth opportunity.
- A thread that runs through Greiner's model is the style of leadership and degree of control that is imposed. Collaboration and communication is important at every stage and is a key to growth.

Note

1 Greiner, LE (1972) Evolution and revolution as organizations grow, *Harvard Business Review*, July–August

Importance-performance matrix

29

Improving the effectiveness of any business initiative

What the model looks like and how it works

This framework was proposed by John Martilla and John James and uses attributes that are measured in order to find out the importance of different aspects of service and how well they are performed. The framework is especially useful in assessing customer satisfaction. Various elements of customer service are rated in terms of importance and satisfaction and analysed in a grid that shows where to improve performance.

In a customer satisfaction survey various factors are chosen that are considered important to a company's business success. These may be determined by qualitative research with customers, by the management in the company, or they may be regular attributes that are used in a customer satisfaction tracking survey. Once the attributes have been chosen, a questionnaire is developed using a scale asking the importance of each.

In the framework from Martilla and James, customers were asked to state the importance of attributes using a five-point Likert scale. This is a verbal scale ranging from not at all important through to extremely important. Having established the importance of different attributes using measurements of this kind, respondents were then asked their satisfaction with the performance of the company on each. Again, a five-point scale was used.

The data is plotted on a grid showing which attributes need attention because they are important and have low performance. The grid indicates actions that are needed for the different attributes. Some will be high priority and need concentrated effort while others can be set aside for a watchful eye.

The origins of the model

In 1977, Martilla and James (respectively a marketing professor and a consultant out of Washington DC) wrote a paper in the *Journal of Marketing* called 'Importance-Performance Analysis'.[1] It was based on a study for a car dealer that attempted to find out how it could improve the loyalty of its service department customers. Fourteen attributes were measured to find out the importance of different aspects of service and how well the dealer performed on each. The results were analysed in a grid that showed where to improve performance.

Developments of the model

There is no rigidity about the 14 attributes suggested by Martilla and James. In customer satisfaction surveys, attributes should be used that are relevant to a particular company. The importance-performance framework has a lot of similarities to the SERVQUAL model that was developed by Parsu Parasuraman, Valarie Zeithaml and Len Berry, following research they carried out between 1983 and 1988. The SERVQUAL model similarly is designed to find out the match between a company service performance and customers' expectations. (See Chapter 50 in this book.)

The model in action

In their paper in the *Journal of Marketing*, Martilla and James listed 14 attributes that were measured in terms of importance on performance. As is evident from the list, they are relevant to the business of a car dealer:

1 Job done right the first time
2 Fast action on complaints
3 Prompt warranty work
4 Able to do any job needed
5 Service available when needed
6 Courteous and friendly service
7 Car ready when promised
8 Perform only necessary work

9 Low prices on service

10 Clean up after service work

11 Convenient to home

12 Convenient to work

13 Courtesy buses and rental cars

14 Send out maintenance notices

The measurements from the survey showed clearly the attributes that were important and which needed improvement. These were 'job done right the first time' and 'fast action on complaints'.

A number of attributes proved to be important and were also where the dealership performed well. These were attributes 3, 4, 5, 6, 7, 8 and 10 in the list. Because these were important to customers a clear action point was to keep up the good work. Also, since they proved to be strengths of the company, they could be used in building a differentiated brand – one that could be trusted and friendly to deal with.

Sending out maintenance notices and being in a convenient location didn't appear important to customers and therefore required no action.

Some things to think about

- What are the attributes that are considered important to your customers when they decide to do business with you or your competitors?
- What is the mean score of importance and performance on these attributes?
- When plotted on an importance-performance grid, where do the attributes fall and what actions do they suggest?
- How do these measures vary between loyal customers and not so loyal customers?
- What strategies are needed to bring the not so loyal customers closer on board?

Note

1 Martilla, JA and James, JC (1977) Importance-Performance Analysis, *Journal of Marketing*, **41** (1) (Jan), pp 77–79

Kano model   30
Identifying purchase motivations

What the model looks like and how it works

When people choose a brand or product, they do so using both conscious and subconscious thought. A model developed by Noriaki Kano focuses attention on what is of value to the customer. This is a model that helps the business develop products that only offer features that matter because they delight customers. This focus makes sure there is no overdelivery and that the product is profitable.

The tool has two axes. The vertical axis measures satisfaction ranging from low at the bottom to high at the top. The horizontal axis measures the degree to which the service or product delivers against what is expected. Poor ability of the product to meet needs is at the left of the axis and excellent fulfilment of meeting needs is at the right.

The Kano model plots products (or services) against three types of properties or attributes:

- **Basic attributes**
  Basic attributes are the features in products (or services) that, when provided, are regarded as neutral because they are expected. When we put fuel in our car and we achieve the expected miles per gallon and performance, we are neutral in terms of satisfaction. If we sit in a meeting room in a hotel and the air conditioning is perfect, we don't think about the room temperature. It is the temperature we require and expect. However, if the room is too cold, it would create a high level of dissatisfaction. A mobile phone that needs charging every 24 hours is considered basic since this is the norm. These are examples of basic attributes that have to be part of any offer if a company is to play in a market. They are sometimes referred to as hygiene factors.

- **Performance attributes**

  Performance attributes are the requirements that customers have from a service or product that can vary and their satisfaction with the product varies in proportion. When checking into a hotel a customer would be satisfied if it took five minutes. They would be dissatisfied if it took 10 minutes and very satisfied if it took only two minutes. If there is a 10 per cent improvement in the performance of the product or service and this results in a 10 per cent improvement to the level of satisfaction, it is considered a performance attribute. Satisfaction increases in a linear way to the improvement in performance.

- **Excitement attributes**

  Excitement attributes are the things that we get from services or products that are unexpected and that delight us. For example, a phone that never needs charging would undoubtedly delight customers. It should be noted that excitement attributes eventually become performance attributes and ultimately basic ones over time. Wi-Fi in coffee shops was at one time different and special and created excitement, but over time it has become a basic part of the offer. These excitement attributes are often innovations and important for any company that wants to become world class.

Kano recognizes that the position of attributes changes over time. The performance features on mobile phones that once delighted us are now assumed as standard and taken for granted. The complimentary shampoo, body wash and hand cream in hotels no longer excites us. There is a need to constantly launch innovations because, if they have any value, they will almost always be copied by competitors and so remove the unique advantage.

In addition to the three attributes of excitement, performance and basics, Kano identified two more sets of attributes:

- **Indifferent attributes**

  Kano's model has a zone of indifference that contains attributes that people don't care about. If they exist, they are unnecessary in a product, especially if they raise the cost of manufacture. Removing them would have little impact on sales but would increase the profitability of the product.

- **Reverse attributes**

  Sometimes features are present in an offer and they decrease satisfaction. Take for example the clock in a modern car that is controlled by a computer program that makes it difficult to adjust and change the time. This may be considered too complicated and unnecessary by an elderly technophobe. A car with a simpler analogue clock that is controlled with a button may be preferred, even though it has fewer attributes. Understanding customers' needs is a vital part of the Kano tool. If some of the product features are identified as not only unnecessary but unattractive they could be eliminated from the offer, improving its appeal and reducing its cost.

In order to determine how attributes play together on the two axes, Kano asks two questions about each attribute:

- *If (name the attribute) improved in its performance, how would you feel?* This question is aimed at determining the functional appeal of the attribute.

- *If this product did not have (name the attribute), how would you feel?* This question is to establish the dysfunctional appeal.

A response scale such as the following could be used to capture the answers:

- *Like it*
- *Expect it*
- *Don't care*
- *Can live with it*
- *Dislike it*

For example, if someone dislikes the functional attribute and says that they would be happy if it was not there (they liked the dysfunctional aspect), then quite clearly this attribute could be labelled 'reverse'. The product would be better without it.

Analyses of the answers to the two questions enable them to be plotted on the axes of satisfaction and implementation, namely:

- **Performance attributes**: these are the attributes that people like having and dislike not having.

- **Basic attributes**: these are the attributes people expect to have and would be upset if they were not there.

- **Excitement attributes**: these are the attributes that are unexpected and would delight the customer.

The origins of the model

Noriaki Kano, a professor of quality management at the Tokyo University of Science in Japan, published his model in 1984.[1]

In the late 1970s Kano challenged the belief that every attribute in a company's offer must deliver customer satisfaction. His premise was that not all the attributes are equal and some are far more critical in building customer loyalty. Living and working in Japan it is no surprise that he was steeped in total quality management (TQM). This led to the publication of his most famous treaty, *Guide to TQM in Service Industries*.[2]

Developments of the model

A suggestion from people who use the Kano methodology is to include an additional question after the functional/dysfunctional pair. The question asks customers how important a particular feature is to them. Answers to the question for all the attributes will help determine which attributes, amongst all the ones that are tested, are really important in affecting customers' decisions to choose the product.

The Kano model has proved itself over time. It is better suited to an on-line data collection method than telephone interviews because of the potential length of the interview. Every attribute needs at least two questions (the functional and the dysfunctional) and possibly a third question to determine its importance. Asked over the telephone, this type of interview can be tedious and lengthy as there could be many attributes, each requiring two or three questions.

The model in action

The first thing to do when applying the Kano model is to decide who should be interviewed. The target audience must be those who use the product or potentially could do so.

Now the questions need to be developed for each single attribute. For example:

- Functional question: 'If you could use your iPhone to locate your car keys, how would you feel?'

- Dysfunctional question: 'If your iPhone cannot locate your car keys, how would you feel?'

- Importance question: 'How important is the key location feature on your iPhone on a scale from 1 to 10 where 10 is extremely important?'

Answers to the questions can be given a numeric score so that it is easy to graph. For example:

- scoring the functional questions: −2 (Dislike), −1 (Live with), 0 (Don't care), 2 (Expect it), 4 (Like);
- scoring the dysfunctional questions: −2 (Like), −1 (Expect it), 0 (Don't care), 2 (Live with), 4 (Dislike);
- scoring the importance of the attribute: 1 (Not at all important), 10 (Extremely important).

It should be noted that with the dysfunctional questions, if someone dislikes something, the offer would be better without it. For this reason, it gets the higher score.

Let us imagine that a computer manufacturer commissioned a survey of teachers to find out the features and attributes that are considered necessary in computers used by high-school students. In such a survey teachers would be asked functional and dysfunctional questions about many features and attributes. The various attributes of the computer can be plotted to indicate which would drive choice. In the analysis the importance of the attributes is indicated by the size of the circle (see Figure 30.1).

Let us imagine that the results from teachers showed they were concerned about how much is carried in a student's bag. Bags that students take to school are already heavy and it is important that the computer does not unnecessarily add to this burden. Lightweight is certainly a desirable function

Figure 30.1 Attributes considered important in computers for high-school students (fabricated example)

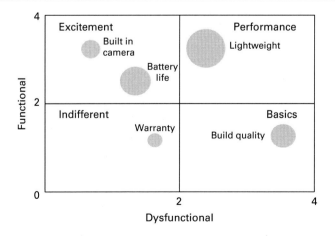

for a student's computer but it is something that is improving all the time. It would be considered a performance attribute.

Build quality is a given. All reputable brands of computers have acceptable quality so to some extent this would be discounted and considered a basic attribute.

Computers are becoming more and more reliable in which case the warranty becomes less relevant. This being the case, warranty is not such an important driver of choice.

A computer with an extended battery life would be highly desirable for students. It would mean that they would not have to take their charger to school and it would be one less thing for the students to worry about. This could be an excitement feature.

Highly desirable and an exciting attribute in the computer is a built-in camera. Students need to capture photos and interview conversations by video, which can be used in presentations. Although the feature may not be that important, it could be an increasingly useful tool for student learning and would be an attractive part of the value proposition.

Some things to think about

- The Kano tool can play an important role in innovation. It can be used to find out the improvements or innovations that could excite people about the product. They are the things that would make the product special and differentiated.

- An alternative tool for the same purpose could be SIMALTO (see Chapter 51).

Notes

1 Kano, N (1984) Attractive quality and must-be quality, *Hinshiuu*, **14** (2), pp 147–56 (in Japanese)
2 Kano, N (2001) *Guide to TQM in Service Industries*, Asian Productivity Organization, Tokyo

Kay's distinctive 31 capabilities

Adding value by identifying your distinctive capabilities

What the model looks like and how it works

The benefit of this framework is its simplicity. According to Kay there are three capabilities within a company that can give it a distinctive capability. These are architecture, reputation and innovation.

- **Architecture** – by this Kay means the structure of the company in the way it is organized. It needs clear corporate objectives and people within the company who are focused on achieving these. Its distribution channels and networks are also part of the architecture.

- **Reputation** – this is how customers and potential customers see the company. It is clearly important to companies that sell quality products and very often is determined by experience. Advertising messages help build the reputation and warranties promise that it will be kept.

- **Innovation** – innovation is a great way of creating a distinctive position and a source of competitive advantage. However, true innovation is quite rare. Many companies promote minor improvements as innovation, and these are seldom sufficient to create the perception of a distinctive capability. It is hard to constantly innovate and so improve products or reduce costs.

If these three capabilities are plotted in a Venn diagram (Figure 31.1), where they overlap are the distinctive capabilities of the company.

Kay makes the point that companies can achieve market dominance because they have ownership of a particular resource – such as a utility network, or a licence, or a very expensive asset. These are monopolistic companies that own a structural resource rather than because of their distinctive capabilities.

Figure 31.1   Kay's framework for identifying distinctive capabilities

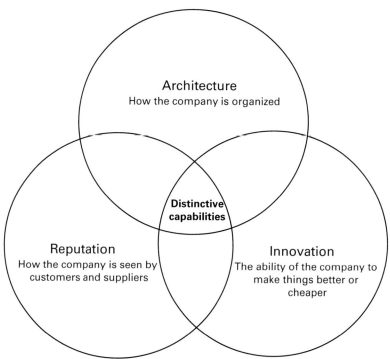

A company can beat the competition and prove successful even if it doesn't fulfil the three capabilities. If it works harder, sells more efficiently, produces more efficiently, and advertises more profusely, it may well gain a competitive advantage. However, distinctive capabilities give a competitive edge that is likely to endure longer.

These three capabilities are difficult to build and maintain. This means that they are also hard for competitors to copy. For them to be effective they need to endure (Kay calls this 'sustainability') and be 'appropriable' in benefitting the company (Kay calls appropriability the capacity to retain the added value it creates for its own benefit).

The origins of the model

John Kay is an economist. He has held many academic and business positions which prompted his first book, *Foundations of Corporate Success* (1993).[1] He describes the strategy of a firm as a match between its internal capabilities and its external relationships. A company has to respond to suppliers, customers, competitors and the environment in which it competes. Corporate strategy requires companies to make choices between their internal capabilities and what is happening in the marketplace.

Developments of the model

Kay's model has some similarities and some differences to those of Michael Porter. Porter argues that success comes from cost leadership, differentiation and focus. Porter's generic strategies model is more based on strategic intent rather than building distinctive capabilities.

Kay's framework is appealing because it brings our attention to just three important elements of a business. In practice it is more complicated. In order to understand the architecture of a company it will be necessary to investigate a large number of factors, for example its organizational structure, its special relationships with suppliers and partners, its geographical strengths and weaknesses, any unique and patented processes, and its workforce. Its reputation also requires a thorough drill-down showing strengths and weaknesses on various attributes with customers and suppliers. An examination of the innovation capability would need consideration of subjects such as the frequency of new product launches, the strengths of the new product development department, and the number of patents. As is the case with many frameworks, Kay's distinctive capabilities could be used with other frameworks such as the balanced scorecard (see Chapter 7).

The model in action

Kay uses BMW as an example of his framework. He argues that BMW's position is built on its reputation for high-quality engineering and the way it has educated and maintained a skilled labour force. BMW cars have established a reputation for engineering quality and have also become popular amongst young, affluent professionals. In this way it has become an aspirational brand.

BMW as a company is structured to take advantage of this position. Its retail margins are relatively high. It tightly controls its distribution network and its image. It has strong relationships with its suppliers. It is a company that has built a distinctive capability and has used this to establish a strong position at the top end of the automotive market.

Some things to think about

- What is your company known for that is better than the competition? What if anything is your company's distinctive capability?

- If you had to choose just one thing that makes your company distinctive, would it be the structure of the company (its architecture), its reputation, or its innovation?

- What can you do to build upon your distinctive capability to make it more difficult for the competition to copy?

- To what extent does this distinctive position follow through to produce a high market share, high profits, or good growth?

Note

1 Kay, J (1993) *Foundations of Corporate Success: How business strategies add value*, Oxford University Press

Kotler's five product levels

Adding value to a product or service

What the model looks like and how it works

Throughout this book various terms are used to describe a company's offer. An offer is sometimes a product, a service, or a product with a service. A strategy model proposed by Philip Kotler provides a useful understanding of what constitutes a 'product'. Kotler recognized three components that lead to the consumption of products:

- Need: there has to be a basic requirement.
- Want: someone must desire the product, believing it will satisfy the need.
- Demand: this is the desire established through the 'want' plus the ability to pay for the product.

Customers therefore choose products that they value. If that value is met or exceeded, then the customer will be satisfied. The customer must be satisfied on all of the product levels.

Kotler proposes five levels of a product:

1 **Core product**: the starting point of Kotler's concept is the core product. This is the product with its benefits as seen by the customer. An airline passenger would see the core product as the ticket to fly from A to B.

2 **Generic product**: this represents the qualities that are associated with a product. In the case of the airline customer, the generic product includes that the airline keeps to the schedule and it is safe.

3 **Expected product**: these are the things that customers anticipate they will receive when they buy a product. The airline customer will expect a degree of comfort. They may also hope and expect that they will enjoy a friendly experience.

4 **Augmented product**: these are the things that add value to a product and are often intangible. They set the product apart from the competition. Most notably the augmented product is the brand and the perceptions that come with it. The airline passenger may feel reassured by choosing an airline with a reputable brand. If they are frequent flyers they may feel that their journey will be augmented by air miles that are credited to their account.

5 **Potential product**: this is the product of the future. In the case of the airline, the future product could include a limousine pick-up and drop-off service. There could be changes made to the on-board service that also improve the product. (Note that the potential product is assumed to be a better product but it could also be a stripped-down version of the existing product.)

The product is the essence of why a company exists within a market. However, the product is not the only basis on which a company competes. It may do so through augmenting the product with a strong brand and services. The product is packaged, delivered and supported by commercial and technical services, all of which will be of value to the customers.

All products have a price. This should be based on their perceived value, though often prices are simply built on costs plus a margin. The product (in its broadest sense) and the price have to be in equilibrium if the company is to be successful.

The origins of the model

Philip Kotler, in his book *Marketing Management*,[1] published in 1967, describes the five levels of a product. He noted that competition takes place more at the augmented level than at the core level. It is the things that 'wrap around' the core product such as packaging, delivery, promotion and advice that people value above all else and that differentiate.

Developments of the model

Kotler built on earlier work by Theodore Levitt. In Levitt's paper entitled 'Marketing myopia',[2] he described manufacturers of buggy whips as short-sighted in that they believed they were simply selling products with which to whip mules that pull carts. When carts were replaced by motor vehicles, the whip manufacturers went out of business. If they had positioned themselves as producers of a 'generic' product or an 'expected' product, they may have still been in business making components for the vehicle industry and using their technology to make fan belts.

The model in action

A supplier of bitumen for roads operates in a very competitive market. In order to rise above the competition it considered Kotler's five levels of product.

Bitumen (also known as asphalt) is used to build new roads or repair existing ones. Technically bitumen is a black sticky residue from the distillation of petroleum. In the application described here, it is mixed with road stone of different sizes to create a smooth, flexible surface for vehicles to drive on. Sometimes relatively small amounts of bitumen are required to cover a hole dug to repair a water main, or fix something dug up for a faulty gas pipe or some other utility. Equally the bitumen may be used in much larger quantities for the surfacing of a new road or an airport runway, in which case a high-specification product is required.

Bitumen has a short shelf life. It needs to be laid quickly and while hot. The workers who prepare the road and lay the bitumen need the product at a specific hour otherwise they are waiting around, wasting their valuable time. For the bitumen supplier Kotler's five levels are considered as follows:

- **The core needs**

  Bitumen fills holes in roads or is used for a new road surface. Although technically bitumen is tar, it normally refers to a mixture of asphalt (the black tar) and stone chippings. This mix of bitumen and stones is then poured onto a road and levelled with a roller.

- **Generic product**

  In addition to the core product, it is critical that the bitumen is delivered to the right specification in the right quantity and at the time requested. This can sometimes be a problem, as the vehicles carrying the bitumen have to contend with road congestion and cannot always meet promised timeslots.

- **Expected product**

  People who buy bitumen do so regularly. They like to deal with the same company and the same person within that company who knows them and their requirements. The 'expected product' is built around relationships.

- **Augmented product**

  Research with buyers and specifiers of bitumen indicated that often people want to call by at the bitumen plant and pick up small quantities of product. This need arises when the quantity required is relatively small and the customer is not buying in a quantity that allows them to demand a specific timeslot for delivery. A pick-up service means the customer is guaranteed to have the product when they need it.

- **Potential product**

  Bitumen is a very old product. It has been in wide use in road making since the late 19th century. There have been developments in the use of bitumen. Bitumen surfaces can be made whisper quiet. Mixes can incorporate waste glass or plastic to be more environmentally friendly. It is also possible to modify the bitumen with polymers to make it more hard wearing and more frost resistant.

The bitumen company decided to launch a fast and flexible asphalt collection service. They piloted a pick-up depot that guaranteed a 30-minute turnaround time with a comfortable seating area supplied with free coffee and newspapers for waiting customers. The express collection centre proved a great success and 40 depots were rolled out nationally with extended opening times. The augmented product created a new and profitable revenue stream for the company in what had for many years been a traditional market.

Some things to think about

- Improvements that are made to a product are unlikely to be around core needs or the generic product. The improvements will be to features or services that enhance the product.

- All products can be enhanced. In order to work out what the enhancement should be, it is worth considering ethnographic research to see how customers actually use the product.

Notes

1 Kotler, P (1967) *Marketing Management: Analysis, planning, and control*, Prentice-Hall, New Jersey

2 Levitt, T (1960) Marketing myopia, *Harvard Business Review*, July–August

Market sizing   33

Assessing the size and value of a served or potential market

What the model looks like and how it works

Marketing strategies need to be based on a good understanding of the market size. The starting point has to be the definition of the market. There are two measures of market size – the total available market (TAM) and the served available market (SAM). The SAM is that which a company supplies with its products and in which it competes against other companies producing similar products. The TAM is wider and includes competitive and substitute products.

A supplier of instant coffee would define its SAM as the market for instant coffee as supplied by the company itself and other competitors. The TAM for instant coffee could be widened to include the market for fresh ground coffee and even the market for substitute beverages such as hot chocolate, tea, etc. The TAM is not necessarily a pushover. Someone wanting instant coffee will only move outside of that closely defined need and into the wider market if instant coffee is not available or if they fancy a change of taste. We need to be aware of these definitions of market size before setting out on the calculation.

Market size estimations are required for strategic planning purposes (Table 33.1).

The market size figure alone will not answer the strategic questions. It will also be necessary to understand the channels to market, the levels of competition, customer loyalty, prices, etc.

There are three different approaches to assessing the size of the market:

Demand-side

This is the bottom-up approach where research from end users is applied to statistics on the market. For example, a company wanting to assess the size of the market for workers' overalls carries out a survey to find out how

Table 33.1   Market size

Market size solves these strategic questions...	By answering these specific questions...
• Should we invest in this product/market?	• Is the market big enough to interest us?
• Should we increase our investment in this product/market?	• Is the market moving in the right direction?
• Should we decrease our investment in this product/market?	• Is the market moving fast enough?
	• Is the market profitable enough?

SOURCE B2B International (2014)

much is spent on overalls per year per employee and then applies this data to publicly available statistics on the number of employees in industry that may wear them. Calculating the market size in this way is useful because, as in the case of the overalls, it is possible to assess the market size in different industry verticals. Effectively a model of demand has been created. Models are particularly useful as they explain things. In this case they show where most potential lies for the overalls.

Top-down

This is the opposite of the demand-side method of market size assessment. It takes a bird's-eye view of the market from published reports and macro data. Sometimes industry experts feed their opinion into this type of assessment.

Supply-side

This is the assessment of market size built up from estimates of the revenue of each competitor that supplies the market. An assessment of this kind is useful as it shows the size and strength of the competition. It is also a good logic check as any company that appears to have a market share that looks strange, probably is wrong. There are obvious difficulties in carrying out a supply-side assessment. The revenues of companies by product group are not usually publicly available. From a survey of users of a product it may be possible to determine the market shares and revenues of the different suppliers. If the revenue of one of the suppliers is known (for example the company that has sponsored the research) it can be used as a reference point by which to judge the market revenues of other suppliers.

The assessment of market size is almost always an estimate. It is helpful to carry out the assessment in more than one way to obtain a cross check on accuracy. If the estimates are wide apart, they would be challenged and refined.

The origins of the model

No one can claim to be the originator of market sizing. In the 1920s and 1930s Nielsen in the United States began audits of products, effectively assessing sales through grocery stores. This provided market-share data, which was used to calculate market size.

In the post-war period, marketing became structured and market size data was required for marketing plans. In 1968 Aubrey Wilson wrote a book entitled *The Assessment of Industrial Markets*,[1] in which he described the processes for calculating market size.

Developments of the model

In general, a wide tolerance on the assessment of market size is permissible under the following conditions:

- When an investment is very small within the total market.
- When the study is a preliminary scan of the market.
- When the chief objective is to answer the question 'Where are we going?' rather than 'How are we going to get there?'

Businesses can be over-obsessed with the calculation of market size. A company that has a very small position within a market does not need to know with precision the size of the market. If a market is obviously huge and the company has a very small percentage share, then spending time and money obtaining a precise figure on market size will not help the strategic thinking. Equally, a company that knows that it is a very large player within the market will have a good feel for its market share. What may be more relevant to a company in this dominant position is to know the share of wallet it has with its customers. For example, a company could have a 10 per cent share of a market. However, this 10 per cent market share may be the result of having very few customers but ones that are amongst the largest buyers of the product. This is a very different situation to a company with a 10 per cent overall share achieved by having small shares of wallet of lots of companies in the market.

High levels of accuracy are sometimes necessary where:

- The investment is large within the total market and the investor aims to achieve a significant share within it.
- Market sizes from different years are needed to show a trend.

- When a company is operating within a niche. The marketer preparing the plan in this narrow market has to have some feel for the size of the ultimate prize.

The model in action

Warehouses are becoming ever more sophisticated. Large warehouses, especially those storing food or supplying online customers, occupy very large spaces. Products within the warehouses are kept in bins with electronic tags. People working in the warehouses are given pick lists of orders to fulfil and they are routed from one bin to the next by voice systems or electronic instructions. The software and hardware used to manage the warehouses is a rapidly growing market. A supplier to this market wanted to know the global market size.

The study began with an assessment of base statistics – the number and the size of warehouses around the world. Patchy data exists on the numbers and size of warehouses, with excellent statistics in North America and Europe and sketchy data elsewhere.

Expensive warehouse management systems are only used in facilities of more than 100,000 square feet. A picture was built up of the number of warehouses of this size in North America and Europe and estimates were made for countries elsewhere. The number and size of warehouses bore some relation to the gross domestic product (GDP) of each country, which made it possible to fill gaps in the statistics using ratios. There was a pattern of size and use of warehouses in southern Europe and a different pattern in eastern Europe. The North American situation mirrored the warehouse distribution of western Europe.

A survey was carried out with 500 operators of large warehouses around the world. A basic question for everyone interviewed was the size of their warehouse in square feet/metres and the number of 'pickers' employed. These are the staff who fulfil the orders by pulling products from the bins. Knowing the number and size of warehouses and the number of pickers, it was possible to determine the number of pickers per square foot. This figure could then be applied to the square feet of warehouses around the world to determine the number of pickers. Pickers use headsets and carry portable computers that instruct them what products to collect and where from. With the knowledge of the number of pickers, and the average cost of the software and equipment per picker, it was a relatively simple task to assess the global market size.

The global estimate of market size was broken down country by country and by different verticals – grocery, food service, third-party logistics, fast-

Figure 33.1   Served available market and total available market

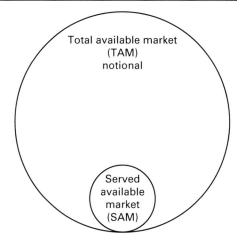

SOURCE B2B International (2015)

moving consumer goods and so on. The company was able to see the size of the global market at the present and how much it would be worth if all the hand picking was changed to automated picking (see Figure 33.1). The assessment of market size provided a forecast of demand for the next five years.

Some things to think about

- Market size estimates seldom need to be precise. It is good practice to obtain triangulation on the assessment by using a top-down (macro or high-level) and bottom-up approach (modelled from end-user intelligence and market statistics).

- It can be helpful to assess market size in number of units. This avoids the problem of products having different prices as they move through the value chain.

- If the value of the market is assessed in currencies, it is important to state whether the figure is at manufacturers' selling prices or consumer buying prices.

Note

1 Wilson, A (1968) *The Assessment of Industrial Markets*, Hutchinson, England

Maslow's hierarchy

34

Differentiating market positioning

What the model looks like and how it works

Every business needs to understand what drives the behaviour of its customers. At a superficial level we can ask people what motivates them to do something and we receive an answer. But can we believe what they have told us? Do people really know what made them choose that Porsche, join that gym, or train as a nurse? Maslow's hierarchy of needs (Figure 34.1) helps us to understand motivations. It is a theory described as five levels in a pyramid. Each level is a need fulfilled and leads to the desire to reach the next level and move upwards through the pyramid.

In its simplistic form, Maslow believes that the levels in the hierarchy follow in sequence. This can be observed in early life stages of a child. When a baby is born its only needs are physiological – food and warmth. Up to the age of five, children have a need for all the physiological requirements plus safety, love and belonging. When they start school between the ages of five and seven, they start to show that they care what people think of them. This progression from one level to another is obvious in a young child. As we mature, the five levels are still recognizable but they can appear in a different order or be absent altogether. In fact, Maslow was of the view that very few people make it to the highest level – that of self-actualization. This does not detract from the wide appeal of the theory, which describes the complications of behaviour in a very easy-to-understand way.

The most basic needs, those that sit at the bottom of the pyramid, are required for our physiological functioning. These are the need to eat, drink, have sex, stay warm and sleep.

Once our basic needs are met, there is a desire for personal safety, including health and well-being. Financial security is also part of this need.

Figure 34.1   Maslow's hierarchy of needs

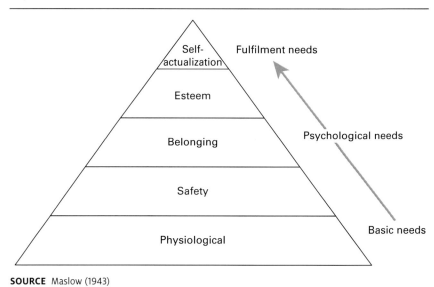

SOURCE Maslow (1943)

When we feel safe and secure we are in a position to seek love, friendship and company. This is a tribal instinct; a need to belong. It is why people feel patriotic, join clubs and support sports teams.

Moving up through the pyramid there is now a search for social recognition, status and respect. These are the values of esteem and they give a person a sense of value. There are two levels of esteem. A lower level yearns for respect from other people and could come from a desire for status and recognition. A higher level of esteem and self-confidence comes from an inner strength that follows the mastering of a skill.

At the top of the hierarchy is self-actualization. This is achieved when people reach their full potential. It is a poet and their poetry. It is a fêted artist. At this level a person has achieved everything they are capable of achieving. Maslow claimed that only 2 per cent of the population reach this level. In 1970 he published a list of a small number of people who had achieved self-actualization, living or dead, and he came up with just 18 names, including Thomas Jefferson, Albert Einstein and Maslow himself.

The origins of the model

Abraham Maslow was born into a Brooklyn slum in 1908. His parents were Russian Jews and he faced anti-Semitism as a child in New York. It is claimed that he had an IQ of 195.[1]

He published his theory of human motivation in a paper in 1943.[2] It followed the work of previous psychologists who were more concerned with psychology dominated by the psychoanalytic and behavioural approaches. Maslow focused on the human potential rather than the negative emotions. He believed that behaviour is not driven by external forces but rather internal ones that motivate us to do better and improve. His model does not assume that we do things because we have been conditioned to do so by our parents and our upbringing; it is based on aspiration and a desire to improve.

In many respects, his pyramid describes levels of achievement towards the American dream. His psychology was based on optimism and the ability of human beings to move onwards and upwards. As a psychoanalyst, he differed from many of his colleagues in that he was not interested in finding out what goes wrong for people; he focused on what could go right for them.

Unlike other psychologists, who wrote for their colleagues, Maslow wrote for the general public. His theories have practical uses, particularly in business.

Developments of the model

As with many sequential models, life is never that simple. Not everyone moves up through the pyramid in a neat and orderly way. Maslow's theory was based more on observations and ideas rather than empirical evidence. After Maslow's death in 1970, research by Clayton Alderfer suggested that Maslow's five groups of needs could be reduced to three – existence, relatedness and growth (the ERG theory).[3] The argument here was that human beings need to be satisfied in all three areas and, if this is not the case, then there would be a natural inclination to boost one of the categories.

Consultants and business writers have embraced Maslow's model and modified it to relate to organizations rather than individuals. Figure 34.2 shows a pyramid developed by B2B International reflecting the hierarchical needs of businesses.

Level 1: survival needs

A successful company needs the basic physiological requirements of an offer – the right product, at the right price, at the right place, with the right promotion.

Level 2: development needs

Once established, the company must now become sustainable. The business that began with a product focus must think about adding value to its offer.

Figure 34.2 Maslow's hierarchy in a business context

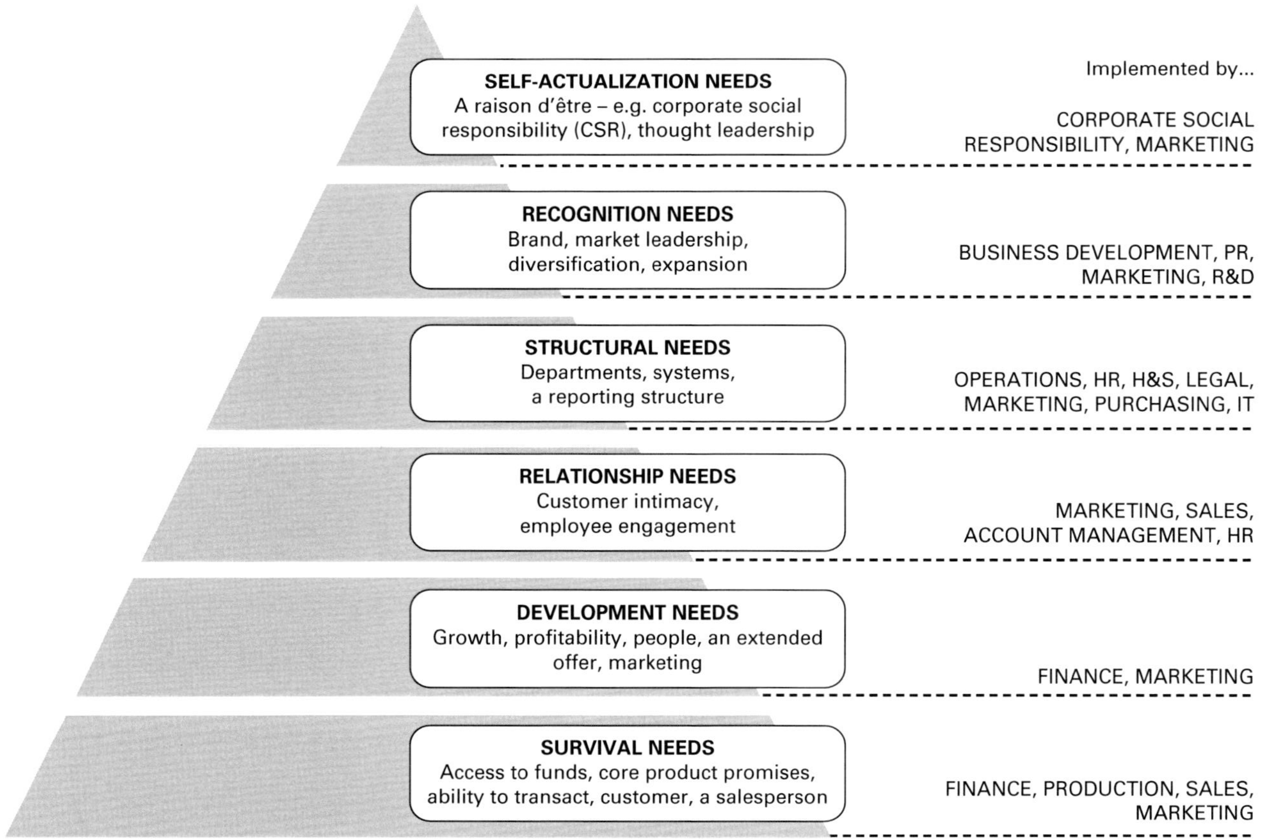

Implemented by...

SELF-ACTUALIZATION NEEDS
A raison d'être – e.g. corporate social responsibility (CSR), thought leadership

CORPORATE SOCIAL RESPONSIBILITY, MARKETING

RECOGNITION NEEDS
Brand, market leadership, diversification, expansion

BUSINESS DEVELOPMENT, PR, MARKETING, R&D

STRUCTURAL NEEDS
Departments, systems, a reporting structure

OPERATIONS, HR, H&S, LEGAL, MARKETING, PURCHASING, IT

RELATIONSHIP NEEDS
Customer intimacy, employee engagement

MARKETING, SALES, ACCOUNT MANAGEMENT, HR

DEVELOPMENT NEEDS
Growth, profitability, people, an extended offer, marketing

FINANCE, MARKETING

SURVIVAL NEEDS
Access to funds, core product promises, ability to transact, customer, a salesperson

FINANCE, PRODUCTION, SALES, MARKETING

SOURCE B2B International (2015), based on Maslow (1943)

If the company does not develop at this stage, like many start-ups, it will fail within the first year or two, or at best stagnate.

Level 3: relationship needs

At the time of the start-up, sales are everything. As the business matures, there is a greater focus on tactical marketing and key account management.

Within the business itself, employee engagement becomes important. An engaged workforce is more likely to work harder and satisfy customers.

Level 4: structural needs

The growing business needs to slough its informal ways and impose structures and reporting hierarchies. IT systems and customer relationship management (CRM) systems are installed. Middle managers are appointed with responsibilities for departments, which in turn reinforce the need for reporting structures.

Level 5: recognition needs

The company is now large and has a brand that must be cherished and protected. There will be vision and mission statements that ensure that the company is seen to have a clear direction. The brand will be recognized as an important asset and a 'guiding star' for employees.

Level 6: self-actualization needs

Just as Maslow believed a very small percentage of people reach self-actualization, so too we can surmise that there are very few businesses that reach this level. This is the level where a company places great emphasis on corporate social responsibility (CSR). Profit may still be important but not at the expense of the brand and what it stands for.

The model in action

In business, the hierarchy of needs has many applications. It is used by managers to identify the needs of staff and help them feel fulfilled. In marketing it is used to segment customers who buy products and services to meet their different needs. It is used by advertising companies who want to develop messages that resonate and trigger actions.

Engaging with staff

A large mining company was finding it difficult to recruit staff. The company had a number of mines and processing plants scattered around the country. The products mined and processed were not particularly inspiring compared to working for a finance or digital company in a large city. The mining company commissioned a survey of employees and potential employees to find out what motivates people to seek employment at a company of this type.

Two factors emerged as basic requirements. The salary and the location of the company had to be acceptable. However, beyond these two basics, there was a strong appeal for joining the company if it could offer opportunities for career growth. Also job security and work–life balance proved to be important drivers. These motivational needs, beyond the basics, became the focus of the recruitment campaign and proved highly successful.

Segmenting customers

A major manufacturer of caustic soda found itself under pressure. Caustic soda is considered by many customers as a commodity. It accounts for a high proportion of a product's cost and the manufacturer of caustic soda came under severe price pressure. Customers were classified as small, medium or large. As might be expected, larger accounts received more attention. However, this size-based classification was also used by other suppliers of caustic soda and so it gave no advantage.

The manufacturer commissioned research to identify the more subtle needs of its customers. The research showed that price was a significant driver influencing the choice of caustic soda supplier but it was by no means the most important. Other than price, the biggest challenge facing customers was logistics, particularly the planning of deliveries of the product. Customers of all sizes faced logistical challenges.

Using the findings from the research the company segmented its customers according to their needs for the better planning of volume deliveries. Safety also proved to be an important driver of supplier choice because caustic soda is an aggressive chemical. Safety was made a watchword for customers of all sizes. Improved planning of logistics enabled the company to better serve large, medium and small companies and to do so with greater efficiencies. The new segmentation was delivered at a higher level than the basic delivery of product and price. By meeting the higher-level needs for safety, the caustic soda manufacturer significantly improved levels of customer satisfaction and its own profitability.

Developing messages that resonate

Advertising agencies know it is a waste of time promoting features and benefits around the bottom of Maslow's hierarchy. These are basics that every company supplies if they play in the market. Ad agencies know that customers are motivated by emotional factors higher up the pyramid. Meeting psychological needs or self-esteem needs are much stronger draws than hitting on the basics.

David Ogilvy is sometimes referred to as the grandfather of ad men. He was recruited by Rolls-Royce to design a campaign to promote one of the company's new cars. Ogilvy did not talk about the amazing quality of the car. He did not talk about its reliability, which was legendary. He never mentioned status. His headline ran: *'At 60 miles an hour the loudest noise in this new Rolls-Royce comes from the electric clock.'*

The message was clear. The car itself had reached self-actualization. There was nothing more to be said about the perfection of the car other than the noise of the clock. The ad, quite rightly, became world famous.

Some things to think about

- Marketers must, of course, get the basics right. They must have the right product, at the right price, in the right place. However, emotions are what distinguish companies and drive demand. The most effective communications and segmentations are based on the top end of Maslow's hierarchy. They address psychological and fulfilment needs.

- Use focus groups and qualitative research to understand emotions and use quantitative research to measure and quantify how important these emotions are for your customers.

Notes

1 Kremer, W and Hammond, C (2013) Abraham Maslow and the pyramid that beguiled business, *BBC World Service*, 1 September
2 Maslow, AH (1943) A theory of human motivation, *Psychological Review*, 50 (4), pp 370–96
3 Alderfer, CP (1969) An empirical test of a new theory of human needs, *Organizational Behavior and Human Performance*, 4 (2), May, pp 142–75

McKinsey 7S   35
A company 'health check' audit tool

What the model looks like and how it works

Every business needs to know whether it is on track. There are lots of obvious metrics that can help in this regard. Financial targets such as sales and profits are obvious indicators of the performance of the company. However, it is possible to have a financially successful company that is heading for the rocks. For example, a company may make money for a time, but if it is overcharging customers, or if it has not invested in the right systems, or if employees are overworked and are beginning to feel disgruntled, it will eventually hit the buffers.

The consultancy firm McKinsey developed a model with seven elements, each an indicator of the health of the company. The seven elements all begin with the letter S and so the model is known as the McKinsey 7S framework. Three of the seven elements of the model are referred to as hard elements. They are called hard elements because they are easier to define and management can affect them directly. They are strategy, structure and systems.

Alongside these hard elements are four soft elements. These soft elements are so-called because they are less tangible, more influenced by culture but just as important. In fact, because they are harder to identify, they are harder to copy by the competition and so can be important in giving the company a competitive advantage. They are skills, style, staff and shared values. All the elements are interrelated so that the change in performance in any one of the components will influence another:

Strategy

This is the overarching direction of the business and the plan that the management has laid down to grow the company over the medium to long term.

Structure

This describes the way the organization is put together. It could be a description of the organizational hierarchy or the strategic business units and how they report to the centre.

Systems

The systems refer to the procedures for measuring things that happen in the company. They include financial processes, IT systems, HR procedures and the like. These are critical components of any company going through organizational change.

Shared values

The shared values describe the culture and the DNA of an organization. They are the recognizable traits that enable someone to say 'You can tell this person works for company x'.

Style

This describes the behavioural attitudes of the top management team, which in turn will be influenced by the management style of the company leader.

Staff

These are the employees, their number, how they are recruited, how they are trained, their demographic make-up and their attitudinal characteristics.

Skills

These are the core competences of the employees.

The 7S tool has found favour amongst change consultants for providing a structure to:

- improve the performance of a company;
- account for the effects of changes within a company;
- align departments and processes during a drive to greater efficiencies or following a merger or acquisition;
- work out how to implement a strategy.

The origins of the model

In the late 1970s, the consultancy firm McKinsey sponsored a number of projects to examine successful strategies in business. Tom Peters led the project. In 1980 Bob Waterman, Tony Athos, Richard Pascale and Tom Peters, a mix of McKinsey consultants and academics, hid themselves away in what

Peters referred to as a two-day séance and arrived at the 7S framework.[1] In the same year, Peters, Waterman and Phillips wrote an article called 'Structure is not organization', which introduced the McKinsey 7S framework.[2] Peters and Waterman developed this further in 1982 in their book *In Search of Excellence*.[3]

Two more McKinsey consultants, Richard Pascale and Anthony Athos, contributed to the model, recognizing from their research with Japanese companies that they were linked by the 7S framework.[4]

Developments of the model

The model is a useful tool for carrying out an audit of the company to determine where its strengths and weaknesses lie. However, the model does not provide benchmarks and triggers that indicate what should be done. It points to where the focus of attention should lie – that is on any of the seven elements that are not aligned with their counterparts.

The 7S model is widely employed as a strategic planning tool and as such it is often adjusted and amended by the consultants who use it.

The model in action

This is a flexible tool pointing to seven elements of a business that drive excellence. It is a step beyond a SWOT as it identifies the elements of success from the start. The model can be put into practice in five steps:

Step 1: audit the 7S elements for alignment

Each of the 7S elements are examined to see how closely they are aligned with each other. The purpose of the audit is to spot any gaps or inconsistencies. Consider a Yes/No notation to indicate if there is alignment with the other interconnected elements. This is not something that requires huge precision but to indicate whether alignment exists or not. The tool does not require every element to be addressed – only those that are not in alignment. To this extent it is a prioritization tool.

Step 2: determine what the 7S elements should look like

Following the audit and knowing the gaps between the elements, a plan is needed to show what the optimal organization should look like. This should begin with the hard factors. There needs to be agreement at the top as to the goals and the strategy of the company. The leadership team need to sign off the structure and systems to achieve the goals.

Step 3: decide what changes must be made

This is the detailed plan of 'how to do it'. The plan has to be a practical match between the resources that are available and the aims. Crucial to the plan is 'getting the right people on the right seats on the bus'.

Step 4: implementing the plan

As always, implementation is usually the most difficult stage of all. It takes time, resource and there needs to be an appetite for change. Not least, there needs to be a positive attitude towards change and the achievement of the goals if the plan is to succeed. This process is unlikely to be quick. It will take at least a few months and most likely at least a year.

Step 5: monitor and review

Every plan needs to be checked against targets. This is the period over which monitoring will be carried out and adjustments made.

Some things to think about

- Every successful business has to be aligned with the needs of its customers. This should be borne in mind when examining the strengths of the 7S elements. To what extent does each of them deliver against customers' needs?

- Companies are made up of people and they are involved in every one of the seven elements. When reviewing each of the 7S elements it is worth asking 'Have we got the right people? Are they connecting successfully with their colleagues?'

Notes

1 A Brief History of the 7-S ('McKinsey 7-S') Model, http://tompeters.com/docs/7SHistory.pdf (archived at https://perma.cc/HQJ7-HQ6W)

2 Waterman, RH, Peters, TJ and Phillips, JR (1980) Structure is not organization, *Business Horizons*, 23 (3), 14

3 Peters, TJ and Waterman, RH (1982) *In Search of Excellence: Lessons from America's best run companies*, Grand Central Publishing, New York

4 Pascale, RT and Athos, AG (1981) *The Art of Japanese Management*, Simon & Schuster, New York

Mintzberg's 5Ps for strategy

36

Devising a competitive strategy

What the model looks like and how it works

Strategies are vitally important to businesses. They are the grand plan of action that enables a company to achieve its overall goal. It is seldom possible for a company to achieve an overall goal in weeks or months and so strategies are nearly always longer term, usually a year or more. Tactics are the shorter-term devices that are used to achieve the grand plan. In military terms the strategy is how you win the war and the tactics are how you fight a battle.

Henry Mintzberg, an academic and a business thinker, developed a model for helping classify and understand business strategies. He recognized five different types, each named with a P:

Strategy as a **P**lan: an intended course of action

The most usual type of strategy is a master plan – one that states a goal with a course of action that sees it is achieved. It is a plan developed consciously and purposefully. It is prepared in advance to guide the actions that follow. Most strategies have a plan. They may also have one of the other distinctive attributes of a strategy recognized by Mintzberg.

Strategy as a **P**loy: a manoeuvre to beat the competition

A strategy can be an action designed to frustrate or even mislead a competitor. Chapter 26 described the Lanchester strategy. It tells of a manoeuvre by the copier company, Canon, who beat Rank Xerox in the UK copier market by first concentrating on a region that it knew was not core for Xerox. It focused on Scotland where, little by little, it built up a 40 per cent market share from which it had a springboard to move south to the bigger pickings.

Had Canon attempted to attack London at the outset, it would almost certainly have failed.

Strategy as a **P**attern: a strategy that emerges, perhaps by accident

Successful strategies have a consistency in the way they are applied. The plan is the intended strategy and the pattern is what actually happens. In fact, what actually happens may not be part of the original plan. Patterns can often be recognized amongst market leaders. They can be predictable in the way that they act. They put their prices up once or twice a year and they expect competitors to follow. If they are attacked on price, they may well have a reaction that is anticipated.

Strategy as a **P**osition: a brand that stands out against competitors

Companies may choose to fight within a market by taking a low-cost position, or a differentiated position based on its brand, or play within a niche. These different positions are described by Porter in his generic strategies (see Chapter 43). Harley Davidson's strategy as a manufacturer of motorcycles is an example of a company fighting from the strong position it has carved out for itself. It has focused on a niche (albeit a big niche) amongst customers who want a heavyweight luxury bike, with a highly differentiated brand that signifies their lifestyle.

Strategy as a **P**erspective: the unique way the company works within its market

Many companies have a culture, a view of the world that defines them and the way they work. Southwest Airlines would be such an example. It is a company that has been successful through limiting the types of planes it uses, it has concentrated its geographical operation on the south-west of the United States, and it has focused on a low-cost reliable service. It is, however, the spirit of the employees that sets the company apart. The book *Nuts!* tells the story of Herb Kelleher, the founder of Southwest Airlines,[1] whose unorthodox leadership style created a company with a certain perspective. The subtitle of the book is *Southwest Airlines' crazy recipe for business and personal success*. The book describes the positively outrageous service that makes the company successful and that is so difficult for competitors to copy.

The origins of the model

Henry Mintzberg is a professor of management studies at McGill University in Montréal. He is a prolific author on management and business strategy and has published 150 articles and 15 books on the subject. He developed the 5P model of strategic thinking in 1987 under the title 'The strategy concept I: five Ps for strategy', which was published in *California Management Review*.[2] His model was aimed to give more precision to the definition of strategy.

Developments of the model

Mintzberg's model is descriptive and provides a good explanation for the strategic management process. It is useful for describing a type of strategy and bringing the focus on to how managers can pursue a strategy to survive within a market. It is less useful for helping a business determine which strategy it should use. However, other models can be used within the Mintzberg 5Ps. Porter's generic strategies can help a company decide how it should position itself in the market.

The Mintzberg model places its emphasis on the competition within the market. In many markets, strategy will be influenced by factors other than the competition, and a better balance of understanding what will affect the strategic plan could be obtained by a PEST analysis or Porter's five forces.

The model in action

Mintzberg tells the story of Honda when it entered the US motorcycle market.[3] Its plan (i.e. its intended 'position') was to enter the market as a supplier of low-cost large bikes. The US market was principally made up of domestic and European bikes of 250cc and more. The company set up distributorships throughout the country and by 1965 it had covered two-thirds of the US market.

However, the strategy that led to Honda's success in the US was not as originally intended. Honda's larger bikes developed faults as they were not designed for the wear and tear caused by the US roads. The company had made little effort to sell its small 50cc bikes though they were used for running errands by Honda staff. Honda was left with no alternative but to sell the only machines it had, the small bikes. They proved extremely popular with people who previously had never bought motorbikes. This led to an advertising campaign that claimed 'You meet the nicest people on a Honda'.

Honda's small 50cc motorcycles became the cornerstone of its new strategy – based on 'pattern' – a strategy that emerged by accident. Through trying various attacks on the market in those early years, Honda found out what worked for it and this gave rise to a pattern and, later, to perspective.

Mintzberg makes the point that although patterns and positions can change a strategy, a perspective, once established, becomes immutable. It is what makes Southwest Airlines so strong.

Some things to think about

- Strategies are critical for the successful growth of any company. However, strategies have to be flexible and may change. The strategy of a company must align with its strengths and the needs of the target market.

- Although strategies require some flexibility, it is important that they do not change too frequently. A company has to give a strategy sufficient time for it to bear fruit.

Notes

1 Freiberg, K and Freiberg, J (2001) *Nuts! Southwest Airlines' crazy recipe for business and personal success*, Texere Publishing, London

2 Mintzberg, H (1987) The strategy concept I: five Ps for strategy, *California Management Review*, 30 (1), pp 11–24

3 Mintzberg, H (1989) *Mintzberg on Management: Inside our strange world of organizations*, Free Press, New York

MOSAIC   37

Setting objectives for current and potential opportunities and how to reach them

What the model looks like and how it works

One of the oldest and simplest frameworks for addressing problems and opportunities in a business is to achieve answers to the following three questions:

- Where are we now?
- Where are we going?
- How can we get there?

The MOSAIC model is an extension of these three questions. It is a framework for addressing macro and micro business issues. MOSAIC is an acronym for mapping, objectives, strategy, action, implementation and controls (Figure 37.1).

Mapping

A map is an essential part of any journey. It tells you where you are, where you could go and the routes by which you can get there. No one would think of venturing up an unknown mountain without a detailed map. A map is just as vital in business.

In the same way that a spatial map locates roads, towns and the physical geography of an area, a business map contains the economic equivalent – the competition, the size of the market, growth trends, an analysis of the customers, their needs, the route to market, pricing structures and so on. The amount of detail required at this mapping stage depends on the subject in hand. A detailed and accurate map will be needed for a complex and important project.

Figure 37.1   The MOSAIC framework

M   Mapping. Assessment of the market, future trends, the competition and your position in the market

O   Objectives. These should be SMART: specific, measurable, actionable, realistic and timely

S   Strategy. The long-term, high-level means by which you will achieve the goals

A   Action. The detailed ways you will achieve the strategy and respond to competitive pressures

I   Implementation. Who will do what, by when and with what resources

C   Controls. The measures you will put in place to make sure that you achieve your goals

SOURCE B2B International (1998)

Mapping the market takes time. It is also a job that is never finished. It is important that the mapping stage does not bog down the process through the obsession with finding 'just one more piece of information'.

The mapping process usually results in the clarification of thoughts. It is an occasion to locate the problem or the opportunity within a context and, in so doing, it helps show the way forward.

Objectives

Objectives are a statement of the way forward. The acronym SMART defines the setting of the goals:

S – the objectives should be specific, significant and stretching.

M – they should be measurable, meaningful and motivational.

A – they should be achievable and agreed with colleagues.

R – they should be realistic, reasonable and relevant.

T – They should be time based and trackable.

Strategy

A strategy is the blueprint for meeting the objectives. The strategy describes the plan of action rather than the detailed tactics as these could change on a day-to-day basis.

A good strategy is one that is based on a competitive advantage. It should be grounded on the core competence of the company and play to its strengths. It should also be very clearly targeted and focused on a particular audience.

Day-to-day decisions and tactics in the implementation of the plan will be made by a variety of people. It is important, therefore, that the strategy is straightforward and obvious, providing a clear view of the direction of travel.

The strategy should have some flexibility. We often hear people talking about Plan A and Plan B. If there isn't a Plan B, and there is no flexibility in the strategy, the project could fail if it hits a problem.

Action

The strategy has to be turned into an action plan. This is where tactics, people, resources and timing come into play. The action plan will comprise steps to achieve the objective. Against each step it will be necessary to show who will be responsible and the date by which that milestone will be completed.

'*The best-laid plans of mice and men often go awry.*' This being the case, it is important to foresee what problems will be faced and how they can be overcome.

Implementation

Implementation is the process of putting the plan into effect. It is almost always the most difficult part of the MOSAIC model as it is here that the plan on paper proves to be more difficult than expected. Implementation requires action, and whoever is responsible for that action may find that the effort and time is more than they anticipated. Optimism at the time of preparing the action plan very often means that during implementation things take longer and cost more than was budgeted.

Recognizing the difficulties of implementation is crucial. Whoever is responsible for each part of the plan will need constant monitoring and motivation. The plan should allow for small steps, which can be readily achieved and lead to intermediate progress points. It is seldom possible to jump quickly and straight to the objective. Keeping things simple and straightforward during the implementation stage is critical.

Controls

The implementation is unlikely to go exactly as planned. The plan will have a critical path, which must be tracked so that if a problem is faced it can be solved. Controls are necessary to spot these problems and take corrective action. The controls must be determined at the outset and built into the plan. Usually this means some form of measurement that ascertains whether a milestone has been achieved.

The origins of the model

The MOSAIC framework was developed in 1996 by B2B International as a tool to drive action from market research studies. At about the same time, Paul Smith, a marketing consultant, developed a planning tool that he called SOSTAC® (or, in full, PR Smith's SOSTAC® Plan). This is a similar and equally useful framework for business planning and is supported by a book by the author. SOSTAC® stands for:

- Situation – where are we now?
- Objectives – where do we want to be?
- Strategy – how do we get there?
- Tactics – how *exactly* do we get there?
- Action – what is our plan?
- Control – did we get there?

Paul Smith also offers a book on how to use SOSTAC® in writing a marketing plan.[1]

Developments of the model

The MOSAIC and SOSTAC® models are planning tools. There are many other tools that can work within these frameworks. At the mapping stage it may be helpful to carry out a PEST and SWOT analysis to identify forces that are shaping the market and the strengths, weaknesses, opportunities and threats that face the company.

It may be instructive to understand the cause and effect of relationships at this early stage and there are various interrelationship tools that can be

Figure 37.2   Prioritization matrix

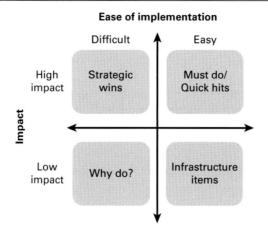

used for this purpose. They aim to analyse the links between different aspects of a complex situation and show the underlying drivers.

At some stage in the planning it will be necessary to prioritize actions. For this purpose it can be useful to plot the actions against the difficulties of implementing them and the impact they will have (Figure 37.2).

The model in action

Flexydie (the name is made up to hide the identity of the company) makes flexible dies for printers. Flexible dies are thin sheets of metal that wrap around a cylinder and are used by printers to produce folds and perforations in paper or card. The flexible dies sell at between €60 and €600 depending on their complexity. Most are towards the bottom end of this range.

A customer (a printer) will email the design for the die and request shipment of the finished product the next day. Flexydie is a small regional player and wanted to grow its business within Europe. It used the MOSAIC model to develop its business plan:

Mapping

The company estimated that there are around 5,000 potential customers for flexible dies in the major markets of Europe. Competition comes from a small number of large German manufacturers and a large number of regional players. The market is relatively static and so growth for Flexydie could only be achieved by stealing market share.

Objectives

Flexydie calculated that it had a 5 per cent share of the European market and set itself the goal of achieving a 10 per cent share over a five-year period.

Strategy

The company aimed to achieve its objective by offering an extremely fast turnaround supported by excellent customer service.

Action

An action plan was developed that included the recruitment and training of customer service personnel who would deal with the orders.

Implementation

The implementation did not go to plan. Despite a strong marketing push, printers were loyal to their existing suppliers of dies and proved reluctant to switch to a new supplier unless their incumbent let them down. Prices were already tight and there was no room for reducing them to win business.

Controls

It would have been easy to back off from the original plan in the face of the disappointing response to the sales push. However, the company regrouped. It developed a sales proposition based on both speed of turnaround of the order as well as product innovations such as non-stick coating of the dies. The original plan had anticipated that sales would increase in a linear fashion but in fact they followed the shape of a hockey stick. There was relatively little movement in sales for two years and then a rapid increase. The company achieved its goal within four years.

Some things to think about

- The MOSAIC template can be used to drive action in a wide range of marketing and promotional plans.
- Mapping a market takes time and is a critical part of any plan. Once the market has been mapped, the objectives, strategy and implementation plans can be devised quickly.

- The most difficult part of the MOSAIC process is implementation. There will be inevitable push backs, which need to be dealt with using the control mechanism.

Note

1 Smith, PR (2015) *SOSTAC®: The guide to your perfect digital marketing plan*, PR Smith, England (SOSTAC® is a registered trade mark of PR Smith. For more information on SOSTAC® Planning and becoming a SOSTAC® Certified Planner visit www.SOSTAC.org (archived at https://perma.cc/ME2G-D22U)

Net Promoter Score® 38

A tool for driving customer excellence

What the model looks like and how it works

The Net Promoter Score® (NPS) is a measure of customer satisfaction and loyalty and is used to determine how likely customers are to recommend and promote a company. The score is based on answers to the following question:

How likely are you to recommend brand X to a colleague using a scale from 0 to 10 where zero means not at all likely and 10 means very likely?

It is argued that a 'likelihood to recommend' score equates with loyalty. The NPS is computed by taking the percentage of people who give a score of 9 or 10 out of 10 (called promoters) and subtracting the percentage of people who give a score of 6 or below (detractors). Those giving a score of 7 or 8 are ignored in the calculation (passives) (Figure 38.1).

In answer to this question most respondents who know a company or brand and have used it choose an answer between 6 and 10. In fact the

Figure 38.1 Calculation of the Net Promoter Score® (NPS)

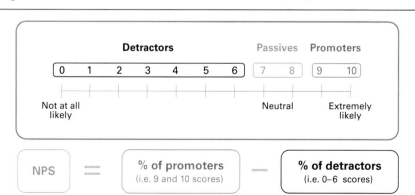

Table 38.1 NPS scores

NPS score	Types of companies typically achieving this score
Less than 20	Utility companies, monopolists, chemical companies, commodity suppliers, most western airlines
20–30	Manufacturing companies of all types, large corporates
30+	Service companies and companies with a high service content in their offer, high-tech companies, professional services companies, small and medium-size companies, good merchants and distributors

majority often choose a score of 7 or 8 out of 10. This means that the real width of the scale is narrower than it appears. The NPS score only uses responses from people who give extreme scores of 9 or 10 and 6 or below. These are people who feel some passion about a brand or company and will talk positively or negatively about it.

A high NPS correlates strongly with loyalty and future growth. Tracking the NPS is important to determine trends in loyalty. Promoters are advocates of a company and become a company's best salespeople.

In B2B markets the average NPS is between 20 and 30. The scores shown in Table 38.1 are reasonable benchmarks.

For many companies the best way of improving an NPS is to work hard to increase the 'likelihood to recommend score' amongst those giving a score of 7 or 8 out of 10. If a company or brand has more than 20 per cent giving a score of 6 or below, there is something wrong with the offer or the offer is being targeted at the wrong segment.

Companies and brands achieving high NPS scores (50+) always have an excellent product. They are also likely to excel at one or more of the following:

- A strong brand that delivers against its promise.
- Good relationships with customers through frequent contact and with staff who are friendly and empowered.
- Responds quickly to requests.
- Is easy to do business with.

The origins of the model

For many years companies have measured the satisfaction people have with their products and services using scales that run from 1 to 10, or 1 to 5, or 1 to 7, where a high number means very satisfied and a low score means not satisfied at all. Such surveys usually have a large number of questions that explore satisfaction across different aspects of the product, the delivery, the sales service and price. These satisfaction surveys and questions are still widely employed.

The NPS has found appeal because, according to its inventor, Fred Reichheld of Bain & Company, it is the '*One Number You Need To Grow*'. This was also the title of an article by Reichheld in *Harvard Business Review* in 2003.[1] The 'one question' concept is appealing to senior managers of companies who may find the traditional plethora of customer satisfaction questions confusing and too much detail.

It should be pointed out that Reichheld does not suggest that the only question posed is 'likelihood to recommend'. He believes, quite rightly, that it is followed up with the supplementary question 'Why did you say that?' Insights from the answers to this open-ended question often point to actions required to improve loyalty.

Developments of the model

The appeal of the NPS is its simplicity. As the name of the tool suggests, it delivers a metric on the net number of people who are advocates of a brand or company. Many large consumer brands have integrated the NPS into their customer loyalty programmes. It is often used in employee research to establish staff loyalty to the company where they work.

Despite its popularity amongst large corporates, research by Hayes (2008),[2] suggests that the 'likelihood to recommend' question is no better a predictor of growth than other customer loyalty questions such as 'How satisfied are you with Brand X?' or 'How likely are you to buy Brand X again?'

A weakness of the tool is where there are only a limited number of re-spondents. In many B2B markets it may only be possible to obtain 100 completed surveys on the NPS question from customers. If the majority of the responses give a score of 7 or 8 out of 10, the NPS will be calculated from a small base of promoters and detractors. This makes the score volatile as it is tracked over time. The movement of just one or two customers in and out of the promoters and detractors categories will cause the NPS metric to change drastically. It is an unreliable score when sample sizes are small.

It is best to assume that there is no single question that can be used to monitor customer loyalty and satisfaction. NPS is certainly a useful measure enabling changes to be tracked over time. More questions should be asked to get a true understanding of customer loyalty and to find out what is driving a high or low score. A question that asks *'How likely would you be to repurchase a product from this company?'* may be just as good a measure of loyalty. So too, many companies like to ask a company effort score because they know that ease of doing business is a key driver of satisfaction and loyalty – 'How much effort is required to do business with this company?'

Customer loyalty comes from the complex relationship with the product, service, price and channel and it cannot be fully understood by asking one question.

In 2021 Fred Reichheld, together with Darci Darnell and Maureen Burns, wrote an article in *Harvard Business Review* proposing a new metric which he called the 'net promoter 3.0'.[3] He claimed that this was a better system for understanding the real value of happy customers.

The centrepiece of this new thinking is that delighted customers return again and again and also promote their favoured company to others. This results in something that they call 'earned growth'. Imagine one of your customers tells five people about your wonderful company and they in turn become customers; how do you measure this? These are new customers you have earned through great customer experience. They are quite different to new customers who you may have bought through expensive promotions and marketing. Earned customers cost you less, they spend more, give more recommendations and are likely to be more loyal. The argument goes that it is earned customers that we must seek.

The problem with this very worthwhile metric is that it isn't easy to measure. A customer who increases purchases from your company may be doing so because their business is growing and not necessarily because you are doing an amazing job. A new customer that comes on board may have seen one of your adverts and not joined as a result of a recommendation. The best way you can find out how and why they have become a customer is by talking to them. Understanding the earned growth rate means having a dialogue with the customer. There is nothing wrong with that – but it isn't easy.

Measuring the 'earned growth rate' requires us to find out the primary reason a customer is doing business with us. This has its difficulties as some customers may struggle to give an appropriate answer. It is suggested that customers are presented with some options such as 'trustworthy reputation', 'recommendation from friends', 'seen an advert', 'helpful salesperson', 'good price deal'. The first two of these options would put the customer in the 'earned' bracket while the others suggest that it has been 'bought'. But is that right? Someone who opts for 'trustworthy reputation' may say this, not knowing quite why they think that way. In fact it may be that they have been influenced by brand advertising that has subliminally moulded their perceptions over many years. This isn't an earned customer; they have been bought.

The model in action

Molson Coors brews beers and lagers. It also has a distribution division that sells and delivers soft and alcoholic drinks to a wide range of independent pubs, clubs, bars and restaurants.

In 2011 the company in the UK had a strategic vision to become first choice for customers of its distribution division. In order to become first choice the company interviewed customers to find out what type of experience they were receiving and how it could be improved. It devised a simple programme based on asking customers how likely they would be to recommend Molson Coors following a recent business transaction. Every year thousands of short telephone interviews are carried out to obtain feedback.

Key results from the customer interviews are emailed to managers so they can address any issues. Audio recordings are played to the business managers so they can hear the voice of the customer at first hand. Quarterly strategic reviews track progress.

The company witnessed a significant increase in its NPS from a market average of +25 when it started the programme, to a market-leading score of +60 today. This improvement was achieved by more and better interactions with account managers and the credit control service.

The importance of customer experience within the organization was made clear when the customer loyalty scores were used to calculate the bonuses of regional directors. This created high engagement and focus with staff who were in a position to implement change and make a difference to the customer experience.

There were many benefits to the customer experience programme. The increase in customer loyalty resulted in a reduction in customer churn. Customers began purchasing a wider range of products from Molson Coors and the financial results improved all round.

The most important part of this programme was the effect of using the NPS in making Molson Coors a more customer-focused organization. As a consequence it was easier to introduce other customer-engaging initiatives such as an online community called the 'Promoter Club'. This is an online blog in which customers can share and discuss improvements that Molson Coors can make to their service. One such improvement that was suggested through the Promoter Club was to the online website, which now allows customers to pay online rather than having to wait for a call from credit control.

Some things to think about

- There is an enormous interest in building customer loyalty – and for good reason. Once the expense of finding a new customer has been met, it makes complete sense to keep them for as long as possible. The NPS is a simple metric that correlates strongly with customer loyalty.

- The NPS is best used when there is a sample of at least 50 and ideally 100 responses. This is because many people give scores of 7 or 8 out of 10, which means that the NPS score is calculated on a low sample size (the percentage of promoters minus the percentage of detractors) and can fluctuate wildly when tracked.

- It may also be worth considering asking other questions that drive loyalty such as overall satisfaction, satisfaction with different parts of the company's offer, and likelihood to repurchase. All these questions will benefit from a supplementary question: 'Why did you say that?'

Notes

1 Reichheld, FF (2003) The one number you need to grow, *Harvard Business Review*, 81 (12) (December)

2 Hayes, R (2008) The true test of loyalty, *Quality Progress*, 41 (6) (June), pp 20–6

3 Reichheld, FF, Darnell, D and Burns, M (2021) Net Promoter 3.0: A better system for understanding the real value of happy customers, *Harvard Business Review*, November–December

New product pricing (Gabor– Granger and van Westendorp)

Pricing new products

39

What the model looks like and how it works

A well-thought-out pricing strategy is crucial for optimizing both sales volume and profit. It is surprising, therefore, according to data from the Professional Pricing Society (the world's largest organization dedicated to pricing) that fewer than 5 per cent of Fortune 500 companies have a full-time function dedicated to pricing.[1] Every company needs to ask itself the question 'Am I charging optimum prices that will generate the maximum profits for my sales?'

The consulting group McKinsey carried out a famous exercise that determined a price rise of 1 per cent at an average company in the S&P 1500 index (which covers small through to large companies) would generate an 8 per cent increase in operating profit if sales volume stayed steady.[2] With just a 1 per cent price increase, sales are unlikely to waver much and the extra profit flows directly on to the bottom line. The leverage of price is substantial. All overhead costs have been met and so the additional gross margin that is obtained (somewhere between 40 per cent and 60 per cent depending on the product or service) contributes completely to net profits. It does of course raise the question 'Why not increase prices by 5 per cent, 10 per cent or even 15 per cent?'

Launching a new product and pitching it at the right price is critical. A price that is too high will kill sales and a price that is too low will jeopardize profits. Many companies set the price of new products by looking at competitive products already on the market and make a judgement as to where the new product fits. The sales teams have a strong contribution in this discussion and there is more than a possibility that they will push for a price that is relatively low, on the grounds that it will make their job easier. It is worth using independent research and tried-and-tested pricing tools to make sure that the optimum price is chosen.

The only sure way of obtaining an accurate and realistic understanding of how price works for a new product is to carry out a test market – in other words to create a situation where customers are exposed to real price changes with real demand pressures. However, it would still be necessary to decide on what price to launch into the test market and, in any case, test markets are expensive and difficult to organize. For this reason, we turn to pricing models that simulate buying situations.

Gabor–Granger

The Gabor–Granger pricing tool is often used to establish price perceptions of new products. It was developed in the 1960s by two economists (André Gabor and Clive Granger). The proposed new product is shown or described to target customers who are asked if they would buy it at particular prices. The prices that are presented to customers are changed and on each occasion respondents say if they would buy or not. In theory, customers should be given random prices but in practice the first price they are presented with starts high and subsequent prices are lowered. Levels of demand can be calculated at each price point (the demand curve in Figure 39.1). Using this estimate of demand, the price elasticity (or expected revenue) can be calculated and so the optimum price-point is established. The demand curve in Figure 39.1 shows that a price of around $3.50 would be good for the launch as it would capture almost 80 per cent of target customers. Of course, it would be necessary to check whether an acceptable profit can be achieved at this price.

van Westendorp

A more sophisticated variation of the Gabor–Granger technique is a tool developed by Peter van Westendorp. Respondents are shown or told the features and benefits of a product (or service) and the price sensitivity measurement (PSM) tool determines pricing options based on four questions:

Figure 39.1   Price volume curve from market research

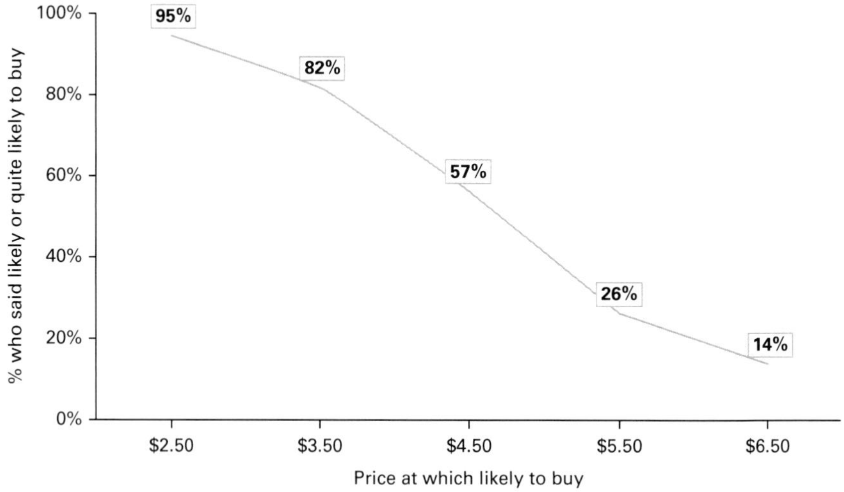

SOURCE After Gabor and Granger (1965)

- At what price would you consider this product/service to be cheap?
- At what price would you consider this product/service to be too expensive?
- At what price would you consider this product/service to be priced so cheaply that you would worry about its quality?
- At what price would you consider this product/service to be too expensive to consider buying it?

As with the Gabor–Granger tool, van Westendorp is often used to set the price of a new product or service and can also be used for price-testing existing products. Analysis of the data yields four demand curves, as shown in Figure 39.2. The various intersections on the curves describe the pricing options:

The indifference price point (IPP)

This is where the number of respondents who regard the price as cheap is equal to the number of respondents who regard the price is expensive (see Figure 39.2). According to van Westendorp, this generally represents either the median price actually paid by consumers or the price of the product of an important market leader. IPP is based on customers' experiences with price levels in the market and will change with market conditions.

Figure 39.2   Using van Westendorp to determine the price of workplace ear defenders

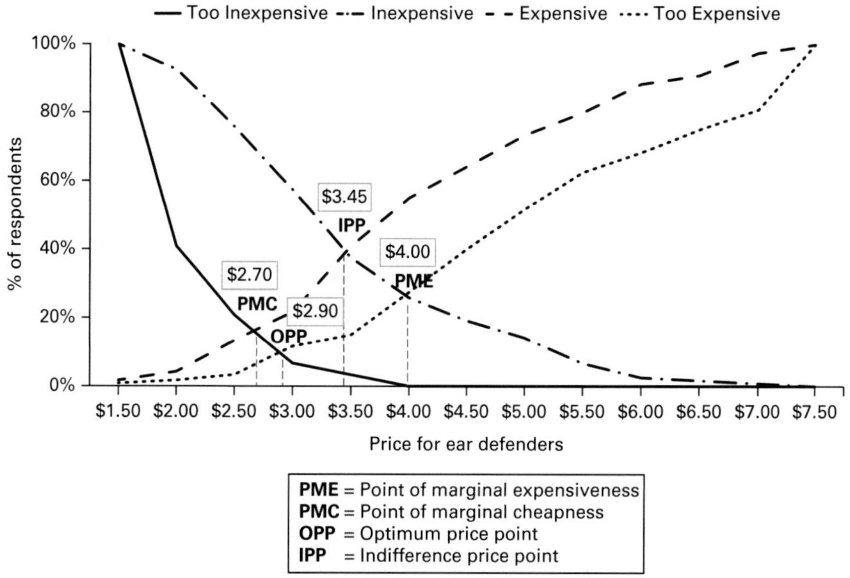

SOURCE Based on van Westendorp (1976)

The optimum price point (OPP)

This is the price at which the number of customers who see the product as too cheap is equal to the number who see the product as too expensive. This is typically the recommended price.

The range of prices between the point of marginal cheapness (PMC) and the point of marginal expensiveness (PME) is the range of acceptable prices for a product. According to van Westendorp, in established markets, few competitive products are priced outside of this range.

The origins of the model

Clive Granger and André Gabor, professors of economics at the University of Nottingham in the UK, developed their pricing tool for new products and services in the 1960s.[3]

Peter van Westendorp, a Dutch economist, developed his price sensitivity measurement tool in 1976.[4]

Developments of the model

Although Gabor–Granger and van Westendorp pricing tools have been around for more than 40 or 50 years, they are not so often used. There may be a number of reasons for this:

- Conjoint analysis (see Chapter 16) is much preferred by market researchers as a more scientific approach. Conjoint calculates the optimum price and the utility values of the different features of the product without having to ask specific questions about people's perceptions of what is too cheap or expensive.

- There is something intuitively worrying about asking people if a product is too cheap or lowering the price until someone says 'Yes, I will buy it.' People don't seem to worry about buying an airline ticket for as little as $25.

- Interpreting the findings from Gabor–Granger and van Westendorp is not always straightforward. van Westendorp offers us a number of options where the demand lines intersect. Which of these is the one we should choose? The Gabor–Granger tool may worry people if they feel that respondents will latch on to the fact that the price keeps dropping and so hang on to choose the lowest price possible.

These concerns may have held back the two tools. That said, in circumstances when the tools have been used alongside conjoint, they have delivered surprisingly similar results. Also, when sample sizes are small, as is often the case in B2B markets, Gabor–Granger and van Westendorp deliver very believable results. Conjoint tends to be unreliable with sample sizes of around 100 respondents or fewer.

The model in action

A manufacturer of ear defenders used in noisy workplace environments wanted to test a new product against competitive products; 120 companies were recruited to take part in a test. All had workforces that used ear defenders daily. All the products were stripped of their brands and identified as product A through to C. Each product was used for up to a week in the workplace. Guidelines were given to the companies that did the tests to ensure that the ear defenders were used in a controlled way and to rule out exceptions that could skew the results.

At the end of the trial the buyer at each company was interviewed and asked their views on the ear defenders, including the four van Westendorp questions:

- At what price would you consider this ear defender to be good value?
- At what price would you consider this ear defender to be priced so low that you doubt its quality?
- At what price would you consider this ear defender to be getting expensive, but at a price that you would still consider paying?
- At what price would you consider this ear defender to be so expensive (i.e. too expensive) that you would never consider buying it?

The results were analysed and graphed (see Figure 39.2). The new product was well received and the van Westendorp tool suggested three possible prices. A price of $2.90 was indicated as the optimum price point. This price also fitted the perceptions of the company's salesforce.

However, it was decided to launch the new ear defender at $4 a pair, knowing that many of the companies taking part in the test were large users of these products and would expect significant discounts from the list price. If the ear defender was launched at $2.90 a pair, there would be no room for manoeuvre in price negotiations. Furthermore, the ear defenders were tested without disclosure of their brands. The new ear defender was to be launched with a strong brand and this would have a value in the minds of many buyers.

The pricing strategy proved successful. The new ear defenders were launched at $4 a pair and actual prices achieved amongst buyers were around $3.50 per pair. The ear defender company was reassured by the product and pricing test. It could have used its own judgement to arrive at a launch price for the ear defender but, had it done so, it would have been at a lower value than the one suggested by the research and 'money would have been left on the table'.

Some things to think about

- Establishing the price of a new product is critically important as it determines the success of the launch and the profitability of sales. The Gabor–Granger tool can be used to test concepts before prototypes are made. Once a prototype is developed and can be shown to respondents, the van Westendorp tool will indicate the optimum price.

- Both Gabor–Granger and van Westendorp have proved to give realistic price levels for new products. It is worth considering launching at a slightly higher price than that which is suggested by the tool if it is a market that expects discounts.

Notes

1 Mitchell, K (2011) The current state of pricing practice in US firms, opening speech at Professional Pricing Society Annual Spring Conference, Chicago, 3–6 May

2 Marn, M, Roegner, E and Zawada, C (2003) The power of pricing, *McKinsey Quarterly*, February

3 Gabor, A and Granger, CWJ (1965) The pricing of new products, *Scientific Business*, 3, August, pp 3–12

4 van Westendorp, P (1976) NSS price sensitivity meter (PSM): a new approach to study consumer perception of price, Proceedings of the ESOMAR Congress

Personas   40

Improving the focus of marketing messages

What the model looks like and how it works

Marketing has a high cost. Promotion is expensive and much of it can fall on stony ground. Salespeople too are expensive, especially if they are talking to the wrong people. It is very easy to cast the marketing net wide but this means that we waste a very large percentage of our time and resources. We avoid this by identifying groups of people who have needs that we believe we can satisfy. Segmentation allows us to serve their needs better and more efficiently.

The ideal segment from the customer's point of view is just one person. This is unrealistic. We have to communicate to broader groups of people and we need to do so in such a way that it seems personalized and relevant at the receiving end. In order to achieve targeted communications that are effective, we should have someone in mind. One-to-one communications allow us to engage fully. The more empathetic we are with customers, the more likely we are to understand their preferences. It is this principle that underpins the idea of developing personas.

A persona is a particular character. It is a description of someone, not just anyone. It is the image, the face and personality of a person. If we can characterize a persona within a group of customers, it becomes easier to target them. Persona development is important in advertising in order to give a focus to the promotional efforts. With the persona in mind we know who we are talking to, who we are designing for and who we want to do business with. Persona development nearly always focuses on the buyer of the product. We can develop personas other than customers. For example, it may be helpful to build a persona of someone who is an influencer rather than a customer, or even a 'negative' persona – someone we want to exclude from targeted communications.

The starting point in building a buyer persona is to be very clear about the goal. What is it that we want to sell them? This may lead to a discussion on the composition of the decision-making unit:

- How are decisions made to buy the product?
- Which groups of people are involved in the decision-making process?
- At what stage do these different people get involved in the decision?
- What does each person look for to help them arrive at a decision?
- What role do they play in the decision? Who is the key decision maker?

The discussion about the decision-making unit will require hard choices. Just one person will be selected from the number of decision makers and influencers that are involved. If there are a number of key decision makers it may mean that two or three personas have to be developed.

In building a persona it is good to use a name and a job title. All this is made up, of course, but it is part of the process of characterizing the person we expect to find in a segment. A photograph of someone helps. It is now possible to add details on their demographics, their goals and challenges in life, their values and fears, and the messages that resonate with them. The list in Table 40.1 is by way of example. There is no limit to what could or should be included in the list. If the persona that is being developed is for targeting breakfast cereals, for example, attributes will be included that would be quite different for someone who buys industrial raw materials.

When creating a buyer persona it is useful to brainstorm and to use as many sources of information as possible:

- **Market research reports**: these provide a good background on the key decision makers. The market research reports might have limited information on the personal background of the buyers and influencers but much can be inferred. Focus groups and quantitative surveys can provide insights on the composition of people within the decision-making unit.

- **Sales teams**: customer-facing people speak to buyers and influencers all the time and will be able to provide detailed descriptions.

- **Internet searches**: viewing images on a Google search for people of a certain trade will show dozens of pictures that characterize the audience.

- **LinkedIn**: a search for job titles on LinkedIn shows photos and profiles of people in that role. An examination of these will show ages, education levels and career paths.

- **Google analytics**: Google analytics provides statistics on the demographics of people who visit your website, including the interest that people have in external activities.

Table 40.1 A template for developing a buyer persona

Persona	
Name	
Company role	
Job title	
Work responsibilities	
Company	
Size	
Industry	
Location	
Demographics	
Age	
Gender	
Education/qualifications	
Salary	
Marital status	
Number of children	
What keeps them awake at night	
Challenges at work	
Challenges at home	
Ambitions in life	
Guiding values	
Empathy	
Model of car they drive	
Music they listen to	
Favourite books	
Where they go on holiday	
Pets owned	
Favourite sport	
Media	
Newspapers that are read	
Journals that are read	
Favourite websites	
Blogs that are visited	

Once the persona has been developed, the real work begins of developing the communication messages. The persona will show:

- messages and images that grab attention;
- messages that resonate and mean something;
- words that indicate you speak the same language;
- compelling arguments that make someone want to do business with you.

The origins of the model

The concept of personas goes back to the early 20th century and Jungian psychology. It has been adopted by marketers relatively recently. In the 1980s, Alan Cooper, an American software designer and programmer, pioneered the use of personas as a tool to help create high-tech products.[1]

In the 1990s advertising agencies started to talk about 'a day in the life of your customer'.[2] In doing so they created fictional characters that represented the customer segments they were targeting. Advertising agencies are still today the major users of personas.

Developments of the model

A criticism of personas is that they can be too narrow. They focus on just one person and exclude others who may be involved in the buying process. It may be that insufficient thought has been given to the decision-making unit and more than one persona should be developed, each a focus for different marketing messages.

It is easy to get carried away when building personas. Where possible the characterization of the persona should be grounded in reality. The personas are fictitious but they should be based on as much of a factual or statistical background as possible.

It is sometimes difficult for people to 'walk in their customers' shoes'. In developing personas, managers tend to project themselves. This egocentricity results in people ignoring objective data and creating subjective personas. It is a reminder to check all aspects of the persona with as much factual knowledge as possible. Also, to remind the persona development team to acknowledge their biases so that they can deal with them.

Personas are not static. The attitudes and needs of personas change as they move through the customer journey, acquiring knowledge on a company through to eventually becoming a customer, even a loyal customer. Their hopes and challenges will be different as they move through the stages. It is a strong argument for regularly revisiting the personas.

Something has happened since I penned the first edition of this book. Facebook has changed its name to Meta in the belief that personas (for that read avatars) are going to be the centre of its universe in the future. Avatars are representations of a person, originally in video games and internet forums but according to Meta they will be increasingly used as icons to represent personas in business and domestic life. The jury is out on just how far this concept can be pushed. There is no doubt that avatars and personas can simplify and brighten up our lives. However, I have a sneaking suspicion that human beings like human beings and although cartoon characters might be quite nice occasionally, I am not so sure that they will dominate our lives. (I may have to retract this if we get to the third edition of this book!)

The model in action

Molson Coors Brewing Company UK and Ireland is a distributor of alcoholic and soft drinks to pubs, clubs and restaurants. It places significant importance on the Net Promoter Score® (NPS) (see Chapter 38). The NPS is driven by achieving a high percentage of customers who give scores of 9 or 10 out of 10 in answer to the question 'How likely would you be to recommend this company on a scale from 0 to 10?' The NPS is the percentage of people who give a score of 9 or 10 (promoters) minus the percentage who give a score of 6 or less (detractors). For the purposes of the calculation, those who give a score of 7 or 8 are ignored (passives).

In order to bring the promoters, the passives and the detractors to life, Molson Coors developed three personas. These characterized the promoters, passives and detractors by making them specific to a person. There was Promoter Pat, Passive Pete and Detractor Dave. A poster was made of each person with a summary of their views on Molson Coors, and with background demographic data on their age, gender and location (see Figure 40.1 for an example of a persona).

The persona crucially built a picture of what type of outlet they represented. For example, it showed the number of suppliers used, the share of

Figure 40.1   Example of a persona

One minute interview with...

PROMOTER
PAUL

IN A NUTSHELL

- I am always short of time and need my suppliers to be responsive.
- If a supplier looks after me and makes sure I am never short of product, I will be forever loyal.
- I don't want lots of chat, just someone to help me grow my business.

FACT FILE

Name: Paul   Title: Founder of marketing services company
Age: 60   Location: Manchester, England

WHICH SUPPLIERS ARE YOU RESPONSIBLE FOR CHOOSING?

I have a say (not always the final one) in choosing suppliers that are strategic to our business – software platforms, accounting firm, legal, promotional agencies. I also interview all our senior recruits.

WHAT DO YOU LOOK FOR?

I want suppliers (and employees) that really care – about other people, their own business and the world.

WHO DO YOU BENCHMARK AGAINST?

Our IT contractor. Is rated 10/10 on everything. I would definitely recommend him. He is ALWAYS available. He almost always can fix our problems. He will work through the night or at weekends if necessary.

HOW OFTEN DO YOU SPEAK TO YOUR SUPPLIERS?

Not as often as you may think. Maybe once a month. If I am not speaking to them I know that all is going well.

IMPROVING YOUR EXPERIENCE

I would recommend all these great suppliers and very little needs to change. Their service is great and I feel supported. Maybe they could be a bit more proactive in coming to me with ideas for making my company different and better.

business held by Molson Coors, the type of drinks that were important in their outlet, and a summary of what the persona judged to be important in improving their experience with Molson Coors. Large posters were made of each of the personas and placed around the office as a constant reminder of what Molson Coors needed to do to improve its NPS. Over the period of the campaign, the company's NPS rose from +25 to +60 today – an incredibly high score for any company and helped by the persona development.

Some things to think about

- When developing persona, make it personal. Give the person a name. Imagine what sort of person this is – their age, where they live, their family background, their aspirations at work, the type of car they drive, etc. This person should be as close as possible to the bullseye in the range of people you target.

- The persona you have developed is your customer. Consider making a large cut-out model of this person and bring it into your marketing meetings. This is your customer and they are listening to what you say!

Notes

1 Cooper, A (2004) *The Inmates Are Running The Asylum: Why high tech products drive us crazy and how to restore the sanity*, Sams Publishing, Indianapolis
2 Gouillart, F and Sturdivant, FD (1994) Spend a day in the life of your customers, *Harvard Business Review*, January–February, 72 (1), pp 116–25

PEST   41

Assessing four major macro factors that shape a company's future

What the model looks like and how it works

PEST is an acronym that describes four external forces that shape the business environment – political, economic, social and technological.

The PEST tool is used to examine the macro and micro factors that determine threats and opportunities within the marketplace. Like Porter's five forces or a SWOT analysis (see Chapters 42 and 54), PEST is used to assess the market environment for a business when planning a strategy, writing a marketing plan or thinking about future scenarios. It is normally used before a SWOT as it provides an understanding of the opportunities and threats. The PEST framework can be used to examine the market for a company, product or brand. It is an analysis worth carrying out at least once a year (more frequently if some forces have changed).

Political

There are very few markets that escape political influence. Political influences affect the costs and ease of doing business within a country and can be imposed in any of the following ways:

- The political stability of a region – including the risks of war and military action.

- Taxes on goods – these affect the price of domestic goods and imports. The taxes can be value-added tax, sales tax and import duties. Taxes raise the price of products and can slow sales.

- Taxes on people and companies – the taxes that we pay on profits and earnings can alter the dynamics of the market. High taxes limit the availability of cash for spending and investment.

- Government policy – most governments have policies that influence businesses. Some encourage free trade and investment from overseas. Some policies are nationalistic and favour local suppliers. Some governments like state control while others encourage free enterprise.
- Labour laws – these affect issues such as hiring and firing, pension rights, maternity rights, minimum wages, etc.
- Pricing regulations – including anti-trust laws.
- Environmental laws – these affect waste disposal, product labelling, chemicals that can and cannot be used in processing, etc.

Economic

Economic factors influence the attractiveness of a market from the point of view of costs and growth. These include:

- the GDP of the region – its economic prosperity;
- the GDP per head;
- average incomes and disposable incomes;
- employment and unemployment rates;
- labour skills and costs;
- distribution and channels into the market;
- comparative cost advantages of the region (which are derived from labour costs as well as the costs of raw materials);
- the economic system in the country including government interference with businesses;
- the growth of the economy in the past and forecast growth for the future;
- credit availability;
- exchange rates and their stability;
- inflation;
- interest rates.

Social

Social factors are those forces that affect the workforce and buyers of products. They include:

- population size and growth rates;
- language;
- the demographics of the population: age, gender, religion, education, job skills, household composition, etc;
- the class structures within the country;
- the media that reaches the population;
- the average length of life and the health of the population;
- attitudes to safety;
- the culture of the population and its willingness/ability to work;
- ethical considerations.

Technological

Technological factors can influence the costs of doing business within a region or a market. They are important because they affect the ability of a company to innovate. They vary in importance depending on the nature of the business. Factors to be considered here include:

- technical infrastructure in the region (e.g. broadband distribution and strength);
- speed of technological change within the market;
- types of technological change that are taking place;
- technological skills and interest that exist in the region;
- the willingness of the population to adopt innovations at home and in the workplace;
- research and development spend;
- patent protection.

The number and type of factors that can be built into a PEST analysis are almost unlimited and are business dependent. For example, a food company will place different weights of importance on factors compared to an IT company.

The aim of the PEST analysis is to determine what the future scenario will be for a business by examining each macro and micro factor in the past and the present. The PEST analysis is best used when examining the attractiveness of the market. It is a complement to a SWOT analysis, which focuses on a specific business unit. The PEST usually precedes the SWOT as it feeds into the SWOT's opportunities and threats (see Figure 41.1).

Figure 41.1 The relationship between PEST and SWOT

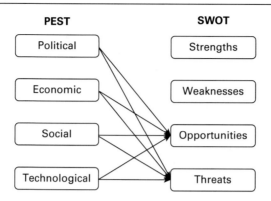

The origins of the model

The origins of the PEST model are vague. One of the first mentions of the four factors was by Francis Aguilar, a professor at Harvard Business School who, in 1967, wrote a book entitled *Scanning the Business Environment*,[1] in which he discussed various factors affecting a business. He gave them the acronym ETPS, referring to economic, technical, political and social factors. It was left to others to reassemble the order of the acronym into the more memorable PEST.

Developments of the model

The simplicity of the PEST model has prompted many variations. Those who believe that the acronym has a negative connotation sometimes refer to the same four factors as STEP.

Others have felt that the model needs extending and have included additional factors, the most common being *legislative* and *environmental*. These additions turn the acronym into PESTLE.

The legislative and environmental factors are arguably already contained within the original PEST model. For those who want to separate them, they could include:

Legislative

Legislative factors can be separated out or included under the 'political' and 'social' headings. They include factors that affect the costs and ease of doing business such as:

- Employment law, including discrimination law, health and safety, etc.
- Company law, including restrictions on directors and company share-holders.
- Anti-trust law and those affecting competitive practices.

Environmental

Environmental factors include:

- Geographical location: a country's location, especially in a global econo-my, can offer a considerable advantage.
- Infrastructure: the roads, railways, airports, water supply and broadband availability give certain environments an advantage.
- The weather and climate change: the availability of sunshine, rainfall and the possibility of hurricanes, tsunamis and wind can all influence the business opportunity.
- Pollution: air pollution and water pollution.
- Raw materials: energy, minerals, fuel, water, etc.

The model in action

The Coca-Cola Company is very visible around the world and makes a great case study for analysis. For example:

Political factors

- Coca-Cola products are regulated by the Food and Drug Administration (FDA) in the United States. These regulations ensure that the product is fit for the United States and also for virtually every other country in the world.
- Political disruption in certain countries of the world has an inevitable negative effect on Coca-Cola revenues.
- Anti- or pro-American feelings could influence Coke consumption.
- Governments may choose to tax sugary drinks.

Economic factors

- The economic growth of a country significantly affects opportunities for Coca-Cola. The financial crises of 2009 adversely impacted Coca-Cola around the globe (though not to the extent it affected other businesses).[2]

- Higher income per head, and an increase in disposable income, provides more opportunities for people to buy indulgent drinks such as Coca-Cola.

- Exchange rates can have an effect on Coca-Cola's performance. For example, the devaluation of Venezuela's currency reduced Coca-Cola's profits in that market by 55 per cent in 2014.[3]

Social factors

- In developed countries there is a trend towards a lower consumption of carbonated drinks as people are becoming concerned about obesity and health. Diet or low-sugar versions of the drink now account for over 40 per cent of the company's cola sales in the UK.[4]

- Coca-Cola has a high appeal as an acceptable alternative to alcoholic drinks for those who want to be abstemious and in countries where alcohol is not available.

- Coca-Cola is a drink for all genders and people of all ages. It is a classless drink.

- In the United States there has been a decline in the consumption of soft drinks over the last 15 years while the consumption of bottled water and sports drinks has increased.[5]

- Media attention and blogs are not always kind to Coca-Cola, mentioning health issues or the experiments with Coke that make a dirty penny shiny.[6]

Technological factors

- There have been significant changes in the way Coca-Cola promotes, especially through social media and digital channels.[7] This is an important shift as digital is a different medium reaching a younger audience.

- The technology for filling cans and bottles has increased enormously such that it is now possible to produce cans of Coca-Cola faster than a machine gun can fire bullets.[8]

Some things to think about

- Take time to build up a deep understanding of each of the PEST factors. Work out which of these forces are the most important influences on your company. Set up alerts to inform you of any changes to these factors.

- Pay particular attention to the threats and opportunities that arise from the analysis. Work out an action plan in response to these.

Notes

1 Aguilar, FJ (1967) *Scanning the Business Environment*, Macmillan, New York

2 NBC News, Recession Takes Fizz Out Of Coke's Profit, www.nbcnews.com/id/29161172/ns/business-us_business/t/recession-takes-fizz-out-cokes-profit/#.WkzrWVVl_xU (archived at https://perma.cc/TWM3-VUQT)

3 McGrath, M (2014) Coca-Cola takes $247 million hit from Venezuelan currency devaluation as Q1 profit, revenue fall, *Forbes*, www.forbes.com/sites/maggiemcgrath/2014/04/15/coca-cola-takes-247-million-hit-from-venezuelan-currency-devaluation-as-q1-profit-revenue-fall/?sh=33b0ef5a3225 (archived at https://perma.cc/F6AU-HML8)

4 Coca-Cola (nd) Which is CocaCola GB's best-selling cola?, www.coca-cola.co.uk/our-business/faqs/which-is-your-bestselling-brand-coca-cola-or-diet-coke (archived at https://perma.cc/RTC7-4WBX)

5 Kell, J (2016) Soda Consumption Falls To 30-Year Low In The US, https://fortune.com/2016/03/29/soda-sales-drop-11th-year/ (archived at https://perma.cc/PPN5-4NDH)

6 Penny Cleaning Experiment, http://sciencewithkids.com/Experiments/Chemistry-experiments/penny-cola-cleaner-experiment.html (archived at https://perma.cc/7NYZ-ZRD4)

7 Mortimer, N (2016) Coca-Cola Has Just Hired Its First Chief Digital Marketing Officer And Here's Why, *The Drum*, www.thedrum.com/news/2016/12/12/coca-cola-has-just-hired-its-first-chief-digital-marketing-officer-and-here-s-why (archived at https://perma.cc/862T-UG2G)

8 Foodprocessing-technology.com, Coca Cola Bottling Plant, United Kingdom, www.foodprocessing-technology.com/projects/coca-bottling/ (archived at https://perma.cc/79PF-VMR6)

Porter's five forces 42

Assessing five economic factors for competitive intensity

What the model looks like and how it works

Life would be easy for a business if it was not for competitors. Is that true? Certainly competitors can be a nuisance. They steal customers, they force down prices, they sometimes produce better products. However, competition does have a positive side. The plethora of coffee shops on the high street has raised our interest in fresh coffee. As a result, all the coffee shops benefit including Starbucks who launched the concept of the Wi-Fi coffee lounge with easy chairs. Competitors may be a nuisance with their improved products but that is a stimulus for us to perfect ours. Pressure from competitors on prices drives us to be more efficient. In the end, it could be argued, everyone benefits.

Michael Porter recognized five forces that bear down on companies. These five forces are not macro factors such as those described in the PEST model (political, economic, social and technological), rather they are micro factors much closer to a business. The forces are likely to have an immediate effect on the company and influence its ability to serve its customers and make a profit.

Industry rivalry

The central force, the one that is usually in the face of every business, is the rivalry that exists with other competitors in the market. Markets can be highly aggressive with all the suppliers attacking each other on price, quality and delivery. Sometimes in mature markets there are a limited number of suppliers (an oligopoly) and the rivalry resembles an orchestrated dance.

This is not necessarily collusion (this would be classed in most countries as illegal), rather they are actions that are taken through years of learning the best moves to make following a change made by another supplier.

Bargaining power of suppliers

Suppliers can have a huge influence on competitiveness. For example, 60 per cent of the world's known cobalt reserves are in the Democratic Republic of Congo. Cobalt has become a vital material in the manufacture of batteries for electric cars. As car manufacturers ramp up their electric car production lines, speculators have amassed large stockpiles of cobalt, driving up its price.[1] Companies such as Tesla that require batteries for its electric vehicles are being forced to pay the premiums caused by restricted supply.

It is not just raw materials that can influence a company's competitive position. A supplier of power tools could disenfranchise one of its dealers, removing a major product line from the distributor's portfolio and putting its business under threat.

Threat of substitutes

A company's competitive position can be weakened by substitutes. Almost all products have some form of substitution. If coffee becomes too expensive, people can turn to tea, hot chocolate or other beverages. If rail fares become too expensive people can consider travelling by road or air. Metal can be replaced by plastic; coal can be replaced by oil, gas or renewables (wind power, solar power, hydroelectric, nuclear). Substitution is not always easy. People get hooked on coffee and will not readily change. Advanced composites offer significant advantages in the manufacture of the airframes and interiors of new jetliners but they can only be built into new models, as the designs of existing aircraft are approved and cannot easily be changed.

Threat of new entrants

The cosy position enjoyed by suppliers to a market can be disrupted by new players. Any new supplier will steal some share. They could have a lower price, a superior product or a completely different way of serving the market. In some cases the cost of entry is low. A Chinese manufacturer of steel can sell its products into Europe relatively easily. It already has a manufacturing base in China and all it has to do is to transport the material and pay the import duties. In other markets it may be more difficult. It would be difficult for just anybody to enter the electric car market, as the cost of manufacturing electric cars is extremely high. The investment in manufacturing facilities and marketing will limit entry to established car companies or rich billionaires who are brave and committed enough to break the traditional mould.

Bargaining power of buyers

In some markets there are a limited number of large buyers who can dictate prices and terms. Dairy farmers supplying supermarkets and grocery stores find themselves dictated to by their large customers. Service companies wanting to do business with large corporate companies are seldom in a position to strike a hard bargain as buyers have a wide choice of often quite desperate suppliers. Many small and medium enterprises find themselves in a position where they are dependent on one or two customers for the bulk of their revenue. These companies are highly vulnerable to the loss of one of these large customers and are likely to yield to pressure from them simply to keep the business.

Porter referred to the threat of substitutes, the threat of established rivals and the threat of new entrants as 'horizontal' competition. The bargaining power of suppliers and the bargaining power of customers he considered to be 'vertical' competition.

The five forces model will not, on its own, point to a strategy. The model will show the weight of influence of each micro force that surrounds the company. It may be helpful to also carry out a PEST analysis and understand the higher-level forces before examining the five forces. Armed with this understanding of what is shaping the business, a SWOT would complete the strategic overhaul.

The origins of the model

As a young associate professor at Harvard Business School, Michael Porter published an article in the *Harvard Business Review* in 1979 entitled 'How competitive forces shape strategy'.[2] There has been the inevitable analysis and criticism of the model since then but its wide use and appeal is testimony to the significant contribution it has made to strategic thinking. In particular, the five forces are those that influence the profit structure of an industry as they determine how the economic value is apportioned. It can be drained away by any of the forces – rivalry between competitors, the power of suppliers, the power of customers, new entrants or substitutes.

Developments of the model

In the mid-1990s, a suggestion was made to add a sixth force.[3] The sixth force was 'complementary products' – that is, the impact of related products and services that are already in the market. For example, sodium hydroxide (also known as caustic soda) is a significant raw material used in paper making. Any rise in the price of sodium hydroxide would potentially raise the prices of paper and accelerate its decline. Similarly, fuel is a significant cost in public transport. A bus company uses a considerable amount of fuel. If the price of fuel increased significantly, it would ultimately result in an increase in ticket prices and cause customers to seek alternatives such as cycling, walking, car sharing, etc.

The model in action

The Swedish furniture retailer IKEA has more than 400 stores across 60 countries. In 2021 the company had total sales of €42 billion.[4] Applying Porter's five forces to the company we can recognize the following:

Rivalry amongst existing competitors (very strong)

The retail furniture market is aggressive. Competition exists from small and large companies and there are many of them. Some specialize in certain types of furniture and to that extent can meet customers' needs better than IKEA. Although rivalry is fierce in the retail furniture market, IKEA has carved out a position for itself as a modern value-for-money supplier. There are few companies with the same differentiated position.

Threat of new entrants (strong)

New entrants are always a threat to IKEA as there are few barriers preventing companies setting up as furniture retailers. Admittedly they are unlikely to do so on the size and scale of IKEA. Even so, the aggregate number of new competitors could be a nuisance. Furthermore, it is easy for companies to set up online retail operations and these too could threaten parts of IKEA's business.

Bargaining power of buyers (moderate)

People who shop at IKEA are price conscious. Individually buyers have not a great deal of power though collectively they are a big force. Anything that IKEA does to upset its customers (such as raising prices significantly) would be highly disruptive to the company.

Bargaining power of suppliers (weak)

IKEA has over 1,000 suppliers in more than 50 countries.[5] The huge purchasing power of IKEA means that suppliers do not have a great deal of power and IKEA has sufficient alternative sources if any single supplier proves difficult. Indeed, IKEA sets standards for its suppliers and insists that they work to its exacting specifications.

Threat of substitute products (weak)

The home furniture products sold by IKEA are unlikely to be substituted by anything significant. People will always want to sleep on a bed and sit on chairs. Beds and chairs can change in shape and style but IKEA is capable of adjusting to meet those changes. The products it sells are likely to be in demand for many years to come.

Some things to think about

- Competition is a threat but it can usually be managed. Use the five forces to work out where the main threat comes from so that it can be minimized.

- Consider also carrying out a PEST analysis (see Chapter 41), which will take account of the macro factors shaping your business.

Notes

1 Stevenson, D (2017) Batteries could power up your portfolio, *Financial Times*, 20 April

2 Porter, ME (1979) How competitive forces shape strategy, *Harvard Business Review*, 57 (2) (March–April), pp 137–45

3 Six Forces Model, Investopedia, http://www.investopedia.com/terms/s/six-force-model.asp (archived at https://perma.cc/Q4YP-KLXY)

4 IKEA, About Us, https://about.ikea.com/en/about-us (archived at https://perma.cc/F6JN-LJ6T)

5 Taneja, NK (2016) *Flying Ahead of the Airplane*, Taylor & Francis Ltd, London

Porter's generic strategies 43

Pinpointing the strongest competitive position

What the model looks like and how it works

There are a number of models described in this book that help a business to develop its strategy. Ansoff offers a model that looks at opportunities within existing markets, new markets and with existing products and new products (see Chapter 6). This is useful when thinking of future areas for expansion. So too the Boston matrix looks at opportunities arising from markets with strong growth prospects and those where a business has a significant market share (see Chapter 10). Mintzberg gives us an understanding of how strategies vary from those that follow a plan through to those that develop a ploy to beat the competition or simply adjust to the ebb and flow of the market (see Chapter 36). Michael Porter with his generic strategies starts at the beginning. He argues that a brand or a business must stand for something if it is to be successful. His thesis is that there are three important positions that a brand can take:

- **Low-cost (cost leadership)**
  Companies that have a cost advantage can use this to compete effectively within a market. Low-cost airlines that strip bare their services and hone their processes to perfection can offer airfares at a fraction of the cost of the legacy airlines. Chinese companies that produce products in immense volumes and with low-cost labour can compete against those who are shackled with higher labour costs and smaller production runs. Porter recognizes that in any market there is a significant minority of people who simply want the lowest possible price. Because price is the key driver of choice, companies that seek this position have less loyal customers. People driven by low prices are likely to flit to wherever they see a marginal price advantage.

A company competing on a low-cost strategy is likely to find that it does not last forever. The low labour-cost advantage of China may be overtaken by cheaper labour in Vietnam or Cambodia. Once the cost advantage has gone, it may be necessary to find a new strategy. A company taking a low-cost position has to ensure that it covers the basic needs of its customers. In order to achieve the low-cost position it is permissible to eliminate the exciting factors and those that differentiate a brand but it would be dangerous to compromise on the fundamental quality of the offer.

- **Niche (focus)**
  Specialization is always a good strategy for competing. People like to deal with specialist brands and companies that they believe are attuned to their own narrow needs. Most markets have a number of companies that carve out a niche for themselves. Porter saw these companies as highly focused, targeting only a small proportion of the total market with their specialist products. They tend to be smaller than the big competitors who work on a cost advantage but they nevertheless can be profitable and develop a loyal customer base. In the motorbike market Harley-Davidson sits in a niche position offering large luxury bikes to people who want a customized product. Admittedly this segment of the overall motorbike market is sizeable and big enough for Harley-Davidson to have achieved revenues of $5.6 billion per annum.[1]

- **Differentiation**
  Companies can develop brands that stand out from the competition be-cause they are seen to have a very distinct value proposition. The big automotive brands such as Mercedes-Benz, BMW, Ford and General Mo-tors all seek a differentiated position. In the industrial market, companies such as Dow, Grundfos and Shell have built brands that people specify because of their strength. A differentiation strategy that builds a strong brand is usually easier to defend than a low-cost strategy. The position that the differentiated brand has in the shelf space of people's minds sticks for a long time.

  This said, a brand can be knocked off its pedestal if it faces a disaster. In 1990 Perrier was a brand synonymous with mineral water. It had a 15 per cent share of the US market. It had a differentiated position, being seen as a pure brand that was healthy to drink. In 1992, it nearly came unstuck when US regulators in North Carolina found contamination with benzene. Although the contamination was minuscule, it required Perrier to recall 160 million bottles across 120 different countries at a cost of more than $250 million.[2] It was a high price but it had to be paid to defend its differentiated position.

Companies competing on low cost can have a strong brand but it is the low-cost part of the offer that prompts people to choose it. Companies in a niche can have a strong brand but in their case it is their specialization that draws customers to them, not just the brand itself. These companies address a broad range of customers within the market, except perhaps those who are simply interested in buying at the lowest price.

A good strategy is one that is solidly located in one of the three positions. The worst place to be is stuck in the middle where a brand tries to stand for everything and, in doing so, achieves nothing. Porter believes that it is difficult but not impossible to address a broad audience with more than one position. This has to be achieved by segmentation. Airlines, for example, offer a strongly differentiated value proposition to business-class customers and a stripped-down offer to those in coach or economy class. While this is possible in some markets, it is more difficult in others. It would be difficult for a car manufacturer to position itself with a single brand that in some cases offered a differentiated product and in other cases a low-cost one. Many B2B companies find it difficult to deal with customers who want a low price alongside those who are prepared to pay a premium. They find themselves falling into the trap of giving everyone the same product and service but at different prices and with different levels of profitability.

Determining which strategy is the right one should begin with a SWOT analysis. This will show the company's strengths and weaknesses and the opportunities and threats that it faces. It would also be helpful to carry out an analysis using Porter's five forces to see how these are shaping the company. Against this background, a generic strategy can be chosen that is right for the company and that plays to its strengths.

The origins of the model

Michael Porter is a professor at Harvard Business School. In 1980 he wrote the book *Competitive Strategy* in which he described the three generic positions of differentiation, cost leadership and focus.[3] In 1979 he published an article in *Harvard Business Review* titled 'How competitive forces shape strategy'.[4] This was the genesis of his other big theory, the five forces that influence the market.

Developments of the model

Not everyone agrees with Porter and his generic strategies. Some criticize it because it is not based on empirical evidence. Others say that it is not necessarily a bad thing to be 'stuck in the middle'. In today's environment where flexibility of response is necessary, it may be possible to combine two strategies successfully. It could be argued that Southwest Airlines with its low-cost offer is also a highly differentiated company because it takes considerable care over its brand position. Porter later revised his thinking and accepted the possibility of a successful hybrid business strategy. So too, it may be incorrect to position Harley-Davidson as a niche supplier when it has such a strong differentiated position.

The model in action

McDonald's provides an interesting case study. It has grown to be the biggest fast-food restaurant chain in the world and has enormous economies of scale. It has achieved these through its massive buying power but also vertical integration. The company owns facilities that produce many of its food ingredients.

Although it can be argued that McDonald's has a cost leadership advantage, its generic strategy is differentiated. The company has extremely competitive products but they do not seek to be the lowest cost or cheapest in their market. Indeed, the company is prepared to spend money putting a 50 cents small toy in kids' meals to build the Ronald McDonald brand. The overall aim is to compete on service, quality and convenience. Competitive prices are thrown in to add value.[5]

Walmart is a good example of a company that has successfully chosen and maintained a low-cost leadership position. Founded in 1962 by Sam Walton in Bentonville, Arkansas, the company now has over 10,000 stores worldwide. It has always had the philosophy of pile it high and sell it cheap. Its prices are highly competitive with other outlets.

These low prices are achieved by massive purchasing muscle. Walmart buys direct from source and cuts out intermediaries. The scale of its purchases enables it to command lower prices than any competitor. It uses analytics to predict supply and demand and drive efficiencies. It has its own fleet of trucks to move goods from the manufacturer to warehouses and retail outlets. Its huge stores are located on the outskirts of major cities where rates and property costs are low.

Some things to think about

- Clarity is really important when developing a strategy. It is why Michael Porter argues in favour of building a strategy based on differentiation, cost leadership or focus. Don't get confused about the strength of your brand. You can have a strong brand in cost leadership and also in a niche. What is it in overall terms that gives you a competitive strategic advantage?

- Once you have established your strategic advantage, make sure that your customer value proposition and your messaging emphasizes it. This will give resonance to your communications.

Notes

1 Harley-Davidson Revenue 2010-2022 | HOG - Macrotrends, www. macrotrends.net/stocks/charts/HOG/harley-davidson/revenue (archived at https://perma.cc/XJN5-CVDU)

2 Caeser-Gordon, A (2015) Lessons To Learn From A Product Recall, *PR Week*, www.prweek.com/article/1357209/lessons-learn-product-recall (archived at https://perma.cc/H3JA-8HKW)

3 Porter, ME (1980) *Competitive Strategy: Techniques for analyzing industries and competitors*, Free Press, New York

4 Porter, ME (1979) How competitive forces shape strategy, *Harvard Business Review*, **57** (2) (March–April), pp 137–45

5 Mourdoukoutas, P (2016) How McDonald's Keeps Bouncing Back, *Forbes*, www.forbes.com/sites/panosmourdoukoutas/2016/12/18/how-mcdonalds-wins/?sh=40f5d39c65d0 (archived at https://perma.cc/BHD2-ZAQJ)

Price elasticity   44
Outlining opportunities for raising or lowering prices

What the model looks like and how it works

Most businesses have a good understanding of their customers. They know the number of customers they serve, they understand their needs, they know the competition and they have a good feel for the opportunities and threats. What most businesses do not understand is the price elasticity of their products.

Price elasticity is an important concept in business. It describes the relationship between the price of the products and the demand for those products. Products have high elasticity if a small change in price results in a large change in demand. Think of this small price change as stretching (like elastic) the market considerably. Products that have a high level of elasticity are foodstuffs, particularly basic food items. These are products people need and so a reduction in their price encourages purchases in greater volume. Discount coupons and special deals abound in supermarkets, encouraging people to buy two for the price of one.

When a change in the price of a product has very little effect on its demand it is inelastic. There is no change, no stretching. Typical products here are those used in industrial applications. People buy nuts and bolts and motors and chemicals to use as components in things they make. If the price of nuts and bolts changes, they cannot consume more because their need is determined by the volume output of whatever they are used in.

At this stage it is important to make the distinction between the price elasticity of a generic product and the price elasticity of a specific brand. Take for example the fuel we use in our cars. Most of us are so dependent on cars for transport that we will pay a heavy price for fuel. The elasticity of demand for petrol is therefore inelastic (up to a certain point). However, if two fuel stations face each other across a road, people will be drawn to the station that offers fuel at just a few pence a gallon less. The price elasticity of a brand of petrol is highly elastic and that is why most fuel stations charge approximately the same price.

While it may be true that a company will not buy more nuts and bolts simply because they are cheaper, they may consider changing their supplier if an alternative supplier has products that are at a lower price. It is this price elasticity in a competitive environment that interests us.

It should also be remembered that price elasticity has its limits. If the price of butter is reduced relative to margarine, it will steal share. People will use butter in applications where previously they used margarine. However, there will come a point at which people can consume no more butter, even if its price was to drop to a ridiculously low level. There is only so much someone can eat.

Price elasticity works within common-sense bounds. Strange things happen outside normal bounds. For example, during the potato famine in Ireland in the mid-19th century, people bought more potatoes despite a heavy increase in their price. This is counterintuitive but it was the result of potatoes being an important part of the staple diet of people in Ireland at the time. It was more efficient to feed families on potatoes, despite their higher price, than to pay even more for the meat, chicken and other vegetables that were on offer. This is known as the Giffen effect, after the economist who described it.[1]

The relationship between price and volume is critical to all marketers. Price is one of the important levers that affect sales. It is also the only one of the 4Ps that collects value; the other 3Ps incur costs.

If we get the price of our products wrong, for example if the price is too low, money is left on the table. Equally, there will be a level at which the price will be too high and sales will be lost. For every product in every market there is an optimum price and we should know what this is.

Most managers in business think that they have a good understanding of price elasticity. In fact, it would be hard to believe that a company offers products at a price that they believe is wrong. However, surveys show that most managers price their products too low. Managers are constantly berated by their customers who tell them that their prices are too high (they would, wouldn't they?) and they are fearful of losing sales by overpricing. They may also be guilty of failing to communicate to the customers the real value of their products. A product will seem overpriced if the customer does not understand its true value. A company that sells features rather than benefits will find itself in such a position.

The formula used to determine price elasticity is based on the change in volume demand relative to the change in price of the product:

$$\text{Price elasticity} = \frac{\text{percentage change in volume}}{\text{percentage change in price}}$$

Data for calculating the price elasticity is not always available. Whenever a business changes its price it does not usually keep a record of the change in the volume of its sales. The change that takes place in sales may not be immediate. It may take time for customers to realize what has happened to the price. Sometimes customers may not react immediately because they are tied into a contract. The effect of the price change could therefore be delayed.

When the price elasticity is −1.0 (note that the negative sign indicates that price and quantity are inversely related), it is neutral in that the degree by which the volume for the product increases is in direct proportion to the price decrease. A 10 per cent decrease in price results in a 10 per cent increase in volume. When the price elasticity is more than −1.0 the product demand is elastic. This means that a fall in price will be more than compensated for by a proportionately greater volume of sales. Airfares for leisure purposes are elastic with a price elasticity of −1.5.[2] Lower prices encourage people to travel who otherwise would not have considered it or been able to afford it. The demand for Coca-Cola is highly elastic at −3.8.[3] A small reduction in price encourages people to buy it in preference to another beverage. Equally a price increase will result in the loss of a disproportionately large number of customers.

When the price elasticity is less than −1.0 it is inelastic. Most industrial products have a price elasticity of around −0.7 or −0.8. This is because buyers of industrial products know that they are made to a specification and the specification may be written into the products that they buy. Changing a supplier of products could result in the buyer getting involved in raising new paperwork to change the specification to the new product. The buyer of the products may be reluctant to change, suspicious that the price advantage will be short-lived and it will not be long before the new supplier raises prices to those that were previously paid. There may also be a concern about a new supplier as to whether they will be able to live up to their promises and deliver on time, provide the same service, deal with complaints quickly, etc. There is a strong incentive to stick with the devil you know.

The origins of the model

The economist Alfred Marshall in 1890 is credited with defining the elasticity of demand in his book *Principles of Economics*.[4] He referred to elasticity as the responsiveness of a market to the change in demand for a product, given a change in price.

Developments of the model

A company that does not have historical data showing the effects of price changes on volume may consider using market research to determine the elasticity of demand. A crude indication of elasticity of demand can be determined by asking a buyer of products the likelihood of making a purchase at a specific price. If the starting price is high and the purchaser says that they would not purchase, they would be asked a series of further questions at lower prices until they finally agree on a price that would trigger the purchase (see Chapter 39). This is only an approximate measure as the purchaser is not in a buying situation. Furthermore, the purchaser may hold off on saying that they will pay a certain price, knowing that a lower one is forthcoming. That said, with all its faults, the method gives a good indication of elasticity of demand.

A more sophisticated measure of elasticity of demand is to use conjoint analysis (see Chapter 16).

When a company has no access to data of any kind, it could make a judgement as to the elasticity of demand based on the criteria set out in Table 44.1.

Table 44.1   Factors influencing the elasticity of demand for a product

	Elastic	Inelastic
Easily substituted for another product	✓	
Product has low switching costs	✓	
Considered to be a commodity rather than differentiated	✓	
Strongly supported by patents		✓
Strongly branded		✓
Written into specifications		✓
Limited availability		✓
Someone else pays		✓
Strongly supported by personal service		✓

The model in action

The owner of a group of regional newspapers was concerned about its decline in profitability. Sales of its newspapers were falling. As part of its strategic review it wanted to know if it could redress the declining profitability by increasing charges for advertising space. This was strongly resisted by the internal sales team who said that any rise in advertising prices would kill sales. It was decided to carry out a market survey amongst businesses that advertised in regional newspapers (such as retailers and entertainment) and to measure the elasticity of demand for different types of adverts.

Amongst the many subjects covered in the interview was a question that asked respondents to indicate how important they considered the role of advertising to be for their business. Three-quarters of respondents said that advertising was very important and, of all the different types of media available, newspaper advertising was at the top of the list.

Various newspaper advertising scenarios were presented to respondents, each with different prices. Around 25–35 per cent of respondents said that they would not place an advert in a newspaper at any price. These were classified as a segment of no interest.

Amongst those that were prepared to buy newspaper advertising space, they indicated their likelihood to do so at different prices. Surprisingly, the elasticity of demand proved to be –0.8, indicating that demand was relatively inelastic. If the newspaper raised its prices by 10 per cent, demand would fall but the higher price per ad would mean total revenue would stay roughly the same and the company would increase its overall profitability.

The company successfully raised its prices and did so at the same time as reinforcing the importance of newspaper advertising and making its value proposition more compelling. It also introduced an incentive scheme to advertisers based on a points system that rewarded loyal and high-spending customers.

Some things to think about

- Understanding the price elasticity of your product is vital. Many B2B companies are fearful of losing custom by pricing too high and so they undercharge. Use the checklist in Table 44.1 to get a high-level view of whether your product is elastic or inelastic, and consider using research to give a more precise figure.

- It should also be borne in mind that the price elasticity of your product will be determined by the degree to which you communicate its value. Differentiated products with strong brands tend to be inelastic and can command higher prices.

Notes

1 Giffen good, https://en.wikipedia.org/wiki/Giffen_good (archived at https://perma.cc/4NDE-J6TH)

2 Ayers, RM and Collinge, RA (2003) *Microeconomics*, Pearson/Prentice Hall, New Jersey

3 Ayers, RM and Collinge, RA (2003) *Microeconomics*, Pearson/Prentice Hall, New Jersey

4 Marshall, A (1890) *Principles of Economics*, Macmillan, London

Price quality strategy

Guiding a company's pricing strategy

What the model looks like and how it works

Throughout this book the term 'product' refers to the offer that a business makes to its customers. This offer could be a tangible product or service. When people buy products they have to pay using currency; products have a price. The way that people determine the value of a product is very much determined by its perceived quality.

Quality is a nebulous term. It refers to the build quality, the reliability, the durability, as well as the quality of the service and backup. Even though we may not have a precise definition of what quality means, we have a feeling that high-quality products will be expensive and low-quality products will be cheaper.

The relationship of price and quality is at the heart of the model described by Philip Kotler. He sees three levels of price – high, medium and low. He also recognizes three levels of quality – high, medium and low. The combination of these levels of price and quality result in nine pricing strategies:

- High quality/high price – a premium strategy.
- High quality/medium price – a good value strategy.
- High quality/low price – an excellent value strategy.
- Medium quality/high price – danger of overcharging.
- Medium quality/medium price – middle of the road strategy.
- Medium quality/low price – a good value strategy.
- Low quality/high price – an exploitative strategy.
- Low quality/medium price – a false economy strategy.
- Low quality/low price – a cheap strategy.

It is important to note that this strategy matrix does not consider the cost of manufacturing the product. Many products are sold on a cost-plus basis, adding a profit margin to the cost of manufacture. Kotler's model assumes an ability to charge whatever price is thought appropriate, though this very much depends on the product quality. For example, although it may, in theory, be possible to charge a high price for a low-quality product, this strategy is unlikely to last long as it will quickly be seen as a rip-off. Even a high price for a medium-quality product may be inappropriate if it suggests the company is overcharging. There are six strategies that are feasible within the model. They are those that are high quality (with a high, medium or low price) and those that are low price (with a high, medium or low quality). The three strategies that will not work are high price/low quality, medium price/low quality and high price/medium quality.

The feasible pricing strategies are as follows:

High quality, high price

This is a premium pricing strategy and one that is recognizable in most markets. Rolls-Royce cars, Savile Row suits, finest single malt whisky and Dior gowns all command top-dollar prices and are seen to justify them by their quality. This is also a strategy that usually requires a strong brand to communicate the high level of quality. It is not always the case; it is sometimes enough to know where the product has come from to know that it will be of high quality. It is why the Champagne region of France has protected the use of the word, requiring it to be specific only to those sparkling wines made within that region of France.

High quality, medium price

This is the strategy of Mercedes, BMW and high-end Japanese cars. Stores such as Nordstrom in the United States and Marks & Spencer in the UK have the reputation of selling high-quality products at a medium price. This is an upmarket to mass-market strategy.

High quality, low prices

Many products leaving China and the Far East are of a high quality and have a low price. The reason for adopting this strategy could be to achieve a rapid penetration of the market or to get traction in a market with a brand that is not yet recognized for its high quality. Samsung phones, Lenovo computers and Kia cars are now well-known brands that have adopted a low-price position with their high-quality products in order to achieve penetration in western markets. There are potential problems with this strategy in that a low price tends to signal low quality to most people. It may take time for the market to recognize that the products are of excellent quality and therefore very good value.

Low price, medium quality

Again we see many Asian products positioned with a low price and medium quality. In the high street, retailers such as H&M in Europe and Subway and Costco in the United States offer good value with their low prices and products that meet the needs of their customers. This is very much a mass-market strategy.

Low price, low quality

This is the economy basement. Low quality does not necessarily mean that the products are not fit for purpose; it may simply mean that they are stripped down to a bare minimum. The budget airlines that offer bargain prices but with very little extras beyond a seat on the plane would fit into this pricing strategy. This is a mass-market strategy in that somewhere between 20 per cent and 30 per cent of any population (a significant minority) are so strongly driven by low prices that they will find the offer attractive.[1]

Kotler strategies encourage businesses to pitch a price equal to what the market believes is appropriate. Customers are not disappointed if the right balance of price and quality is achieved. This may appear to be a freewheeling strategy that gives a company permission to grab what they can in order to make the highest possible profit. This is not what Kotler is saying. Any attempt to increase profitability by removing product features or downgrading quality while maintaining high prices will quickly be identified as 'false economy'. The aim is to balance the price and the quality to fit boxes in the north and east of the matrix.

The origins of the model

Philip Kotler is a prolific author on marketing subjects and a professor of international marketing at the Kellogg School of Management at Northwestern University. He presented his price quality theory in 1988 in a book entitled *Marketing Management: Analysis, planning, implementation and control*.[2] The book is now in its 15th edition and is the world's most-used textbook in business schools.[3]

Developments of the model

There are numerous pricing models and many of them have similarities to the price quality strategy proposed by Kotler. A simplified model (author unknown) proposes four, rather than nine, positions, as shown in Figure 45.1:

- Premium: this speaks for itself with a high-quality product at a high price.
- Penetration: the aim of the company using this strategy is to quickly win market share with an aggressive price and an excellent-quality product. Note: at some stage this strategy may have to change if the low prices are not generating sufficient profit.
- Economy: the budget airline strategy; a stripped-down product for a low price.
- Skimming: this could be a misnomer. Skimming can also refer to the strategy of taking high profits within a market from the small number of people who are prepared to pay a very high price. In other words, it could be a subset of the high-quality, high-price segment. In the way it is used in Figure 45.1, the company is extracting a high price from people who may have to buy the product because they have no choice. For example, the last manufacturer of gas mantles may be able to charge a very high price for them because there are no other suppliers. A more frequently encountered example is the high price we have to pay for things at an airport. It is not unusual to have to pay a high price for an indifferent sandwich because we are a captive audience.

Figure 45.1   Modified price/quality strategy

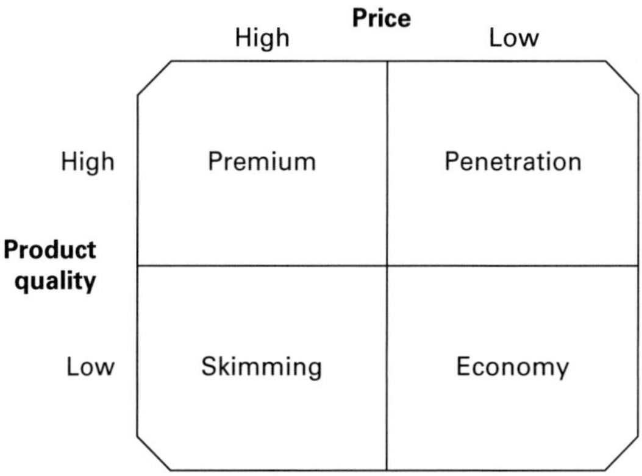

Kotler's paradigm does not cover all pricing strategies. It was never meant to do so as it focuses on the relationship between quality and price. However, the pricing strategist should also be familiar with the other pricing options. These include:

- **Cost pricing strategies**: these are very common strategies used by manufacturing companies who calculate the variable cost of the products they make and add what they think to be a suitable gross margin. There are variations of cost pricing strategies such as marginal cost pricing whereby the manufacturer, eager to fill capacity at the factory, will be prepared to sell some products to certain groups of people (e.g. exports) at a price that barely covers the cost of manufacture but makes some contribution to overheads. Such strategies are employed by product-orientated companies whose main goal is to keep the production line as full as possible.

- **Specialist strategies**: these are pricing strategies to achieve a particular objective. For example, predatory pricing (illegal in many countries) could be employed to undercut competitors and put them out of business, despite delivering no profit.

- **Psychological pricing**: for some products it is not possible for the customer to fully understand the quality of what they are buying. Their perceptions could be manipulated to make them believe a high price is worth it. Psychological pricing can be used with wines, perfumes and luxury goods. Here the company chooses a pricing strategy that is higher than is merited by the quality of the products but which is justified in the eyes of consumers because of the product's status.

It should be borne in mind that Kotler's price quality strategy is set in the framework of a competitive marketplace. The buyer is able to judge price and quality relative to other products on the market. These other products provide reference points in terms of both price and quality by which the product in question is judged. We are therefore talking about perceived prices and perceived quality in relation to other products.

The model in action

Dow Corning is a manufacturer of silicones. There are only a few global manufacturers of the product in the world. It is an aggressive market and one in which Dow Corning believed it was losing share to competitors with lower prices.[4] It researched the market and determined that there was a segment of customers for whom a low price was the main driver of choice. They wanted a quality product but without many of the value-added services that required the premium charged by Dow Corning.

Dow Corning produces high-quality products and it had no intention of reducing that quality. It also provides excellent sales and technical service though it found difficulties in limiting this part of its offer. Problems occurred because companies sometimes extracted a low price from Dow Corning, claiming that they did not need the added-value technical service. However, when these companies requested technical advice, as they often did, it was hard to turn them down.

In the early 2000s Dow Corning decided that the way forward was to segment the market into two groups: 1) those who want a high-quality product and are prepared to pay a high price for all the services associated with it; and 2) those who want a high-quality product without the additional services.

In order to serve the second group with a value offer, Dow Corning created Xiameter, an online website from which people could buy high-quality silicones. Customers signing up to buy online had to agree to the terms and conditions, which said that the product came without the supporting services that were available if they purchased from Dow Corning.

This two-pronged pricing strategy proved to be highly successful. The company earned back its investment in just three months and by 2011 30 per cent of Dow Corning's revenues were generated online.[5] Although there were concerns that the new model would cannibalize the existing customer base, this did not happen. New business came mainly from new customers.

Some things to think about

- Many companies have a pricing strategy built on legacy. Prices have been set a number of years ago and adjusted (usually upwards because of inflation) year on year. Use Kotler's pricing grid to see if your prices are appropriate for your target audience.
- Think about using different brands to address the needs of different audiences (as did Dow Corning with Xiameter).

Notes

1 Estimate from surveys carried out by B2B International Ltd

2 Kotler, P (1988) *Marketing Management: Analysis, planning, implementation and control*, Prentice-Hall, New Jersey

3 Wikipedia (nd) Philip Kotler, https://en.wikipedia.org/wiki/Philip_Kotler (archived at https://perma.cc/3MMR-FGKG)

4 Gary, L (2005) Dow Corning's Big Pricing Gamble, *Harvard Business School*, https://hbswk.hbs.edu/archive/dow-corning-s-big-pricing-gamble (archived at https://perma.cc/6YZB-PC3A)

5 Johnson, M W, Christensen, C M and Kagermann, H (2008) Reinventing your business model, *Harvard Business Review*, December, https://hbr.org/2008/12/reinventing-your-business-model (archived at https://perma.cc/4MZE-84DK); Chief Executive (2011) How Dow Corning beat commoditization by embracing it, https://chiefexecutive.net/facing-the-commoditization-challenge-how-dow-cornings-xiameter-brand-beats-commoditization-by-embracing-it__trashed/ (archived at https://perma.cc/2XVT-36UF)

Product life cycle

Determining a long-term product strategy

What the model looks like and how it works

The concept of a life cycle is easy for us to understand. We face it every day of our lives. Babies are conceived, born, grow up, turn into adults, and eventually age and die. The same concept can be witnessed in products. Through understanding the product life cycle it is possible for a company to develop a marketing strategy at each stage.

Pre-birth

At some stage an idea for a product is conceived. This is a delicate time for the embryo as a significant number of new ideas fail to make it. They may fail because they do not fulfil the needs of potential customers, the competition is too fierce, the costs of manufacturing are too high, or the penetration of the marketplace is too difficult. Pre-birth is not an easy time for a new concept.

Clay Christensen, a professor at Harvard Business School, is on record as saying that 95 per cent of new products fail.[1] It is hard to know whether this figure is correct because many new products never get off the ground. Of those that are launched, there appears to be a consensus that 30–50 per cent fail (depending on the industry).[2] Whatever the failure rate, these figures indicate the difficulty of a new product gaining ground in a market that is already well served. Very few markets have vacuums waiting to be filled and new product launches require true innovation, good marketing support and excellent timing if they are to be successful.

Youth

As stated above, the launch period of a new product can be difficult. The new product needs to acquire a high level of awareness and this in turn must be supported with an appropriate promotional budget. Distributors and re-tailers must be persuaded that it is worth their while listing the new product. If the new product is to win a significant number of customers, it must ap-peal to the innovators who will be happy to trial and experiment, but it must also jump the chasm and become of interest to the early adopters and early majority (see Chapter 21).

During this early stage, sales could be slow before they pick up. Costs will be high and it is quite likely that the new product will face losses. The length of time that a product stays in this youthful stage will vary. Toys, electronic products and digital products can move quickly and gain significant mo-mentum within a few months. Most other products are likely to stay in the youthful stage for a few years.

Growth

After a time, the awareness of the product will increase and sales will grow significantly. The early adopters will begin to buy the product in earnest and the early majority will be showing a strong interest.

Other companies will see the strong growth and competitors will be lured into the market. This is not necessarily a bad thing as the extra competition will also help bring the product to a wider audience.

With greater volumes of sales, costs will be reduced and the product will move into profit. However, the extra competition will put pressure on prices.

Maturity

Eventually the new product becomes mainstream. It will be widely known and widely used within the market. The late majority will now buy the prod-uct and its penetration will be moving quickly towards saturation point. At this point, the many competitors that entered the market during the growth phase will begin to rationalize. Acquisitions and mergers will reduce the numbers of competitors although the competitiveness of these now large companies will be especially fierce as they compete for a market that has gone ex-growth. Prices will be under pressure but the suppliers to the mar-ket will be highly efficient and can be expected to reap good profits. Products in this stage are often cash cows. The suppliers of the products will become more sophisticated turning to brand differentiation, segmentation and value marketing.

Old age

Eventually, the applications for the product will decline or new products will come on to the market that can better serve customers' needs. As a result, sales volumes decline. Inevitably there will be still further rationalization of suppliers. Declining sales volumes and continuing price pressures will put a squeeze on profits. This will be a period when suppliers of products must decide whether they remain in the market, possibly improving efficiencies through acquisitions and mergers, rejuvenate the product with

Figure 46.1   The product life cycle and phases of marketing communications

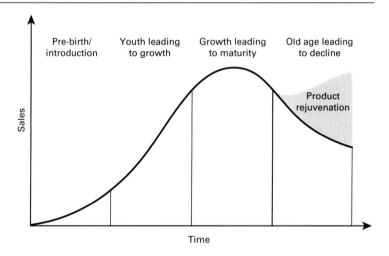

Marketing objectives	Gain trial by early adoption	Establish market share	Strengthen market share	Use product as cash cow
	Minimize learning requirements	Establish distribution	Build dealer and customer loyalty	Consider product extensions
Communications objectives	Create wide awareness	Strengthen brand preferences	Promote frequency of use	Minimum promotion
	Generate interest amongst innovators	Stimulate wider trials	Suggest new uses for product	Maintain brand Create classic niches
Communications strategy	Personal sales	Media advertising	Media advertising	Reduce media expenditure
	Media advertising	Personal sales	Dealer promotions	
	Opening offers	Sales promotions	Sales promotions	

innovations, or exit completely. These phases of the life cycle are shown in Figure 46.1, together with the different marketing and communications objectives that are relevant at each stage.

The origins of the model

In the early 1900s sociologists began to apply the biological concepts of the life cycle to products of industry. Economists took up the theme in the 1920s and 1930s noting that products such as automobiles had life-cycle growth curves.

In 1933 Otto Kleppner, the founder of a New York advertising agency, recognized different phases of a product's growth that required appropriate types of advertising: pioneering, competitive and retentive.[3]

It was as late as 1950 that the term 'product life cycle' received its first mention. This was by Joel Dean in a study of pricing policies for new products published in *Harvard Business Review*.[4] The consultants Booz Allen Hamilton published a paper in 1960 in which they formally described the product life cycle.[5] Since then, marketing gurus such as Theodore Levitt (1965) have popularized the concept, emphasizing its use as a forecasting tool.[6]

In 1966 Raymond Vernon, an American economist, published an article that described how products move through a life cycle. For example, computers developed in the United States were originally made and consumed locally. The cycle moved forwards when they were exported from a manufacturing base in the United States. Eventually, production moved overseas and the computers are now imported to the place where they were invented. As a result of this 1966 article, Vernon is frequently credited with inventing the term 'product life cycle'.[7]

Developments of the model

The product life cycle is conceptual and as such it is difficult to know exactly where a product sits. This is further complicated by the timeline of the life cycle. Some toys have a life cycle of less than 12 months from launch to decline. Electronic products can have a life cycle of three or four years. A car's life cycle is around seven years. However, products such as steel, cement, bricks and basic materials have life cycles that stretch to many years.

It is also difficult to judge when maturity moves into old age in the life cycle. In the later years of the 20th century glass appeared to be entering a period of maturity or old age. A resurgence of interest amongst architects and designers has resulted in glass finding new applications in construction. Some products such as wheels, hammers and nails are likely to survive for many years and will probably never follow the predicted course of decline.

Despite the limitations of being able to state exactly where a product sits in the timeline of the product life cycle, it has proved useful to marketers in explaining how and why sales of the product change over time and the strategies that are needed during the different phases.

The model in action

The Kellogg Company, best known for its Cornflakes and Rice Krispies breakfast cereals, launched a new breakfast bar in 1997.[8] Nutri-Grain was positioned as a healthy snack for people on the move and who may have skipped breakfast.

In the youthful phase of the product launch, Nutri-Grain was highly successful. In just a couple of years it monopolized the cereal-bar market with nearly a 50 per cent market share.

Supported by strong promotion, it grew quickly until 2002. Some repositioning of the brand took place as it changed from being a missed breakfast product to being an all-day healthy snack.

The cereal-bar market quickly matured and saw competition from many branded and own-brand products. By 2004, just seven years after its launch, sales of Nutri-Grain started to decline even though the market continued to grow at 15 per cent per annum. Kellogg had to decide whether to withdraw from the market or extend its life in some way. The company carried out research, which showed that the brand message was not strong enough and some other Kellogg's products, such as *Minis*, had diluted Nutri-Grain's position. The product was in need of more marketing support.

The company developed a soft-bake bar that appealed to people who wanted great taste and also required their snack to be healthy. It was repositioned as a snack for mid-morning – still branded Nutri-Grain with a sub-brand of *Elevenses*.

The relaunch took place in 2005. The product rejuvenation (see Figure 46.1) put the emphasis on health and taste and was a success. The relaunch was supported by strong promotion and the product was relaunched at a competitive price. As a result, the decline in sales was reversed and the Nutri-Grain sales increased by almost 50 per cent. Two decades later Nutri-Grain remains a strong brand and product within Kellogg's product portfolio.

Some things to think about

- Knowing where your product sits in its life cycle is important as it determines your strategy. It is particularly important to know when demand is 'topping out' and moving into decline. This is a stage at which you need to decide whether rejuvenation is possible.

- Remember that your communication strategy needs to change depending on where your product sits in the life cycle.

Notes

1 Christensen, C (2011) Clay Christensen's milkshake marketing, *Harvard Business School Research and Ideas*, February, https://hbswk.hbs.edu/item/clay-christensens-milkshake-marketing (archived at https://perma.cc/GTL2-92YP)

2 Castellion, G (2013) Is The 80 Per Cent Product Failure Rate Statistic Actually True? *Quora*, www.quora.com/Is-the-80-product-failure-rate-statistic-actually-true (archived at https://perma.cc/2HVJ-A3RW)

3 Kleppner, O (1933) *Advertising Procedures*, Prentice Hall, New York

4 Dean, J (1950) Pricing policies for new products, *Harvard Business Review*, November

5 Booz Allen Hamilton (1960) The management of new products, New York, pp 5–6

6 Levitt, T (1965) Exploit the product life cycle, Graduate School of Business Administration, *Harvard Business Review*, November

7 Vernon, R (1966) International Investment and International Trade in the Product Cycle, *Quarterly Journal of Economics*, 80 (2), pp 190–207

8 Extending The Product Life Cycle – A Kellogg's Case Study, http://businesscasestudies.co.uk/kelloggs/extending-the-product-life-cycle/introduction.html (archived at https://perma.cc/7KCC-6CZN)

Product service positioning matrix 47

Positioning products according to quality and service value

What the model looks like and how it works

This framework has been developed to assist companies to match their product and service offer to leverage a price premium. It is particularly suited to B2B companies as it recognizes that a significant component of the brand position arises directly from the experience of the customer with its products and services. The model highlights the options for premium pricing, and where investment would be needed to achieve this. It can be used to check that a company's strategy and alignment of a brand fits with the market perceptions.

The two axes of the matrix are product superiority and service superiority:

- Product superiority: products are considered to be superior if they are of a high quality, reliable, perform well, last a long time, have innovative features and a strong reputation.

- Service superiority: service superiority is judged by the responsiveness of the service team, their knowledge and technical capability, the ability to sort out problems quickly, their proactivity in identifying problems before they arise and the degree to which they are on the customer's side.

There are four important positions that can be identified on the matrix (Figure 47.1):

1 **Premium positioning – high product superiority/high service superiority**
   A company can claim to be in this position if they are a market leader and able to charge premium prices for their offer.

2 **Technical leadership – high product superiority/low service superiority**
   These are companies with strong product offers but that have not
   developed high levels of service. It is possible that some of the companies
   in this quadrant are new to market and have not yet developed the service
   offering.

3 **Service leadership – low product superiority/high service superiority**
   Companies in this quadrant succeed through service excellence. They
   may be distributors selling a range of imported products, which though
   not technically superior may do a good job and have the backing of
   excellent service.

4 **Low-cost leadership – low product superiority/low service superiority**
   Companies in this quadrant are likely to survive through a low-priced
   offer. Their products will be used by companies that either cannot afford
   or will not pay for higher-performing offers.

The matrix enables a company to determine:

- if its prices are right;
- if there is an opportunity to increase prices;

Figure 47.1   The product service positioning (PSP) matrix

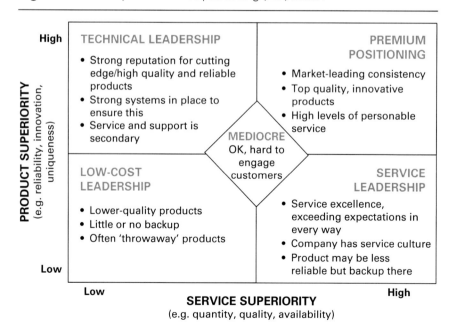

SOURCE Carol-Ann Morgan, B2B International (2016)

- if it is at risk from overcharging;
- if there is a gap in the market in leadership that it has capabilities to occupy;
- where it needs to invest to align and retain its position.

There is only one true 'premium' position, and that is with the consistent offer of a superior product and superior service.

The origins of the model

The model was developed in 2016 by Carol-Ann Morgan, a B2B market-research consultant, as a direct result of working with B2B companies seeking to identify and justify a price premium. It originates from the view that a company's reputation and brand image is born out of the experience customers have with its products and service. This is particularly the position for newer brands that do not have the advantage of a heritage built over years. In recent years, newer brands have emerged to challenge the traditional brands. This has created the imperative for all brands to clearly identify where their advantage lies, whether or not they justify a premium and what future investment is required to maintain their position.

As buyers become more savvy, and markets become more competitive, it is important for brands not to be complacent about their ability to command premium prices. The matrix was developed to encourage suppliers to look at their offers and clearly identify a position in the market that can justify a premium.

The matrix can be populated with data such as customer-experience performance measures and attitudes to brands. A survey of views of managers within a company can be compared with market perceptions. Any gaps will point to strategic adjustments that are required.

Developments of the model

The framework has been developed further to describe the sectors in greater detail and identify opportunities and threats for each of the four market positions, as shown in Table 47.1.

The model positions a company for its product quality and service quality and these will almost certainly be influenced by the strength of the brand.

Table 47.1 Actions for each PSP position

	Premium positioning	Technical leadership	Service leadership	Low-cost leadership
Summary position	Brand strength based on best in class High-quality products with excellent product support Strong, consistent customer service	Product excellence: Industry-leading products Superior, high-quality, reputable products	Service excellence: Average products but excellent service both before and after the sale	Best prices: Based on attention to cost at all stages
Invests in...	Brand People Products Processes to ensure high quality and innovation	Product development Innovation Production processes Supply chain Product quality testing Supplier controls	People and processes Culture of service, 'customer first'	Taking out cost Supply chain efficiencies
Ability to charge premium...	Very high	High/very high	Moderate/high	None
Long-term survival issues...	Need to ensure brand lives up to premium charges Enough customers are willing and able to pay premium to be viable	Rigorous product quality systems – product must outperform competitors Investment in innovation	Maintaining culture of service amongst staff Managing the cost of service backup for products	Staying on top of operating costs to retain low-cost position Accurate cost of sales data
Long-term danger points...	Cost to serve exceeds premium tolerated by market Poor reviews	Product becomes commoditized Product innovation too slow and new entrants emerge	Customers tire of poor product reliability Brand risk of poor product performance	Spiral of low pricing reducing profit for reinvestment in the company

SOURCE Carol-Ann Morgan, B2B International (2016)

It is the brand positioning that really matters in the model as this is a true reflection of the market's view.

The model in action

A chemical company wanted to understand its opportunity to charge a premium. Primary data from a market survey was plotted to show the company's position against those of its competitors. Future positions were also anticipated. The analysis showed that none of the suppliers occupied the premium position.

The research showed that the chemical company that sponsored the study (Supplier X in Figure 47.2) had the highest satisfaction with pricing, suggesting there was some room for increasing prices. It also was seen to have a weakness in its service quality, which could threaten its long-term position in the product leadership quadrant.

Using the matrix, the supplier invested in training its sales force and customer service representatives. The greater empowerment of these front-line service people made a big improvement to the perceptions of the company's service and moved it into the north-east quadrant. With a strong position on

Figure 47.2 PSP used in the chemical industry to identify opportunities and threats

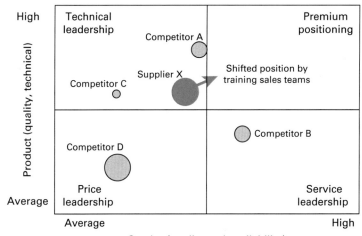

SOURCE Carol-Ann Morgan, B2B International (2016)

both product and service, the company was now in a position to charge premium prices.

In another example, the model was used by a manufacturer of engines sold to manufacturers of large construction plant. The engine manufacturer was suffering falling revenues, competitive challenges and expensive customer complaints in the form of warranty claims and law suits. Historically the company had always occupied a premium position in the market, based on its technically complex and bespoke products in this heavy industrial market. Relationships with customers, the large original equipment manufacturers (OEMs) that made construction equipment, were strained as there was an interdependency of the companies with long-term contracts for product supply and maintenance.

The PSP matrix was used to plot:

- desired and stated position in the market (heritage position, current market communications, website, etc);
- internal company perceptions of its position;
- market perceptions of its position from customers.

Clear differences could be seen, most notably that the company's desired position was a long way from the position experienced by its customers. More importantly, the matrix highlighted the problems with its pricing strategy. The company's pricing was based on its desired position rather than actual position and this was impacting the brand image detrimentally. The company thought that it was failing to meet its premium position, it just did not realize how bad it was.

Using the matrix in internal workshops and supported by external market research, the company was able to consider not only its pricing but the investment and actions required to rectify its position. Product innovation was necessary to iron out product problems and this could not be achieved in a short time frame. This led to a strategy of improving service as a short-term measure until product development would re-establish the product in the premium position in this highly technical market (see Figure 47.3).

Some things to think about

- In B2B markets the product quality and service quality are critically important. Established companies can become complacent about their

Figure 47.3   PSP used in identifying company position and pricing

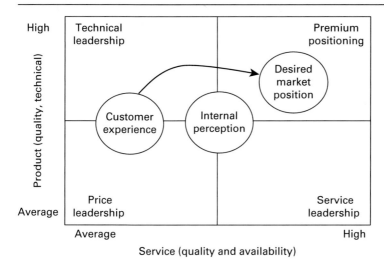

SOURCE Carol-Ann Morgan, B2B International (2016)

position, and charge premium prices that are not justified by their products and services. Use customer feedback from complaints, warranty claims and market research as a reality check. In the short term much can be improved by investing in service quality.

- Ask yourself what makes customers delighted about your products. Use the Kano model to find product features that will delight customers (see Chapter 30).

Segmentation   48

Using customer groups to gain competitive advantage

What the model looks like and how it works

Satisfying people's needs and making a profit along the way is the purpose of marketing. However, people's needs differ and therefore satisfying them may require different approaches. Identifying needs and recognizing differences between groups of customers is the role of the marketer. Different groups of customers are segments. Segmentation is therefore at the heart of marketing.

A common segmentation approach is based on demographics (in the case of consumer companies) or firmographics (in the case of B2B companies). A demographic segmentation is characterized by the physical attributes of the marketplace – age, gender, marital status, family composition (in the case of consumers); and size of company, industry vertical, geographical location (in the case of businesses).

A further sophistication may be to classify customers into those who are identified as strategic to the future of the business, those who are important and therefore key, and those who are smaller and can be considered more of a transactional typology.

These demographic segmentations are perfectly reasonable and may suffice. However, they do not offer a sustainable competitive advantage that competitors find difficult to copy. Nor do they address what customers and potential customers want. A more challenging segmentation is one based on behaviour or needs. Certainly, large companies may be of strategic value to a business but some want a low-cost offer, stripped bare of all services, while others are demanding in every way. If both are treated the same, one or both will feel unfulfilled and be vulnerable to the charms of the competition.

A mechanism is required for determining what customers need. The common-sense approach may appear to be to ask them. However, what questions should be asked and can we be sure of the answers? It is not that people lie, but they may not be able to acknowledge the truth:

- Do people really buy a Porsche for engineering excellence?
- Do people really choose an Armani suit because it lasts so well?
- Do people who say they buy their chemicals purely on price, never require any technical support or urgent deliveries from time to time?

Questions asked in a market-research survey are frequently used to arrive at segments. The classification data on questionnaires provides demographic data, while questions in the body of the interview determine aspects of behaviour. Cross tabulations of data on these criteria allow us to see the different responses amongst groups of respondents. This is market segmentation at its simplest level and every researcher uses the computer tabulations of findings to establish groups of respondents with marked differences.

Statistical techniques and, in particular, multivariate analysis are used for a more detailed analysis of segments. In surveys, respondents are asked to say to what extent they agree with a number of statements. These statements are designed to determine the different needs, interests and psychographic breakdown of the market. Typically there are a couple of dozen such statements, sometimes more. The combinations of groupings from 200 interviews are literally millions and we need some means of creating groupings that have a natural fit.

Factor analysis is used to work out which groups of attributes best fit together. Looking through the different statements or attributes that make up these groupings it is usually possible to see common themes, such as people who want low prices with few if any extras, people who want lots of services or add-ons and are prepared to pay for them, people who are concerned about environmental issues, and so on. Factor analysis reduces the large number of attributes to a smaller but representative subset. The subsets that have been worked out by factor analysis are now run through further computations using cluster analysis to rearrange the data into groupings with common needs. These groups are then given labels such as 'price fighters', 'service seekers' and any other such terms that represent their key characteristic.

The statistical approach to a needs-based segmentation has become extremely popular and it is an important, impartial means of finding interesting and possibly more relevant ways of addressing the customer base. However, the tastes and needs of populations are constantly changing and we should always be mindful of new segments that may not show up as more than a dot on the current radar screen. For example, if Guinness had carried out a needs-based segmentation amongst its customers in the 1960s, it may not have recognized the opportunity to reposition the drink as young and trendy. This segment was developed by a series of astute marketing campaigns.

The origins of the model

Companies have always recognized differences in their customers and targeted them accordingly. In the first instance goods were sold on a local or regional basis. When mass marketing began in the early 1900s, advertising agencies began to see the advantages of targeting different respondents.

It was not until 1956 when Wendell R Smith wrote an article entitled 'Product differentiation and market segmentation as alternative marketing strategies' that segmentation as we know it today was born.[1] He argues in his paper that successful product differentiation addresses a broad and generalized market. For example, Heinz beans have a distinctive product position and sell to lots of different people. He describes this as a layer of the market cake. On the other hand, a company that employs market segmentation carves out a wedge-shaped piece. He cites the example of refrigerator manufacturers who at the time launched fridges without a freezer compartment, because some people owned home freezers and their frozen-food storage needs were already fully met. They were addressing a wedge in the market – a segment. He saw segmentation and differentiation as linked. He suggested that the successful strategy of segmentation would eventually lead to the redefinition of a segment as an individual market and would swing the strategy back to differentiation.

Developments of the model

By plotting the different segments on an X/Y grid it is possible to determine which are worth targeting and, equally important, which are not (see Chapter 22 for the directional policy matrix). The two factors that influence this decision are the opportunities for the segment against the supplier's differential position within that segment. In this way it is possible to identify targets that justify resources in targeting and development. In the example in Figure 48.1 price fighters may be deselected as a target if they offer little

Figure 48.1   Segmentation matrix

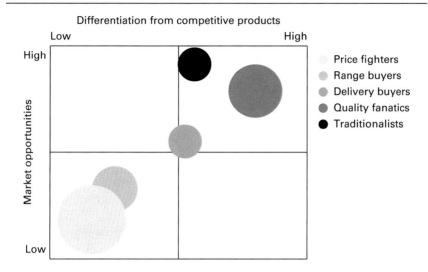

profit, even though they form a large segment. However, the range buyers may be worth addressing to see if they can be moved north and east to join more attractive segments such as traditionalists, quality fanatics or delivery buyers.

Needs-based segmentation has its critics. It is especially difficult to apply in B2B markets because the decision-making unit is so fragmented and changing all the time. Segments that are described physically lack insights into the motivations and emotions that are important in driving sales. Also, segments can change quickly and companies can blindly carry on with a segmentation policy that is long out of date.

All that said, market segmentation is very much about better meeting the needs of customers and is likely to remain an enduring concept into the future. With the advent of digital communications it is now becoming possible for marketers to customize their offer to narrow slices of customers and we can expect that the number of segments served by companies will increase dramatically in the future.

The model in action

Nivea Sun is owned by the German company Beiersdorf.[2] It used a segmentation strategy to address the UK sun-care market. The company had built up a large brand portfolio of products capable of meeting many different needs.

It was of the view that people's attitudes to sun-care products were the most important variable in a segmentation strategy. In order to fully understand these attitudes the company carried out a market-research study. The study identified five segments of customers with different attitudes to sun care:

1 **Concerned consumers**: these consumers are aware of the harmful effects of the sun and buy products with a high sun-protection factor. They do not consider a good tan to be important.

2 **Sun avoiders**: these people avoid sunbathing and see the use of sun protection as a chore. However, they recognize the dangers of too much sun and could be convinced to buy protection products if they were easy to apply.

3 **Conscientious sun lovers**: these people love the sun and buy well-known brands with appropriate protection factors. They know about the different products and purchase whatever they think is suitable for their skin and their family members.

4 **Careless tanners**: these people love the sun but do not use sufficient protection as they are not overconcerned about the long-term damage that can occur. They are occasional buyers of sun protection cream and when they do so it is often with a low skin-protection factor.

5 **Naive beauty conscious**: this group values a good suntan. They know that sun protection is important but they do not have a full understanding about sun protection factors. They have the money to spend on sun creams but need educating as to which type they should use.

Out of the five key consumer segments, three were seen as primary targets because of their interest and concern with sun-care products. These were the conscientious sun lovers, the naive beauty conscious and the concerned consumers. The sun avoiders and the careless tanners were secondary in terms of importance. The attitudinal differences were the main means by which the segments were identified. Within the segments there were consistent demographic differences. Men looked for convenience in sun-care products; women enjoyed more luxurious products. Adults with children had different needs. The attitudes to sun care transcended income and social class.

Important questions to answer about this case study are 'How does a segmentation of this kind help Nivea?'; 'What other options could Nivea have pursued and would they have been better?'

Certainly Nivea was not obliged to develop a segmentation based on attitudes. It had an excellent position within the market and a good product line-up. It had been pursuing Wendell Smith's strategy of product differentiation.

Its wide range of protection products included lotions, sprays, products for sensitive skin and products for children. It had aftercare products of various kinds and self-tanning products. The product range was well positioned to meet the needs of different consumers. Men liked the sprays, women liked the luxury lotions, and there were special products for kids. It would not have been a bad strategy to carry on focusing on products aimed at different demographic groups.

The segmentation based on attitudes added an extra level of understanding about the market. It proved useful to the research and development team who were able to use the findings to develop fast-acting products and easy-to-apply products. It was also useful to the communications team who could develop messages that would resonate with the different groups of customers. Understanding the attitudes of customers brought Nivea closer to the people who buy their products and enabled it to engage more fully with them.

Some things to think about

- Grouping companies together to better meet their needs is not easy. It requires good intelligence on consumers – their demographics, their behaviour, their psychographics and their needs. However, a segmentation based on customer needs and behaviour is important in making a company marketing-orientated. It is also a strategy that is hard for competitors to copy so it gives a competitive advantage.
- B2B companies find needs-based segmentation more difficult as the decision-making unit is complicated and frequently changes. It may be more practical for B2B companies to address company characteristics such as their behaviour. The behaviour of B2B companies is influenced very much by their size and the industry in which they operate.

Notes

1 Smith, WR (1956) Product differentiation and market segmentation as alternative marketing strategies, *Journal of Marketing*, **21** (1) (July), pp 3–8

2 Segmentation – A NIVEA Case Study, http://businesscasestudies.co.uk/nivea/segmentation/introduction.html (archived at https://perma.cc/JF68-XKJL)

Service profit chain

Connecting employee satisfaction and
performance with company profits

What the model looks like and how it works

Company managers know that there are only three ways to increase profits – sell more, charge more, or reduce costs. The service profit chain model
argues that there is a fourth way. Employees who are happy in their work
will not just do a job, they will do a great job, and this will be evident to
customers. As a result, customers will be happy and happy customers become loyal, generating a high lifetime value and high profits. The chain begins with employees and feeds through to increased profits.

The culture of a company plays a large part in determining whether it is a
good place to work. Company culture is set by the chief executive officer
(CEO) and the leadership team. The success of Southwest Airlines is often attributed to Herb Kelleher, the co-founder and CEO.[1] His reputation is as an
empathetic and charismatic leader, whose core values were having fun, focusing on the customer, hiring the right people and doing good for others. He was
a cheerleader for the company's 50,000 employees. As a result of his leadership, Southwest Airlines enjoyed 47 years during which it never made a loss.

Employees who are happy in their work are more likely to go the extra
mile to satisfy customers. Loyal employees reduce the cost to the company
as there is less hiring, less training and higher productivity. The link between
happy employees and happy customers is especially evident in retail outlets.
Nordstrom in the United States and John Lewis in the UK are famous examples of companies that have highly motivated staff feeding through to strong
profits. Taco Bell examined its employee turnover records across its many

stores. It discovered that the 20 per cent of stores with the lowest employee turnover had double the sales and 55 per cent higher profits than the 20 per cent of stores with the greatest employee turnover.[2]

There is an obvious link between satisfied customers and loyal customers, although it is not necessarily linear. Customers must recognize value as well as good service if they are to be loyal. Also, they need to award very high satisfaction scores to be truly loyal. Rank Xerox researches nearly half a million customers a year to determine their satisfaction and uses a five-point scale where 5 is high and 1 is low satisfaction. It found that customers who gave the company a score of 4 out of 5 on satisfaction differed greatly from those who gave a score of 5 out of 5. Those awarding the company a 5 were six times more likely to repurchase Xerox equipment than those giving a score of 4.[3] James Heskett, a professor of marketing at Harvard University, maps satisfaction measures against loyalty measures and determines that in order to achieve a significant loyal following amongst customers it is necessary to achieve scores of more than 4.5 out of 5 on average.[4]

The origins of the model

The service profit chain concept was first proposed in an article in *Harvard Business Review* in 1994 by James Heskett et al entitled 'Putting the service-profit chain to work'.[4] Heskett et al published a book on the subject in 1997 with the title *The Service Profit Chain: How leading companies link profit and growth to loyalty, satisfaction, and value.*[5]

Developments of the model

The service profit chain is a model that can be applied to any size of company – large or small. It is a model particularly suited to businesses where employees have a good deal of access to customers. Airlines, retail and leisure companies are obvious examples. However, the model has an application for all types of businesses.

It is easy to apply Heskett's model of loyalty and satisfaction to market-research findings. In a recent survey for a global engineering company an analysis was carried out of revenue at risk based on the Heskett model. Analysing the scores given by each customer on satisfaction with the company and likelihood to recommend it (a proxy for loyalty), it was possible to show that one-third of the customers were likely to stay loyal and 20 per cent of customers could be at risk (these being the addition of the percentages on the south and the west of the grid, Figure 49.1). An analysis such as this is a big wake-up call for a company that needs to see the link between customer satisfaction and revenue.

The model in action

Nordstrom was founded in 1901 by John Nordstrom. Through to the present day the company has had a family feel to it with great emphasis placed on looking after employees as well as looking after customers. There are many customer service stories told about Nordstrom that emphasize the empowerment of its employees. One is about a man who went into a Nordstrom store in Anchorage returning a set of tyres – a product that the company has never sold. It materialized that the customer had bought them from an outlet that previously occupied the site on which Nordstrom was based.[6] The store manager decided to allow the customer to return the tyres even though they were not purchased from the company. It became one of many legendary stories that are used to encourage employees to keep customers happy and forge relationships with new ones.

Figure 49.1   Example of revenue at risk based on the Heskett model

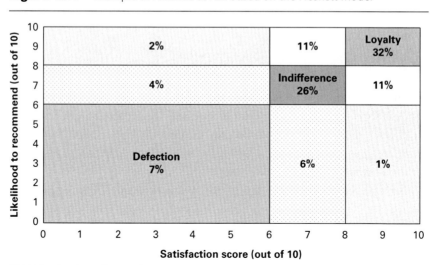

SOURCE Using theory from Heskett, Jones, Loveman, Sasser and Schlesinger (1994)

The employee culture began with John Nordstrom. He set up the store in partnership with Carl Wallin. John was left to manage his new shop on the first day of opening while his partner was out to lunch and no business had been done that morning.[7] When the first customer, a woman, walked into the shop and confronted Nordstrom, he was keen to do business. She had seen a pair of shoes in the window and asked to try them on. Nordstrom looked high and low in his stock for a pair in the size and colour of those in the window. In desperation he asked her to try on the shoes that were in the window and they fitted perfectly. The customer bought them for $12.50 – the only sale of the day. In this single event John Nordstrom set the foundations of 'The Nordstrom Way': 'Do whatever it takes to take care of the customer, and do whatever it takes to make sure the customer doesn't leave the store without buying something.'

More than 100 years later Nordstrom abides by the same principle, which is executed in a very customer-friendly way. Staff are instructed to greet every customer but never apply undue sales pressure and to always make a decision that favours the customer before the company. The company promotes from within whenever possible and more than half of the executive committee are people who started on the shop floor.

Typical of this simple employee/customer engagement principle was the famous Nordstrom's employee handbook, which for many years was a single 5 inch by 8 inch index card that contained 75 words (shown in Figure 49.2) (note that this may be apocryphal but it is oft quoted on the internet).[8]

The happy and empowered employees at Nordstrom have delivered strong profits throughout the years. The company has outperformed almost every other retail company in the United States and it continues to promise high returns as it adjusts to future challenges such as online sales.[9] The key

Figure 49.2   Nordstrom's employee handbook

Welcome to Nordstrom. We're glad to have you with our company. Our number one goal is to provide outstanding customer service. Set both your personal and professional goals high. We have great confidence in your ability to achieve them.

Nordstrom rules

Rule #1: use your good judgement in all situations.

There will be no additional rules.

Please feel free to ask your department manager, store manager or divisional general manager any question at any time.

components of Nordstrom's success have been hiring nice, capable people, targeting high-level customers and offering the very best customer service. These are the key ingredients for the service profit chain.

Some things to think about

- Jim Collins, in his book *Good To Great*, argued that the starting point of any company is good staff.[10] He said that if you get the right people on the bus, the wrong people off the bus, and the right people in the right seats, you can take the bus almost anywhere. This is also the thesis of the service profit chain. Good employees who are motivated will deliver good profits. Ask yourself the question, 'Have I got the right people on the bus?'; 'Have I got them in the right seats?'

- Carry out a revenue-at-risk analysis to see which customers are most vulnerable. Then examine those customers to work out why. Could the risk be minimized by better employee engagement and better customer engagement?

Notes

1 Freiberg, K and Freiberg, J (1996) *Nuts! Southwest Airline's Crazy Recipe for Business and Personal Success*, Broadway Books, New York

2 Heskett, JL, Jones, TO, Loveman, GW, Sasser, E and Schlesinger, LA (1994) Putting the service-profit chain to work, *Harvard Business Review*, 72 (2), March–April, pp 164–74

3 Robinson, S and Etherington, L (2006) *Customer Loyalty: A guide for time travelers*, Palgrave Macmillan, New York

4 Heskett, JL, Jones, TO, Loveman, GW, Sasser, E and Schlesinger, LA (1994) Putting the service-profit chain to work, *Harvard Business Review*, 72 (2), March–April, pp 164–74

5 Heskett, JL, Sasser, E and Schlesinger, LA (1997) *The Service Profit Chain: How leading companies link profit and growth to loyalty, satisfaction, and value*, Free Press, New York

6 LaBonte, D (2008) *Shiny Objects Marketing: Using simple human instincts to make your brand irresistible*, John Wiley & Sons, New Jersey

7 John Nordstrom Facts, *Your Dictionary*, http://biography.yourdictionary.com/
john-nordstrom (archived at https://perma.cc/YW6S-QJWR)

8 LaBonte, D (2008) *Shiny Objects Marketing: Using simple human instincts to
make your brand irresistible*, John Wiley & Sons, New Jersey

9 Lutz, A (2014) How Nordstrom Became the Most Successful Retailer, *Business
Insider UK*

10 Collins, J (2001) *Good to Great: Why some companies make the lead and
others don't*, Random House, London

SERVQUAL 50

Aligning customer expectations and company performance

What the model looks like and how it works

Service quality, shortened to SERVQUAL, is a model designed to find out the match between a company's service performance and customers' expectations. It is a sort of gap analysis (it is also discussed in Chapter 27).

Expectations are built up from what a customer knows about a supplier, past experiences with that supplier and customer needs. In a SERVQUAL study people are asked to rate the expectations they have of various aspects of service from a company and the degree to which these expectations are satisfied. The results show where there are gaps between expectations of the service and the performance of the company in meeting these expectations.

The SERVQUAL model is based around five service dimensions, which make the acronym RATER:

- **Reliability**: these questions examine the importance and satisfaction of meeting promises such as overall satisfaction and likelihood to recommend, etc.

- **Assurance**: these questions examine to what extent customer service and sales staff are knowledgeable and courteous.

- **Tangibles**: these questions determine physical aspects such as cleanliness of the delivery vehicles, appearance of the staff, etc. (Note that SERVQUAL is a service-orientated model and so the tangible factors that are of interest are related to service delivery and not to the product itself.)

- **Empathy**: these questions test the importance and satisfaction of the service provided by people such as sales representatives.

- **Responsiveness**: these are questions about the importance and satisfaction on factors such as speed of response to enquiries, ease of doing business, etc.

Service quality can be reduced to an equation expressed as people's perceptions of the service they receive (P) minus their expectations of that service (E). Namely:

$$\text{Service quality} = P - E$$

Mostly, but not always, expectations are higher than the service that is received, which leads to the identification of gaps in meeting expectations. The identification of service quality gaps enables a company to take action and better meet customers' needs. The gaps that can be identified through SERVQUAL are:

- **Gap 1 – the knowledge gap**: this is the gap between the management's perception of what customers want and what they actually want.

- **Gap 2 – the standards gap**: this is the gap between the standards that the company has designed for the customer and what the customer actually expects.

- **Gap 3 – the delivery gap**: this is the gap between customers' expectations and what they receive.

- **Gap 4 – the communications gap**: this is the gap between the promises that are made and the meeting of those promises.

- **Gap 5 – the customer satisfaction gap**: this is the gap between the satisfaction of the customer and their expectations.

Gaps between expectations and perception are due to a number of factors:

- The supplier may not know what customers expect.
- The supplier offers the wrong service quality standards (usually too low) for customers.
- The supplier has employees who are unsuited to or unskilled in providing the service.
- The supplier has an offer that does not meet expectations.
- The supplier makes promises that are not met.

Using the SERVQUAL results, managers can minimize gaps. They can lift the service levels where necessary and ensure that they do not overpromise. They can train staff to provide suitable levels of service and they can be more effective with communications.

The origins of the model

The SERVQUAL model was developed by three academics, Parsu Parasuraman, Valarie Zeithaml and Len Berry, following research they carried out between 1983 and 1988.[1] The original model identified 10 dimensions of service quality, but after testing these were reduced to five that make up the acronym RATER – reliability, assurance, tangibles, empathy and responsiveness.

Developments of the model

The SERVQUAL model has provided the basis for most customer satisfaction surveys in which customers are asked how satisfied they are with various aspects of a company's performance and how important that aspect is to the customer. Importance and expectations are not quite the same thing but they are closely related. Customers tend to have a high expectation of those things that they think are important when choosing a supplier.

The model is flexible in that a company can develop its own questions to measure reliability, assurance, tangibles, empathy and responsiveness. Usually respondents are asked to give a score for each question (e.g. 1 to 5; or 1 to 7; or 1 to 10) to indicate the degree to which they agree that a company performs well. On a similar scale they then rate their expectations for each of the factors. The model allows flexibility in the composition of the questions. Typical questions are such as:

- Responsiveness questions:
  - The deliveries from the company are always on time.
  - I can always reach someone at the company any time I want to.
  - When I have a problem, the company shows interest in solving it.
- Assurance questions:
  - Employees of the company are knowledgeable about their products.
  - Employees of the company are able to solve my problem satisfactorily.
  - Employees of the company are helpful.
  - Employees of the company are friendly.
  - I have confidence in the employees of the company.

- Tangible questions:
  - The company has modern equipment.
  - The company's products are of a high quality.
  - The company's employees always look smart.
  - The company's promotional material is visually appealing.
- Empathy questions:
  - Employees of the company listen carefully to my needs.
  - Employees of the company give me individual attention.
  - The company has operating hours that are convenient to my needs.
  - The company has my best interest at heart.
- Reliability questions:
  - Overall the company provides good-quality service to its customers.
  - I am satisfied with the company's services.
  - I will continue using the company's services.
  - I will recommend the company to other people.

The above list covers 20 separate questions. Respondents would be asked to rate each in terms of expectations and performance – 40 questions in this particular example. If two companies are rated this would add 20 more questions. The questionnaire also requires classification questions to record the demographics of respondents. SERVQUAL questionnaires are, therefore, lengthy and tedious when administered over the phone. They are best completed online.

The model in action

Over the last two decades, universities have operated in an increasingly competitive environment. They have had to become more 'customer orientated', recognizing the importance of satisfying the needs of students. In order to determine areas that required improvement, a university carried out a SERVQUAL study.

A representative cross-section of more than 2,000 students took part in the survey. Data was collected on the year of study, the subject of study, where the student lived before coming to university, their gender, age, etc.

Figure 50.1 Findings from a SERVQUAL university survey

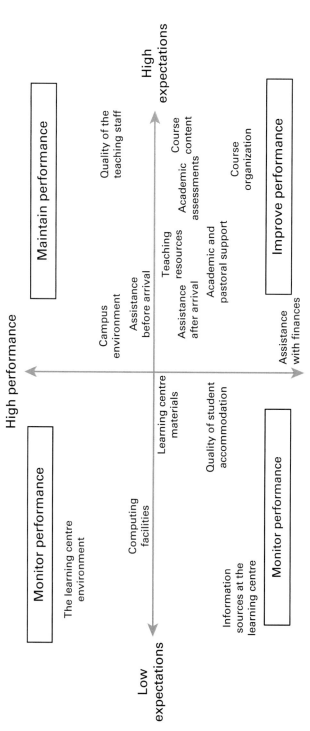

SOURCE Adapted from B2B International (2005)

The questionnaire was devised with SERVQUAL questions covering all the RATER subjects. Under each broad heading of subject there were many detailed questions – 200 in total. Students rated their perceptions on performance and their expectations using a scale from 1 to 7 in an online questionnaire.

A summary of the findings is shown in Figure 50.1. Mapping key RATER factors on performance and expectations, the university was seen to perform well on tangible aspects of its delivery – the quality of the teaching staff and the campus environment. However, its performance was below expectations on a number of 'assurance', 'reliability' and 'empathy' factors (those in the bottom-right quadrant of Figure 50.1).

As a result of the survey the university was able to focus its resources where improvements were most needed. Tracking surveys over the next three years indicated that significant improvements had been made to all the areas of weakness. As a result, students strongly recommended the university to friends and the university has enjoyed a healthy recruitment of new students.

Some things to think about

- Service is a crucial factor in delivering satisfaction. Customers have become increasingly demanding in their expectations of service. Comparisons of your company will be made by customers who enjoy high service delivery in unrelated areas but this nevertheless influences their expectations.

- Delivering good service needs a service 'mindset'. Ask yourself 'Do we employ the right people to deliver good service?' 'Do we train our people to deliver the very best service?' 'Do we give our people the right resources to allow them to deliver superb services?'

Note

1 Parasuraman, A, Zeithaml, VA and Berry, LL (1985) A conceptual model of service quality and its implications for future research, *Journal of Marketing*, **49** (4) (Autumn), pp 41–50

SIMALTO   51

Identifying the customer value placed on product or service improvements

What the model looks like and how it works

Marketers are always asking themselves how their product is performing. They want to know if it meets customers' expectations and, if not, what needs to be changed and by how much. Moreover, they want to know what people would pay for any improvements.

Conjoint is one means by which these questions can be answered. However, conjoint is a statistician's tool. It needs specialist software to set it up and analyse the data. It needs sufficiently large sample sizes if the results are to be believed – 100 interviews as a minimum and more if possible.

SIMALTO is another trade-off model that enables marketers to work out what people value and where they would like to see improvements. The name is an acronym for simultaneous multi-attribute level trade-off. This rather lengthy title describes how the tool works. Respondents are asked to look at a list of different attributes and rank them in order of importance. In this way they are simultaneously trading off a number of attributes that will influence their buying decision. Each of the attributes has different levels. Let's imagine that one of the attributes people want is a face-to-face visit from a salesperson. The different levels of this attribute could be:

- we never receive a visit from a salesperson;
- we receive an annual sales visit;
- we receive a quarterly sales visit;
- we receive a monthly sales visit.

The levels can be varied to suit the subject of study.

Respondents indicate the level of service they receive at present and in the following questions they say what level of service they would like to receive. Finally, they are given a number of points to spend across all the levels to indicate what they would like to be improved. This is the multi-level attribute trade-off in the SIMALTO title.

The SIMALTO tool can best be described with an example. Table 51.1 is a grid showing a selection of attributes that were researched for a power-tool manufacturer. The left-hand column lists attributes that could be considered important when choosing a power tool. The figure shows, for purposes of illustration, only five attributes out of 20 that were covered. Each attribute has different levels of performance, moving from very basic levels at the left of the row through to higher performance levels at the right. Respondents answered questions about what they receive at present and what they would like to receive.

Each level in the row has a number (in parenthesis) that indicates a notional value that people might attach to a particular feature. Towards the end of the interview respondents are given (say) 50 points to spend across

Table 51.1   Selection of attributes from a SIMALTO grid

Attribute	Level 1	Level 2	Level 3	Level 4
Weight of tool	9.3lbs or 4.2kgs (5)	8.4lbs or 3.8kgs (10)	6.7lbs or 3kgs (15)	5.4lbs or 2.5kgs (20)
Durability (time between major repairs)	6 months (5)	12 months (10)	Two years (15)	Three years (20)
Durability, ability of tool to withstand abuse	Will withstand a drop from a short ladder (5ft) (5)	Will withstand a drop from a long ladder (9ft) (10)	Will withstand a drop from a single-storey building (16ft) (15)	Will withstand a drop from a two-storey building (22ft) (20)
Time spent on tool maintenance	60 minutes per week (5)	30 minutes per week (10)	15 minutes per week (15)	5 minutes per week (20)
Battery life	2 hours continuous use (10)	4 hours continuous use (15)	6 hours continuous use (20)	8 hours continuous use (30)

NOTE Numbers in parentheses indicate a value for each level. The numbers can be changed if there is a high cost in offering an improvement (see the row on 'Battery life', which would be expensive to provide).

SOURCE John Green developed the SIMALTO concept and presented it at a market research conference in Oslo in 1977. Table based on Green (1977).

the different levels of performance they have indicated they would like to be improved. The limited number of points they have to spend means they have to make trade-off choices, allocating the points to things they truly value.

The SIMALTO tool can be used with a much smaller sample size than is required for conjoint. In theory a sample of just one respondent is possible with SIMALTO. The single respondent could complete the grid and the analyst could see what they are receiving now and what they would like to receive. This could be used as a discussion point in a depth interview. In practice, sample sizes are selected that cover a cross-section of different types of customers so that in the analysis it is possible to group together respondents with similar priorities and needs. In this way the SIMALTO results can be used to discover different segments.

The 'points spend' question provides a utility value showing people's unmet needs and how much they are prepared to spend to satisfy them. The points spend can be converted to a dollar value as a guide to pricing.

The origins of the model

John Green, a market researcher who began life working for Xerox, developed the SIMALTO concept and presented it at a market research conference in Oslo in 1977. The tool found favour with B2B market researchers who have to deal with small and specialized samples. John Green subsequently became a consultant in the application of the tool.

Developments of the model

The SIMALTO tool has been around for over 40 years. It is a practical tool that can easily be adapted for different products and services. It is surprising therefore that it has not had the exposure or take-up enjoyed by conjoint. SIMALTO can accommodate 20 attributes compared to the usual maximum of seven attributes of conjoint. It uses words to describe the levels of performance of the attributes and these are readily understood by respondents as well as the sponsor of the study. It works with small samples. However, SIMALTO does not have the 'black box' appeal of conjoint, which to many marketers seems more scientific.

The biggest hurdle in developing the SIMALTO questionnaire is creating the grid. Deciding which attributes should go into the grid and working out the clearest way of describing the different levels of each attribute can lead to lengthy discussions.

Analysing the results and presenting them in a clear fashion requires experienced market researchers.

The model in action

A manufacturer of power tools wanted to know which features to focus on in the next generation of products that were being developed. Table 51.1 shows a selection of the attributes that were researched.

SIMALTO questionnaires must be completed online because respondents need to be able to view all the attributes at once in order to decide their rank of importance. They then need to see the different levels of each attribute so that they can say what they receive at the present and what they would like to receive. Finally, they need to be able to review their selections in order to allocate points, which indicate where they would like improvements. These questions cannot be easily answered on the telephone.

The target audience for the research were hands-on users of power tools. These people work on building sites. When they go home at night they do not spend much time on their computers. It is a difficult audience to research and a substantial incentive was required to persuade people to complete the online survey.

A total of 100 completed questionnaires were received and analysed. The results showed that the physical weight of the tool was important and should be an area of focus for research and development. A lightweight tool would be valued because it would improve productivity.

The attribute that would have the greatest appeal in a new tool was a longer battery life. Tradespeople want a tool that will perform for the whole working day. If the tool lets them down, it is not just inconvenient, it is extremely costly. The research showed that a high price would be paid for a battery life of eight hours per day.

The research proved a great success. In addition to the attributes shown in Table 51.1, many more were considered and these provided pointers to the research and development team. Respondents were asked how much they would pay for their ideal tool as chosen from the SIMALTO trade-off. The high price that was given was a reassuring figure that justified the investment of the research and development team in developing the improvements.

Some things to think about

- SIMALTO is worth considering by B2B marketers who, faced with small samples, cannot carry out a conjoint survey. It is a useful tool for establishing unmet needs and which of these are most valued.
- The SIMALTO tool can also be used to find out what improvements employees would like in working practices.
- When developing a SIMALTO grid, think like a respondent. What words would they use? Use the customers' vernacular to describe the different levels of the offer.

Stage gate new product development 52

Planning the development and launch of new products and services

What the model looks like and how it works

New products are the lifeblood of businesses. They provide the opportunity to differentiate, increase prices and steal market share. The proportion of a product portfolio that is made up of new products varies depending on the industry. In the electronics industry the majority of products sold by a company may be less than five years old. In a company selling basic construction materials, the proportion of new products may be less than 10 per cent.

New products that are revolutionary, rather than those that are modifications to existing products, are relatively rare. Most companies can claim that they have a new product if the customer can recognize a significant improvement. Sometimes the product itself may remain unchanged and the 'new' may be the introduction of an associated service.

Stringency is required during the launch of new products. A product that goes to market and fails will incur significant costs in its development and marketing. It is important therefore that the new product's potential success is fully evaluated before the launch. This has led to the development of a stage gate process with a go/no-go decision required at each stage.

The model begins with ideation and is followed by five stage gates:

Idea screen

The process begins with the brainstorming of new product ideas. These may originate from the technical department, the sales team or new product development specialists. It is not unusual at this early stage to have a large number of ideas that are screened on two common-sense criteria:

- Can we make the new product (and at what cost)?
- Will people buy the new product (and at what price)?

At this early stage 100 new product ideas will probably be reduced to just a dozen or so that go forward to the first stage gate.

Stage 1: concept creation

After the initial screening the new product idea is developed into a concept to see if there is a reasonable chance of success if it was to reach the market. The concept will be turned into a picture or graphic so that it can be shown and described to people in order to test their reaction. Potential customers give first impressions of the concept and say whether they see it as truly innovative and beneficial. They would also be asked their likelihood of purchasing such a product if it was available on the market.

Stage 2: business case

An idea that gets through to the second stage requires a business case for it to proceed. This includes the assessment of the size of the opportunity, the competitive environment, the likely price that could be achieved for the product, the revenue potential, the costs and feasibility of manufacturing and the profit potential. Market research plays a role here as it does at every stage. A PEST analysis would prove useful in assessing the forces shaping the market (see Chapter 41). There should also be an assessment of the market size and potential (see Chapter 33).

Stage 3: product development

In this third stage a prototype product is made. The prototype can be shown to potential customers in focus groups to find out their reaction.

Stage 4: test and validation

The fourth stage is an extension of the previous stage. More prototypes are made, possibly in a pre-production run. The products are tested with customers in greater numbers and feedback will show the need for modifications. Customer reactions will prepare the marketing team for the positioning of the new product during the launch.

Stage 5: launch and monitor

If the new product is assiduously reviewed at each of the gates, its launch should be a success. A business plan will be prepared for the launch covering the 4Ps (see Chapter 3). A tracking study may be commissioned to monitor the success of the new product.

Market research plays an important role in the stage gate process, measuring people's attitudes to the new product. A critical question that will be repeated during each of the stages from concept through to test and validation is: assuming the product was offered at a price considered acceptable by your company, which of the following best describes your intent to purchase it?

- definitely would buy;
- probably would buy;
- might or might not buy;
- probably would not buy;
- definitely would not buy.

Typically 25 per cent or more of a target audience will be required to say they 'definitely would buy' in order for the product to pass through the stage gates (see Table 52.1). The response rates shown in Table 52.1 assume that the product has been tested with target customers.

The origins of the model

In the 1940s, stage gate processes were introduced to build new, complex chemical plants. The stages started with research and were followed by an economic study, a pilot plant and, finally, the construction of the plant itself. The gates provided decision points at which time a decision could be made

Table 52.1   'Intention to buy' success criteria

Success criteria in answer to 'intention to buy'	Percentage saying 'definitely would buy'
Fails to clear the hurdle to the next stage	Less than 25%
Standard/minimum response	25% to 34%
Good response	35% to 44%
Excellent response	45% plus

to go forward or not. New product development is often the responsibility of technical and production teams and so it was natural for them to adopt the stage gate approach pioneered by their colleagues.

Developments of the model

The stage gate process is a flexible tool that can be easily adapted. A company can adopt a light-touch stage gate for a product with minor modifications and use heavier and stricter criteria for a new product involving a major investment. Whether major or minor, it is important that metrics and criteria are agreed at the outset that will determine whether the product moves on to the next stage.

The model in action

A manufacturer of workplace gloves recognizes the importance of continuous innovation. In the engineering and chemical industries, gloves are used to protect the product and the hands of workers. Gloves improve productivity and provide the wearer with greater comfort and grip. However, gloves can make it more difficult to grasp small components and they cause sweating if worn for long periods. Modern technology can deal with many of these problems. Gloves are dipped in special polymer mixes that offer protection and good grip. The fabric backing on the gloves allows aeration and wicks away perspiration. Developing the right glove for different applications involves some trial and error. A glove used in a chicken-processing plant needs very different features to one that is used in car assembly. The glove manufacturer uses a stage gate process to ensure the success of each new product launch.

A challenge is the manufacture of the prototype gloves. A sufficient number of prototype gloves must be made for stages 3 and 4. However, the process of manufacturing the gloves in small batches is different to making them in long runs. The prototype products that are tested must be as near as possible the same as those that will ultimately be launched on the market.

Testing the prototype products is another challenge. Gloves are worn by people on the shop floor. The managers of the company where these people work must agree to a product test. They must be assured that the test will not interrupt production or fail and cause harm to their workers.

After the products have been tested, a process is required for the wearers of the gloves to feed back their views and rate the performance of the new gloves against the gloves they normally use. The researchers managing the study must have controls in place so that they know how many hours the gloves have been worn, what they have been used for, and which brand and type of gloves are normally worn (the comparison gloves). There must be a sufficiently large number of tests for the results to be statistically significant. The logistical problem of running a robust trial of this kind is one of the most difficult parts of the stage gate process.

Some things to think about

- Use the stage gate process when launching new products. It is designed to screen out products that will not be successful in the market and whose launch would be a costly mistake.

- When setting up a stage gate process for new products, measures should be agreed at the outset as to what is needed to move to the next gate.

- People who dream up new ideas are extremely valuable in any business. However, like parents of children, they can be very defensive of their ideas. It is why independent research is important in deciding whether the idea can move forward from one gate to the next.

Strategy diamond

Entering new markets

What the model looks like and how it works

The framework recognizes that a number of choices have to be made if a company wants to grow. Decisions have to be taken on what to do and equally what not to do if the strategy is to work. An attraction of the model is its simplicity which means it can be used at any level in an organization.

The strategy diamond has five interrelated components:

Arenas

The arenas are the options for where the company can be active. It is its area of focus. For example, a company could produce different products or operate in different geographies, segments or channels to market. In developing a strategy, it is necessary to decide in which arena the company will compete. The challenge is to focus on that (or those) that offer the greatest opportunities and which fit most neatly with the company's capabilities.

Differentiate

The framework then considers how the company can compete in the marketplace. This is critically important because whatever is selected here will be the means by which the company will attempt to beat the competition. It could differentiate itself on product quality or design, on price or on its brand. This part of the diamond has similarities to Porter's generic strategies as it demands consideration of what will draw customers to the company and that will enable it to beat the competition. Again, there are choices. Do you focus on such as superior quality, attractive price, image or speed to market?

Vehicles

Vehicles are the means by which the company will achieve its objectives. For example, it could decide to do everything itself or it could work with external vehicles such as franchises, licensing or acquisitions. Much will depend on its core competences.

Staging

The strategy has to be launched and this is likely to be in stages. The staging component considers the sequences of launch steps and the speed with which these will be applied. This isn't always easy. On the one hand there will be pressures to move quickly and take advantage of opportunities and on the other hand it is sometimes important that a company paces itself and does not rush into implementation.

Economic logic

The aim of the strategy is to make a profit. The economic logic part of the diamond shows how the pieces fit together to deliver a suitable profit. This may be achieved by economies of scale and low-cost or premium pricing based on any special product advantages.

The origins of the model

The framework was proposed by professors Donald Hambrick and James Fredrickson in an article called 'Are you sure you have a strategy?' in *Academy of Management Executive* in 2001.[1] It is based on a number of choices that can be made about a business seeking to expand.

Hambrick and Fredrickson visualize the framework as a diamond shape. At the top of the diamond sits Arenas and at the bottom are Differentiators. Staging lies in the west and Vehicles in the east. Economic logic sits in the centre of the diamond. The point about the diamond shape is that there is a link between each of the blocks – interdependency.

Hambrick and Fredrickson were of the view that many of the other strategy frameworks failed to consider what constitutes a strategy. This they said draws piecemeal considerations and can result in a fragmented strategy in which a company focuses on low price or large-scale production. The diamond strategy is very much about integrating the various components that will deliver a competitive advantage. It is all about making choices in the five different components of the framework in order to form a unified whole.

Developments of the model

This is a flexible model. It can be moulded to fit any company, especially one that seeks to grow geographically or with new products. The model presupposes that a good deal of research has been carried out on the marketplace. This research will show the size and trends of different segments of the market in different geographies. It will show the size and capabilities of the competition. It will identify customer segments, their needs, and key customers within those segments. Within this depth of understanding of the marketplace the strategy diamond can be implemented:

- **Arenas** will determine the products that will be made and the segments that will be served.
- **Differentiators** will show how the company will succeed against competition.
- **Vehicles** will determine how the offer will be produced and served to the market.
- **Economic logic** will explain how the company will generate revenue and profits.
- **Staging** will describe how the strategy will be rolled out.

The model in action

In the paper that describes the Strategy Diamond, Hambrick and Fredrickson use the example of IKEA.

IKEA's **Arena** is inexpensive Scandinavian-style furniture which it sells to young white-collar customers. It has a widespread geographical footprint. The company has a strong control over product design using many suppliers to manufacture their products.

The **Vehicles** for reaching its chosen arena are its wholly owned stores. IKEA does not make acquisitions and it engages in only a few joint ventures. Top management has tight control over its innovative retailing concept.

There are a number of **Differentiators** that make IKEA different and special. It sells reliable, low-priced products in stores where customers can take their time to compare different items and make their choice. Significantly, the customer can take the furniture home with them or have it delivered the same day.

In terms of **Staging**, the growth of IKEA came through geographical expansion. An early foothold is achieved in a new geography with just one store. Once IKEA learns any special requirements of the geography it rolls out more stores through the region. The **Economic Logic** of IKEA is based on scale and efficiencies. There may be slight differences in products between geographics but the standardization keeps costs low.

All the components of the IKEA strategy diamond fit together. There is an alignment between the targeted arenas, the differentiators, the staging and the economic logic.

Some things to think about

There are lots of things to think about in the Strategic Diamond. Simply developing the five components of the diamond doesn't necessarily deliver a sound strategy. It needs to be tested for its quality. In their paper Hambrick and Fredrickson list a useful checklist of questions for this purpose. They are summarized as follows:

- What are the major changes taking place in the market in which you operate? How does your strategy fit with these?
- What are your key resources? Does your strategy fit with these?
- What are the important differentiators that separate you from the competition? How will you sustain them?
- Does everyone within your organization know the strategy? Are they all aligned with it?
- Do you have sufficient resources to pursue your strategy?
- Is your strategy implementable? Where within your organization could there be any weaknesses that could stop you achieving it?

Note

1 Hambrick, DC and Fredrickson, JW (2001) Are you sure you have a strategy? *Academy of Management Executive*, **15** (4)

SWOT analysis 54

Analysing growth opportunities at product, team or business level

What the model looks like and how it works

The most famous of all business models is the SWOT. This is not without reason. An analysis of the strengths and weaknesses of a company, and the opportunities and threats that it faces, is always insightful. SWOTs are used by business leaders to determine the strategic direction of their business. They are used by marketers to plan campaigns in new territories or with new products. They are used to build profiles of competitors.

The SWOT is a great tool to use at a workshop to brainstorm a solution to a problem or decide on the most effective direction to take. Brainstorming is an important component within the SWOT analysis.

SWOTs are so commonplace they are in danger of being dismissed as a useful tool. Before starting the SWOT it should be clear as to the scope. The SWOT could be limited to:

- a specific brand or company;
- a target audience;
- a product group;
- a geographical region.

Strengths

Strengths are the things that a company does well. When carrying out a SWOT, people find the strengths and weaknesses the easiest parts to complete. The strengths of a company or a product are usually quite obvious. An effort should be made to include all the strengths, no matter how subtle. Some of these less obvious strengths may be differentiators of the company.

Figure 54.1   SWOT analysis grid

	Strengths (internal) • Products • Brands • Promotion • Geographical spread • Distribution • Prices • Processes • People • Profitability	**Weaknesses (internal)** • Products • Brands • Promotion • Geographical spread • Distribution • Prices • Processes • People • Profitability
Opportunities (external) • Market size and growth • Target audiences • Trends and fashions • Competition • Technology • Economics • Politics • Environment • Legal	**Response** • Obvious priorities • Easy and quick to implement	**Response** • Important options • Could be challenging as change and resources are required
Threats (external) • Market size and growth • Target audiences • Trends and fashions • Competition • Technology • Economics • Politics • Environment • Legal	**Response** • Things to address to defend the company	**Response** • Difficult to respond to but a response could be important if the company is at risk

In searching for the strengths, consideration should be given to everything the company does in its markets and business. This includes its products, their quality, special features of the products, prices and the value of the products, the penetration of the market, distribution strengths, the brand, the people skills within the company (including the workforce and the leadership team), the reputation of the company, the geographical footprint of the company, patents or technology leads, infrastructure and modernity of factories, the company culture and its profitability.

Weaknesses

Weaknesses, like strengths, are another internal dimension. These are areas where the company lags behind the competition or is failing in the eyes of customers. They are likely to cover the same subjects as the strengths – products, prices, promotion, distribution, profitability, etc.

Opportunities

The opportunities for a company are those in the marketplace. They are external to the company. They include opportunities that arise from some aspect of the market – its size, its growth, its composition in terms of demographics, the economic situation, the competition, the environment or favourable legislation.

When preparing a SWOT, it is easy to confuse strengths and opportunities. For example, consider a company with a strong brand. This should be listed as a strength and the exploitation of this strength can be in the response box where strengths and opportunities meet (see Figure 54.1).

Threats

Threats are the flip side of opportunities. Threats come from a shrinking marketplace or a highly competitive market. Legislation may pose a threat. Threats could arise from the changing demographic of a company's customer base.

When the strengths, weaknesses, opportunities and threats are laid out in a grid, the meeting point in the centre of the grid prompts responses. This turns the SWOT into an action-orientated tool.

Strengths and opportunities

This is the easiest combination within the SWOT. It quickly becomes obvious how a company can use its strengths to exploit opportunities. It is worth running these responses through a grid to establish the ease with which they can be implemented and the impact they will have. See Figure 54.2.

Weaknesses and opportunities

Where a company has a weakness that is limiting its ability to exploit an opportunity, it becomes a priority for action. There could be factors inhibiting the correction of the weakness such as a lack of finances, insufficient resources, an absence of people skills, etc. The SWOT will identify these and the response will suggest a corrective action.

Strengths and threats

Where a company has a strength but faces a threat in its marketplace, there is a need for defensive action. The threat could be from an aggressive competitor or a declining market and the strength will hopefully suggest how these can be countered.

Figure 54.2 Grid for prioritizing actions

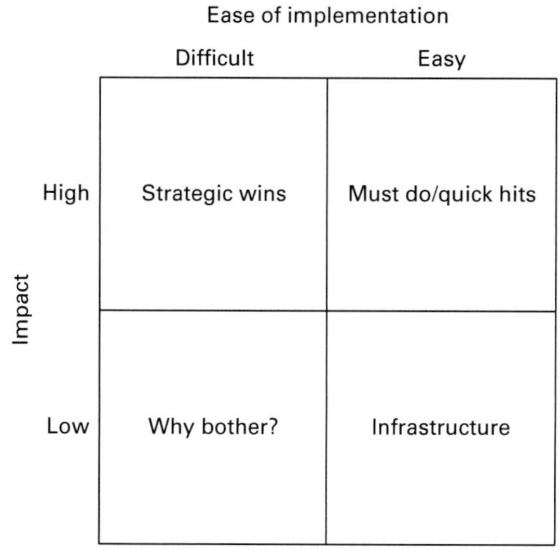

Ease of implementation

	Difficult	Easy
High	Strategic wins	Must do/quick hits
Low	Why bother?	Infrastructure

Impact

Weaknesses and threats

This is the most difficult response within the SWOT. Faced with a threat and hindered by a weakness, it is sometimes difficult to know what to do. Usually the answer lies in correcting the weakness. Until this is rectified, it is hard to see how action can be taken. It may be that the weakness and the threat lead to no action. If the threat does not pose a huge risk, it may not be worthwhile allocating resource to correct the weakness.

The origins of the model

The origins of the SWOT tool began with research carried out by Stanford Research Institute (SRI) in 1960.[1] The research, led by Albert Humphrey, was aimed at finding out why corporate planning was failing in large companies. The answer appeared to be the difficulty companies had in setting realistic objectives and the many compromises that were made when these objectives could not be achieved. There was a missing link as to how a management team within a company could agree and commit to an action programme that would work.

The team at SRI concluded that the first step was to find out what was good and bad about an organization before deciding what it could do. What was seen to be good in an organization was labelled satisfactory (S), what was bad was labelled a fault (F) and these could then be addressed to the opportunities (O) and threats (T) within the marketplace. The team created the acronym SOFT to describe the satisfactory, opportunity, fault and threat components of the tool. In 1964, at a seminar on long-range planning held in Switzerland, the F in SOFT was changed to a W for weakness and the SWOT was born.[2]

Developments of the model

The SWOT analysis tool has proved powerful and popular. It is used in business and marketing to address a company's position within a market, or the future for a product, brand or business idea. It is also used as a problem-solving tool that can be used to guide an acquisition, outsource a service, develop a partnership with a different company, or evaluate an investment opportunity.

The tool can be customized. For example, if there are many components of the SWOT they could be ranked or given a score of importance in order to provide a degree of focus.

As with many of the tools described in this book the SWOT does not have to stand alone. The PEST tool is a useful adjunct (see Chapter 41), especially in identifying the threats and opportunities within a market.

SWOT analysis has come in for some criticism. In the brainstorming that leads to the analysis the strengths and weaknesses of a company may be perceived rather than actual. For example, the people taking part in the brainstorming may think that their products are overpriced whereas a survey of customers could show otherwise. It is important therefore that objective data is collected and the analysis doesn't get overtaken by internal politics.

Sometimes it is difficult to determine whether a company attribute is a strength or weakness. If Sears had done a SWOT, would it have put its retail outlets down as a strength or a weakness? They could be both but then it would be necessary to weight them to indicate whether one was more of a strength or more of a weakness.

There are potential pitfalls with all frameworks if the data put into the analysis is questionable. Most companies using a SWOT framework find it a quick and easy way to get people thinking about where the company stands in its marketplace and where it could go in the future.

The model in action

A supplier of industrial tools had a portfolio of quality products and services that it sold into industrial engineering distributors. It decided to consider the opportunities of selling directly into the automotive body repair-shop market. This is a market made up of many hundreds of small backstreet repair shops that are becoming more professional under pressure from insurance companies. Rationalization was taking place within this market and a number of large automotive repair shops were emerging that were setting standards for smaller competitors. The industrial tool manufacturer believed that there could be an opportunity to market to body repair companies. These tools included hand tools of various kinds, welding equipment, safety products, technical advice, etc.

The company carried out research amongst body shops to establish attitudes to its proposed offer. The research showed that the company had a well-known brand though it was not associated as a supplier of tools to body shops.

The rationalization and mergers within the industry presented opportunities for the company to target the larger body shops. These large body shops were regarded by the smaller repair shops as opinion leaders. The biggest threat within the market came from the motor factors, the traditional source of tools used by the body repair shops.

Repairs to cars were becoming more difficult as a result of the greater sophistication of new models and the materials that are used in their construction. This presented an opportunity for the company to offer a technical service helpline that was unique in the industry.

As a result of the SWOT, the company was able to develop a strong position as a supplier of tools and services to body repair shops. The SWOT analysis provided structure framework, which enabled the tool company to see a way into the market (see Figure 54.3).

Some things to think about

- A SWOT analysis is a great brainstorming tool. Use it whenever you are considering a strategy for a product or a business unit. Use the SWOT grid, which drives action where strengths, weaknesses, opportunities and threats meet.

Figure 54.3   SWOT for a tool company entering the body repair-shop market

	Strengths (internal)	Weaknesses (internal)
	• The company brand is well-known and stands for excellence • The company is acknowledged to offer good products – especially equipment	• The brand is not known as a specialist supplier to body shops • The company is seen as expensive for what it is
Opportunities (external) • A few large body shops are emerging and leaving the traditional shops behind • There is a need for more services to help the body shops focus on what they do best – repairing vehicles	**Response** • Focus on the large body shops who are opinion leaders	**Response** • Run a promotional campaign to build the brand amongst body shops and feature the extensive product range
Threats (external) • Aggressive and well-tuned competition from motor factors • More complicated cars requiring different approaches to body repair	**Response** • Build a service offering that provides advice to body repair shops	**Response** • Position the brand as flexible and friendly so that it is seen to align with body shops

- In developing the SWOT, consider all the detailed strengths and weaknesses, opportunities and threats and then distil them so that the grid contains only those that are most important.

- Place a priority on actions related to the strengths and opportunities and the weaknesses and the opportunities. These will be where the quickest gains can be achieved.

Notes

1   Helyer, R (2015) *The Work-Based Learning Student Handbook*, Palgrave Macmillan, London

2   SWOT analysis, www.b2bframeworks.com/swot-analysis (archived at https://perma.cc/HF3X-W9Z8)

System 1 and
System 2
thinking

Identifying the emotional forces that
drive decisions

What the model looks like and how it works

It is now widely accepted that emotions play a big part in decision making.
Understanding how emotions work within the decision-making process has
become important to marketers.

Behavioural economists recognize two levels of thinking when it comes to
decision making. The first level of thinking is called System 1. It is fast, automatic and arises out of the subconscious. It is a natural reaction to dealing
with a situation. Humans are programmed to respond quickly and auto-
matically for safety. If we were in the jungle and saw a tiger in front of us, we
would not spend much time analysing the situation, we would react immediately. Whether or not it is the right thing to do, we would most probably run.

System 1 thinking is not confined just to decisions related to safety.
System 1 thinking is driven by emotions. The problem with System 1 thinking is that people often do not recognize that they are thinking. The process
occurs in the subconscious and so it is difficult to unpick and describe. Even
if we are prepared to admit that the choice of a product is driven by emotions we may find it difficult to say exactly what those emotions are and
how they are working.

System 2 thinking is easier to analyse. It is the slow, calculating, conscious
and logical way in which decisions are made. People find it easier to recognize and describe them. System 2 thinking is how most of us think we make
decisions when in fact it could be a post-rationalization that follows the true
driver, which was emotions.

Our System 1 thinking, and the actions we take, are influenced by biases. These are also referred to as heuristics. What has happened in the past will almost certainly shape how we think and our actions in the future. There are a number of factors that influence the biases:

Anchoring

Reference points help us in our decision making. If we mention a fact or a figure to someone, it could influence their answer. For example, if we say to people 'How likely are you to buy this product at a price of more than $100?' we have introduced the idea that the product could be worth $100. We may get a much higher proportion of people saying they are likely to buy it at a price of more than $100 than if we were simply to say 'At what price would you buy this product?' The $100 is the anchor.

Availability

We are influenced by things we can quickly and easily recall. Something that has happened recently or something of critical importance will be readily available in our minds and could bias our response. Asking someone how happy they are with a supplier immediately after they have suffered a problem with that supplier is likely to get a strong negative reaction; possibly a harsher reaction than is justified.

Optimism and loss aversion

There is an old saying in business that 'everything costs more than you thought and takes longer than you thought'. This is because of the prevalence of us overestimating the benefits and underestimating the costs. It results in us sometimes taking on projects that are risky, against our better judgement.

Framing

The way a question is asked can materially affect the answer. For example, people could be told that the survival rate of a surgical operation is 90 per cent or they could be told that the mortality rate is 10 per cent. Both figures are correct but people are more likely to happily agree to the operation if they are told that there will be a 90 per cent success rate.

Sunk cost

We are guilty of throwing good money after bad. We make decisions that have a poor outcome and yet we are drawn to continue down the same path, perhaps to try to change the outcome and alleviate any feelings of regret.

The origins of the model

Daniel Kahneman is a psychologist and a professor at Princeton University. He is a Nobel prize winner for his work on behavioural economics. In the 1970s Kahneman worked at Stanford University where, with two other psychologists and behavioural economists – Amos Tversky and Richard Thaler – they developed theories about how we think and to what extent these thoughts are influenced by heuristics and biases. It was not until 2011, when Kahneman published these theories in his book *Thinking, Fast and Slow*,[1] that they became well known and popular.

Developments of the model

People are still working out how to use System 1 and System 2 thinking in business. We know that emotions drive decisions but how do we use this knowledge practically?

We need to figure out exactly how emotions trigger actions. Department stores have long recognized that it pays to put the perfumery department on the ground floor close to where people enter the store. Nice smells put people in a good mood to linger and shop. Smells are used in supermarkets where the aroma of baking produces a queue at the bread counter.

There are other subtle influences on our emotions, some of which we may not be aware of. The use of colour can convert a powerful message. Blue is the colour of trust and reliability. Red is the colour of speed and courage. Orange and yellow communicate cheapness but also fun.[2] Using colour in logos, on packaging and in promotions can carry our emotions down a certain path.

People say that they like innovation. 'New' is a vitally important word in marketing. However, something that is so new it doesn't seem familiar may worry people. Not everyone is an innovator. We therefore need to find ways in which we can make a new idea more acceptable so that people understand it and are more likely to buy it.

The model in action

Market researchers have been guilty in the past of assuming that most decisions have some rationality. In part this has been guided by traditional economics, where it is assumed that the rational buyer weighs value and price when making a decision. Certainly some element of rationality is involved in most decisions. People are fairly rational about how much they can afford to spend on a product and they choose within a price range. Within that price range they may be heavily influenced by emotional factors. Simple products such as lipsticks, foodstuffs and items of clothing are chosen quickly. Someone walking around a supermarket usually gives no more than a few seconds of thought to what they throw in the basket. There is a lot of System 1 thinking here.

So too when we want to measure brand awareness, we rely on System 1 thinking. It is the brands that people mention spontaneously and without a great deal of thought that are usually the strongest. We also know that people forget to mention things and so we prompt by reading out a list of brands and ask which they know. Here we are tapping into protracted thought – System 2 thinking.

There are other things that demand more thought and where decision making is extended. Take, for example, the choice of civil engineer to build a major bridge. It may take months of negotiations and procrastinations with a number of civil engineering companies before one is chosen. There will be many people involved and less room for intuitive decision making. This is not to say that factors such as the brand of the civil engineer will be unimportant. However, if there is a choice between two civil engineers, there will be a good deal of rational scoping until the offers from each look reasonably similar. At that point the brand of civil engineer could swing the balance in favour of one of the companies. When there is nothing else to choose between two companies on rational factors, the emotional factors become important.

System 2 thinking is required to generate ideas. If we ask people what improvements can be made to a product or service, an initial reaction may be 'nothing, it is fine'. System 2 thinking involves effort and people must be pushed to think harder. We could use gamification and say 'you have 20 seconds to mention as many new applications for the product as possible'. In this way we would be forcing the respondent to make an effort and think in a System 2 way.

Kahneman tells us that when people find it difficult to answer a question, they may substitute their own ideas. For example, if someone is asked how their car can be improved, they may answer by saying they cannot think of any improvements (the lazy System 2 option) or they like their car because it does lots of miles to the gallon (substitution of the answer). The person who talks about being happy with the car's fuel efficiency has not answered the question, rather they have substituted an answer for another question.

This means that when we have to get answers to difficult and complex questions we should break the question into a number of parts. For example, we should not ask what improvements should be made to a car, we should ask the car owner what improvements could be made to the comfort of the car, what improvements could be made to the electronics within the car, what improvements could be made to the servicing of the car and so on.

Some things to think about

- Use focus groups and qualitative research to discover what people really think of your products and those of your competitors. Create an emotional profile that shows how your brand is associated with certain words such as happy, pleased, trust, valued, safe, etc – versus stressed, frustrated, irritated, disappointed, unsatisfied, etc. What is the emotional profile of your competitors using the same words? This can develop emotional profiles as suggested by Colin Shaw.[3]

- Use emotions to make your marketing communications more effective. Instead of talking about the features of your products, talk about how the customer will feel after they have bought your product.

Notes

1 Kahneman, D (2011) *Thinking, Fast and Slow*, Farrar, Straus and Giroux, New York

2 Wright, A (2008) Psychological Properties Of Colours, www.colour-affects.co.uk (archived at https://perma.cc/F4DM-KL89)

3 Shaw, C (2007) *The DNA of Customer Experience: How emotions drive value*, Palgrave Macmillan, Basingstoke

Tipping point 56

How small changes to behaviour can result in big achievements

What the model looks like and how it works

The concept of a tipping point has long been used by sociologists. They are of the view that there is a point in time when large numbers of a population suddenly adopt what was once a minority view. For example, scientists in the Rensselaer Polytechnic Institute, a private university in New York, found out that when 10 per cent of a population holds an unshaken belief, this new belief will be widely adopted by most people.[1]

The Canadian writer and thinker, Malcolm Gladwell, is famous for a number of books that help us understand human behaviour. In 2000 he published a book called *The Tipping Point: How little things can make a big difference*.[2] The point of the book is neatly expressed in the title.

Gladwell followed up this theory by arguing that there are three requirements to move an idea from being in a minority to taking a majority position.

1. The right people

People influence people. Obviously it is important to understand your audience. It is especially important to find the right kind of influencers who are prepared to pick up the ideas and spread them. There need to be connectors; people who, as the term suggests, are connected with many others. If something is to spread it needs connected people. Gladwell called these people Mavens. Mavens are information specialists who are particularly good at accumulating and distilling new knowledge. The right people must also include Salespeople because they are able to persuade others that new ideas are worth adopting. In today's world the many influencers that exist in social media would be regarded as Mavens.

2. The idea needs to be sticky

By this, Gladwell means that the message or the idea must be memorable. Various devices can be used to make an idea memorable – repetition helps a lot, so do memory cues (things that are associated with a product or idea). These could be graphics, colours, sounds – things that evoke the senses.

3. The idea must have context

The idea must be right for the moment in time. For example, when vandalism became a serious issue in New York, the concept of zero tolerance for minor crimes was able to take hold as a means of slowing down major crimes. Gladwell has a point here. It is difficult to persuade someone to eat a Chinese meal when they have just had dinner. The time must be right for the idea to be adopted.

In business we can use the tipping point to make marketing messages more effective. The starting point is to work out what message you want to communicate. It is helpful if the message is one with emotional appeal – such as *'our product will last longer because it has 10 per cent more material'*. The message must then be targeted at the right people – the connectors, mavens and salespeople. Devices should be built into the message so that it is memorable. And finally the message must make complete sense to people – *'are you fed up of having to replace the products you are currently using every six months?'*.

The origins of the model

The term 'tipping point' is widely used in epidemiology. It is based on a mathematical insight known as geometrical progression, which is used to predict the speed at which epidemics of contagious disease spread. As we have seen with the coronavirus pandemic, a few infections can suddenly turn into an epidemic. It is not unlike the J curve or hockey stick, often used in business projections. The J curve is where sales begin at a relatively slow pace before gathering speed.

Gladwell was covering the AIDS outbreak for the *Washington Post* in 1991 when he saw how the disease that affected just a few gay men suddenly became a worldwide problem. This is similar to the concept of viral marketing in which a small group of people discussing a subject can find a voice that spreads rapidly through their network of connections.

During the coronavirus epidemic we became familiar with the reproduction number (R), which is the average number of secondary infections caused by a single infected person. An R value of more than 1.0 means that the virus is growing. Viral marketing has the same level of power if it goes past the tipping point amongst people who are well connected and share the subject online. The term viral marketing was introduced by Jeffrey Rayport, a Harvard Business School academic, in a 1996 article for the magazine *Fast Company*.[3]

Developments of the model

Gladwell's 'tipping point' is as much a philosophy as a framework. There are no hard and fast measures to say at what point the penetration of a product within a market will take off and go viral. Tipping points have been studied for many years. Thomas Schelling, an American economist and Nobel prize winner, published articles in the early 1970s in which he showed that if neighbours have a preference to live with people of the same colour it could lead to total segregation. He had introduced a 'general theory of tipping'. In 1978 this was explored in his book *Micromotives and Macrobehaviour*.[4]

Following on from Schelling, in 1978 Mark Granovetter, an American sociologist and professor at Stanford University, proposed a model that assumes individuals' behaviour depends on the number of other individuals also acting in a similar way.[5] This was termed a behavioural threshold. It isn't easy to predict, as the threshold will be dependent on predilections of the population, including their socio-economic status, education, age and personality. It was against this background that Gladwell developed his tipping point theory.

The model in action

In his book Gladwell uses the example of Hush Puppies, the soft and comfortable pigskin shoe made by the Wolverine Company of Rockford, Michigan. The company was founded in 1958 but by 1994 sales had flagged and were down to 30,000 pairs a year. The shoes became popular amongst visitors to the clubs and bars of Manhattan. Fashion designers began featuring them in their collections. Soon they were worn by celebrities. The tipping point was passed and through word of mouth Wolverine sold 430,000 pairs of the shoes in 1995 and four times that number the next year.

The reason for this growth was the surprising and unpredictable acceptance of Hush Puppies as a style item for the hip group in Manhattan. These 'influencers' are critical in the tipping point framework. They are people who are well connected, looked up to, and who readily share their views with a wide audience.

Some things to think about

- What is there about your products that is distinctive and different? With whom does this distinctive/difference resonate?
- What could you do to encourage sales of your products amongst a key target audience? What scope is there for celebrity endorsement?
- How can you make the message about your product more contagious and have greater lasting impact?
- Who are the connectors, mavens, influencers and salespeople that can take your product forward?

Notes

1 Sohn, E (2011) Minority rules: scientists find the tipping point, *NBC News*, https://www.nbcnews.com/id/wbna44021015 (archived at https://perma.cc/B8Q7-ZWMB)
2 Gladwell, M (2000) *The Tipping Point: How little things can make a big difference*, Little Brown & Company, Boston
3 Rayport, J (1996) The virus of marketing, *Fast Company*, www.fastcompany.com/27701/virus-marketing (archived at https://perma.cc/ZX59-DPAL)
4 Schelling, TC (1978) *Micromotives and Macrobehavior*, Norton
5 Granovetter, M (1978) Threshold modules of collective behavior, *The American Journal of Sociology*, 83 (6) pp 1420–43

USP   57

Pinpointing the unique selling point of a product or service

What the model looks like and how it works

A unique product gives a company a distinct advantage, especially if it is desirable. Companies that have unique products may be able to patent and protect them and preserve this big advantage. Most companies have to compete against competitors that have quite similar offerings. This does not mean to say that they cannot find something that stands out as their own 'high ground'. Finding a USP can be difficult. To do so it is necessary to look at the target audience, the customer value proposition, the competitive situation, and the processes by which the product is made. The steps in discovering a USP are as follows:

- Step 1 – select your target audience: the starting point has to be the target audience for the product. Who are they and what do they look like?

- Step 2 – identify the needs of the target audience: the target audience will have a variety of different needs. These should be listed, no matter how big or small.

- Step 3 – identify the unmet needs of the target audience: what is it that buyers of the product would like that they are not receiving at the present? All the unmet needs should be listed.

- Step 4 – rank order the needs and unmet needs: the needs and unmet needs should be placed in order or weight of importance.

- Step 5 – list all the elements of your value proposition: your value proposition is made up of all the different features and benefits of your product, together with supporting services. Weight them in importance from the point of view of the target customer.

- **Step 6 – match your value proposition against those of competitors:** which of your value propositions stand out as different and better than those of competitors?

- **Step 7 – consider the processes by which your products are produced:** list the sources of raw materials that are used in your products, the methods of processing your products, the quality checks that are applied, etc. Which of these could be an indicator of something special to the target audience?

- **Step 8 – select a benefit, a feature or a story that will resonate with the target audience:** following the analysis of customers' needs, unmet needs, the customer value proposition, the competitive situation and the value chain by which the product is made, select a single attribute that will appeal to the target audience.

Various tools and frameworks can be used to help find the USP. A SWOT analysis (Chapter 54), customer journey map (Chapter 18) and Kotler's price quality matrix (Chapter 45) may help.

Developing a USP is not necessarily about finding something at which you are the best. Somewhere there is another company that can probably do it better. Developing a USP is about finding something that matters to customers and that no one else has made their forte. As long as you are able to defend your ability to provide the USP, it can become yours. If another company seeks to use the same story for their USP, they will be regarded as plagiarists.

The USP that is chosen should be checked to see that it successfully drives customer choice. It should also be checked against the fit with the brand position of the company.

The origins of the model

The concept of the USP arose within advertising agencies in the 1940s. It provided them with a tool to develop strong messages to communicate to target audiences. They wanted USPs that fulfilled three things:

- Give the person who saw the advert a reason to buy the product because of the specific factor or benefit (the USP) that was featured.

- Make the USP the property of the company by promoting it in such a way that the competition could not copy.

- Generate a call to action by moving customers and potential customers to want to find out more about the product.

The idea of the USP was introduced by Rosser Reeves of Ted Bates & Company in the United States in 1940.[1] Reeves believed that the purpose of advertising is to sell. Towards this end, he developed television commercials that featured the USP of the product. This was typified in an advert he designed for Anacin, an analgesic for headaches. The ad lasted for seven years, grated and annoyed most viewers and was successful in tripling the product's sales.[2]

Reeves liked delivering his USPs as slogans. He was the creator of the slogan 'melts in your mouth, not in your hand' for M&Ms. The sugar shell around M&Ms made it special and different from other forms of chocolate, which would melt in the hand. The idea of the M&M melting in the mouth also had connotations of delivering taste where it needed to be. By repeating the slogan again and again, Reeves made it a USP.

Developments of the model

The term USP has largely been replaced by the concept of the customer value proposition (CVP). The CVP focuses on the many aspects of the offer for which customers are prepared to pay. (See Chapter 20.)

Al Ries and Jack Trout in their book *Positioning: The battle for your mind* (1981),[3] emphasized the importance of linking the brand position with a strong claim about what makes the company special. The brand-positioning concept has nowadays become more important than the product-positioning concept.

The model in action

Zappos, the online shoe retailer, was led by Tony Hsieh who joined the company in 1999.[4] At that time the company had revenues of just $1.6 million per annum. In 2009 the company was sold to Amazon for $1.2 billion. Tony Hsieh and his team built the company on a culture of passion and excitement. From the customer's point of view, the Zappos staff would do anything to make them happy. They became known as the most convenient, customer friendly online store for buying shoes. They were not known as the company with the lowest prices. It would be hard, if not impossible, to offer both.

Zappos has a big CVP. It offers lots of benefits to customers. But what makes Zappos stand out from the competition is a very simple USP – it has the best return policy ever. As a result, it removes customers' fear of buying shoes online that might not fit.

Developing a USP is about hard choices. Companies with lots of strengths, like Zappos, can be in danger of shouting about all of them. This would dilute the key message. By singling out one thing that matters to customers (the best returns policy ever) a company such as Zappos can carve a unique position for itself within a market.

Some things to think about

- Although the USP is less fashionable than a CVP (customer value proposition), the USP has much to commend it. It focuses on a single factor that makes a company or brand special. In the complicated world in which we live, this simplicity can be a big advantage. It is worth finding your USP.

- A USP that resonates with emotions will be effective. In the case of Zappos there are emotional concerns about buying the wrong size and style of shoe online. With its returns policy and its high level of customer engagement, these fears have been eliminated. What are the emotional triggers and barriers of your customers?

Notes

1 Reeves, R (1961) *Reality in Advertising*, Knopf, New York
2 Anacin (2003) Advertising Age, http://adage.com/article/adage-encyclopedia/anacin/98317/ (archived at https://perma.cc/V5LT-VM86)
3 Ries, A and Trout, J (1981) *Positioning: The battle for your mind*, McGraw-Hill, New York
4 Hsieh, T (2010) *Delivering Happiness: A path to profits, passion, and purpose*, Grand Central Publishing, New York

Value chain 58

Identifying product or service value during the manufacturing process

What the model looks like and how it works

Businesses create value. They do so by taking materials or ideas and making them into something for which they can charge a price that covers the cost of conversion. The value chain is the way that materials enter the company and move through it, increasing in value as they do so.

Michael Porter identified five activities in the value chain within a company:[1]

- **Inbound logistics:** these are the products or materials that enter the company and that will be stored and processed in order to create the finished product. Relationships with suppliers are important as they are the source of materials bought by the company.

- **Operations:** these are the processes that are used to create the products and services. Operations includes the technical department, maintenance, production, testing and packaging.

- **Outbound logistics:** this is the part of the company that deals with the finished product and moving it to customers. It involves warehousing and transportation, including any logistics that are outsourced.

- **Marketing and sales:** products must be sold and for this there needs to be a process for generating interest and executing sales. This part of the value chain covers the internal and external development of promotions, the management of the sales force and the pricing strategy.

- **Service:** the product is supported by a warranty and a service department. This includes the supply of spare parts, product installation, training, repair services, etc.

These five primary activities require support. Porter identified four support activities within companies:

- **Infrastructure**: these are departments responsible for planning, accounting, legal and general management. They are the arteries of the business that enable it to operate.

- **Human resources**: this department recruits, trains and manages the people within the business.

- **Technology development**: this team develops technologies that ensure the product has a competitive advantage.

- **Procurement**: this is the department that sources materials and services that are required in the production of the product.

Both the primary and support activities add value to the business. Inbound logistics, operations and service are activities that are centred on the product. Marketing/sales and outbound logistics are activities that are outward facing and relate to the market.

The difference between the total costs of producing the product and the revenue of the company is its margin. This margin is a measure of the value that has been added and is reflected as a return on the investment.

Porter argues that the competitive position of the company cannot be understood by looking at the firm as a whole. It is necessary to examine each of the primary and support activities to see how they contribute to the firm's relative cost position and create any basis for differentiation.

The value chain model provides a structure for examining the different parts of the company to see which successfully adds value and which does not. In making this examination, care should be taken to note the links between different activities. Broken links destroy value. For example, a sales team could work hard to bring a new customer on board and the accounts team could be overzealous in applying a credit-control rating that frustrates the new customer and causes them to leave before any business is carried out.

The origins of the model

Michael Porter is a professor at Harvard Business School.[2] He is the author of a number of models that help companies establish a competitive advantage. The value chain framework is designed to maximize value creation within a business and it focuses on the business itself. It is often used alongside Porter's 'competitive forces', another framework that is used to assess value creation and that examines external forces influencing a business.

The value chain model was proposed by Michael Porter in his book entitled *Competitive Strategy* published in 1980.[3]

Developments of the model

The value chain framework has become a popular tool within management. It has been extended beyond individual businesses and applied to whole supply chains and distribution networks. The concept of understanding a supply chain allows a business to see where the profit is made and who controls the chain. A simplified value chain for a manufacturer of chemicals is shown in Figure 58.1.

The model in action

An explanation of Porter's value chain can be made with reference to Starbucks. The company was founded in Seattle in 1971 and operates 34,000 coffee shops throughout the world.[4] In 2007 the rapid growth of Starbucks slowed and Howard Schultz, the company's founder, was called back in as president and CEO. Schultz had to work out how to deal with the higher material prices and increased competition from food chains such as McDonald's and Dunkin Donuts as well as the many me-too organizations that had copied the Starbucks formula:

Figure 58.1   Brands in equilibrium in a value map

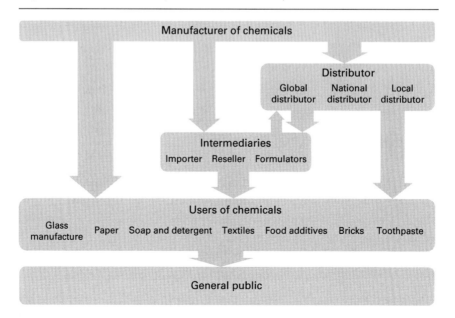

- **Inbound logistics:** Starbucks uses half a billion pounds of coffee beans per annum (3 per cent of the world's supply).[5] The beans come from more than 300,000 growers in Asia, Africa and Latin America. When Schultz reviewed the company and its value chain, he identified the regional and central distribution centres as needing to improve their efficiency. In 2008 only 3 out of every 10 orders of products to stores were delivered perfectly. Schultz reorganized the supply chain operations and quickly improved that figure to 9 out of 10 orders being delivered perfectly.[6]

  The company acquired a coffee bean plantation in Costa Rica and began to grow its own beans.[7] This was not in an attempt to vertically integrate. It was an initiative to help with product development such as the study of disease-resistant beans.

- **Operations:** in February 2008, Starbucks closed 7,100 US stores for 3.5 hours to retrain its baristas on how to make the perfect espresso.[8] Stores were required to grind the beans on their premises and any coffee that was sitting more than 30 minutes had to be thrown away. Schultz invited staff to email him directly with ideas, which he shortly opened up to customers for their thoughts – 93,000 ideas rolled in.[9] He commissioned a redesign of its stores to recapture the coffeehouse feel.

- **Outbound logistics:** an analysis of the supply chain delivering to the Starbucks coffee shops showed that less than half of the store deliveries were arriving on time. Costs of running the supply chain were rising very steeply. The Starbucks supply chain team simplified its structure and reduced the cost to serve its stores. They built one global logistics system.[10]

- **Marketing and sales:** historically Starbucks never spent much on national advertising. When Schultz returned as CEO, one of his first initiatives was to invest in a major national advertising campaign with BBDO. Schultz introduced a customer rewards card that quickly took off and built customer loyalty.[11]

- **Service:** Schultz appointed Chris Bruzzo, chief technology officer from Amazon, to update the technology, the website and to improve the social media presence.[12]

  In addition to the improvements Schultz made to the primary activities, he also addressed secondary activities. He offered a comprehensive health-care package to part-time workers, and new stock incentives and bonuses for partners. Following his return in 2008 and the initiatives he took to improve the value chain of the business, Schultz increased the company's market value from $15 billion to $84 billion in 2016. Schultz has not finished with Starbucks. At the time of writing (December 2022) Schultz has yet again taken the reins as CEO at the company and intends to stay there until his new appointee takes over.[13]

Some things to think about

- A business is a conveyor belt that takes raw materials and labour and converts it into an offer with added value. Every department plays a role in this process and contributes to the value. Where is the value created in your company? How strong are the links between the different departments? Could they be improved in any way that would add value?

- In addition to the value chain within your business, do you know the value chain in your market? What is changing in the way products get from you to the final customer? How are you responding to this change? Who is making the money? How could your business make more money within this value chain?

Notes

1 Harrison, K (2017) What Is A Value Chain Analysis? *Business News Daily*, www.businessnewsdaily.com/5678-value-chain-analysis.html (archived at https://perma.cc/5XDG-2LGB)

2 Wikipedia (nd) Michael Porter, https://en.wikipedia.org/wiki/Michael_Porter (archived at https://perma.cc/A76P-FWDC)

3 Porter, M (1980) *Competitive Strategy: Techniques for analyzing industries and competitors*, Free Press, New York

4 Statista (2022) Number of international and U.S.-based Starbucks stores from 2005 to 2021, www.statista.com/statistics/218366/number-of-international-and-us-starbucks-stores/ (archived at https://perma.cc/5G8C-C2N8)

5 Gruley, B and Patton, L (2014) To Stop The Coffee Apocalypse, Starbucks Buys a Farm, *Bloomberg*, www.bloomberg.com/news/articles/2014-02-13/to-stop-the-coffee-apocalypse-starbucks-buys-a-farm (archived at https://perma.cc/249L-4HYQ)

6 Enz, CA (2010) Case 7: the commoditization of Starbucks, in *Hospitality Strategic Management: Concepts and cases*, ed CA Enz, John Wiley & Sons, New Jersey

7 Gruley, B and Patton, L (2014) To Stop The Coffee Apocalypse, Starbucks Buys a Farm, *Bloomberg*, www.bloomberg.com/news/articles/2014-02-13/to-stop-the-coffee-apocalypse-starbucks-buys-a-farm (archived at https://perma.cc/A7HP-F2C6)

8 Enz, CA (2010) Case 7: the commoditization of Starbucks, in *Hospitality Strategic Management: Concepts and cases*, ed CA Enz, John Wiley & Sons, New Jersey

9 Husain, S, Khan, F and Mirza, W (2014) How Starbucks pulled itself out of the 2008 financial meltdown, *Business Today*, www.businesstoday.in/magazine/lbs-case-study/how-starbucks-survived-the-financial-meltdown-of-2008/story/210059.html (archived at https://perma.cc/KG4J-E3E8)

10 Cooke, JA (2010) From Bean To Cup: How Starbucks Transformed Its Supply Chain, *Supply Chain Quarterly*, Quarter 4, www.supplychainquarterly.com/articles/438-from-bean-to-cup-how-starbucks-transformed-its-supply-chain (archived at https://perma.cc/HQ2R-QHG4)

11 Schultz, H and Gordon, J (2011) *Onward: How Starbucks fought for its life without losing its soul*, John Wiley & Sons, Chichester

12 Schultz, H and Gordon, J (2011) *Onward: How Starbucks fought for its life without losing its soul*, John Wiley & Sons, Chichester

13 Wikipedia (nd) Howard Schultz, https://en.wikipedia.org/wiki/Howard_Schultz (archived at https://perma.cc/7892-JGN4)

Value equivalence line 59

Managing price and product benefits in a business strategy

What the model looks like and how it works

The purchase of a product or service requires a customer to consider the price as a bargain – a price worth paying. Within any class of product there is likely to be a premium offer and an economy offer. The premium offer by its very nature will have more features and benefits than the economy offer and it can be expected to have a higher price. Products or brands can be plotted on a graph in which the Y axis reflects the perceived price and the X axis the perceived benefits. The line that bisects the X and Y axes is the value equivalence line (VEL). This is illustrated in Figure 59.1, which shows a schematic value map of three car brands with different prices, different benefits and all in equilibrium.

Markets are seldom perfect and so it is not unusual for brands to sit either side of the VEL. A brand to the left of the line (e.g. brand 4 in Figure 59.2) will be regarded as having a high perceived price relative to its benefits and can be expected to lose market share. A brand to the right of the line (e.g. brand 5 in Figure 59.2) is perceived to offer significant benefits relative to its price and will win market share.

It is helpful for a company to know where it sits relative to competitive brands on and around the value equivalence line. For example, brand 5 to the right of the line could decide to maintain the 'good value strategy' and build market share. Equally, a decision could be made to raise prices, capture more value and profit, and see the brand move upwards and closer to the VEL. Brand 4 to the left-hand side of the line may want to think about how it can communicate more benefits to customers, or it may recognize it is overpriced and needs to lower its prices.

Figure 59.1 Brands in equilibrium in a value map

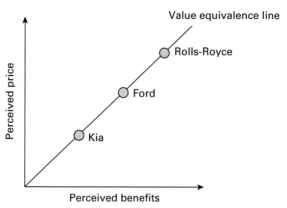

Figure 59.2 Brands 4 and 5 out of equilibrium in a market

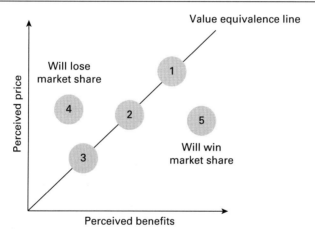

It should be emphasized that the value equivalence model is based on perceptions of price and benefits and these could be wrong. In the above example, brand 4 is thought to offer relatively few benefits for the perceived price. It is just possible that the promotions supporting brand 4 have not communicated the true benefits of the brand and it is being unfairly maligned. If this is the case then a promotional campaign, correcting the perceptions, may be the way forward. So too, a brand could be perceived to have a high price when in fact it offers good value for money because it lasts longer than other products on the market. Again, this could be something that requires addressing through a communications campaign.

Two simple questions can be asked to determine a company's position on the VEL. These are:

- How would you rate Company A on the benefits you get from buying its products and services compared to the benefits you get from other suppliers?
  - *Significantly better*
  - *Somewhat better*
  - *Neither better nor worse*
  - *Somewhat worse*
  - *Significantly worse*
- How would you rate Company A on the prices of its products and services compared to the prices of other suppliers?
  - *Significantly better*
  - *Somewhat better*
  - *Neither better nor worse*
  - *Somewhat worse*
  - *Significantly worse*

The same questions can be asked of other suppliers to the market. The results can be plotted on an XY graph to show the position of the companies or brands and, from these, a brand owner can formulate a pricing and product strategy.

The origins of the model

In 1994 Bradley Gale made the observation in his book *Managing Customer Value*[1] that 'value equals quality relative to price'. He produced a graph that plotted price against perceived quality with a 45-degree line bisecting the two, which he called the 'fair value line'; the precursor of the VEL.

The concept of the VEL was described in 1997 in an article in the *McKinsey Quarterly* by Ralf Leszinski and Michael Marn entitled 'Setting value, not price'.[2] Michael Marn, Eric Roegner and Craig Zawada gave further explanation of the tool in 2004 in the book *The Price Advantage*.[3]

Developments of the model

The theory of the VEL is based on the assumption that people are rational in their actions. For example, it could be assumed that if a major brand makes a significant improvement, offering greater benefits, and its price remains the same, the brand will be repositioned to the right-hand side of the VEL and will gain market share. If the competitors are unable to match the increased benefits of the major brand, we can theorize that they would have to lower their prices to maintain the equilibrium in the market and the VEL would move to the right.

These are changes that are difficult to predict and recognize. The additional benefits offered by a competitor may be insufficient to move the dynamics of the market. Loyalty to companies, and the inertia in buying decisions, may mean that they do not have to move their prices downwards. It cannot be assumed that people will always act in an economically predictable way.

Theoretical concepts can sometimes be difficult to recognize in the marketplace but they are nevertheless useful for developing strategies. The positioning of different players within a market can be achieved by means other than the VEL. B2B International developed the net value score, which is a calculation based on the following question:

- How would you rate company X on the total value the company offers, compared to the total value offered by other suppliers of similar products/ services?
  - *Significantly better*
  - *Somewhat better*
  - *Neither better nor worse*
  - *Somewhat worse*
  - *Significantly worse*

Using the answers to this question, the net value score can be calculated by subtracting the percentage of people who stated 'worse' from the percentage of people who stated 'better' and doubling the percentage of people who stated significantly better/worse. The doubling of the responses that are significantly better or significantly worse adds weight to the factors of greatest importance (see Figure 59.3).

Figure 59.3   Formula for calculating the net value score

$$\text{Net value score} = \frac{\left(\begin{array}{l}\%\text{ of significantly better} \times 2 + \%\text{ of somewhat better}\end{array}\right) - \left(\begin{array}{l}\%\text{ of significantly worse} \times 2 + \%\text{ of somewhat worse}\end{array}\right)}{2}$$

SOURCE B2B International (2011)

The results of the net value score can be converted to a score out of 100. Figure 59.4 shows an example of the results from a survey of companies supplying products to three different vertical markets – the automotive industry, the chemical industry and the construction industry. The competing suppliers within these vertical sectors are numbered 1 to 5. Company 1, the sponsor of the research, performs particularly well in the automotive sector and far less so in construction markets. This is the opposite for company 5, which fares badly in automotive but does well in construction. The net value score shows the distance between the suppliers and points towards the need for action. In the case of company 1 there is a clear requirement for it to adjust its value proposition in the construction industry.

Figure 59.4   Using the net value score to establish comparative advantages

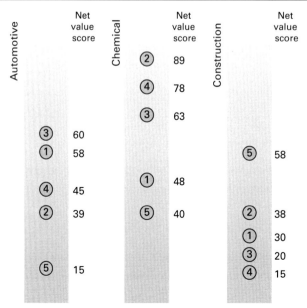

Automotive	Net value score	Chemical	Net value score	Construction	Net value score
②	89
④	78
③	63
③	60				
①	58			⑤	58
		①	48
④	45
②	39	⑤	40	②	38
				①	30
				③	20
⑤	15			④	15

SOURCE B2B International (2011)

The model in action

A manufacturer of hand tools (I will call it brand X) sells to professional trades. It carried out a survey to find out why it was losing market share. The survey showed that the relatively high price of the hand tools was not justified in the eyes of customers. There was not a big difference in the perceived prices of the tools, though some less expensive brands were thought to offer more benefits and even more expensive brands were considered better value for money.

The company could see no reason why its own brand was perceived to offer less benefits. In tests it performed just as well as competing brands, better in some cases.

A further examination of customers showed that brand X had weakened its position with its target audience, professional tradespeople, following the introduction of its products into DIY stores. Its products were now available to the general public. Professional trades did not like using tools bought by the general public, feeling that they diminished their craft and skills. It also led to the perception that the brand was not robust enough for their professional use.

Brand X did not want to give up its rapidly growing sales to the general public. Instead, it relaunched the tools for tradespeople using different-coloured handles, new point-of-sale packaging and a tagline that said 'Professionals Pick Brand X'. Brand X ran a promotional campaign that communicated the high performance of its tools and featuring their use by professional trades.

The repositioning of the brand was sufficient to move the company to the right-hand side of the VEL and it quickly began to increase its market share with professional tradespeople.

Some things to think about

- Understanding where your brand sits on the VEL is important in determining future strategy. If it is to the right-hand side of the line you can carry on winning market share or raise prices. However, if it is to the left-hand side of the line it is necessary to find out why it has adverse perceptions – in order to win back share. A product to the left-hand side of the line could be overpriced, it could lack sufficient features and benefits or it could be failing to communicate them.

- The position of a brand in the market is based on perceptions. Perceptions are created by customer experiences, word of mouth and promotions. What perceptions do your customers have and how are you influencing them in the right way?

Notes

1 Gale, BT (1994) *Managing Customer Value: Creating quality and service that customers can see*, Simon & Schuster, New York

2 Leszinski, R and Marn, MV (1997) Setting value, not price, *McKinsey Quarterly*, February

3 Marn, MV, Roegner, EV and Zawada, CC (2004) *The Price Advantage*, John Wiley & Sons, New Jersey

Value net   60

How to benefit from competitor collaboration

What the model looks like and how it works

Most people see competition between businesses as a war zone. Some business leaders have been known to carry in their briefcase *The Art of War*, a book by Sun Tzu, an ancient Chinese military strategist. Admittedly companies compete with each other but that does not mean their aim is extermination. On many major roads leading out of towns you can see a collection of car franchises lined up next to each other. Each is in competition with the other, but collectively they make a stronger proposition to the car-buying public through the greater choice they provide. In the same way, one successful restaurant in town can encourage others to locate nearby and soon the area becomes known as a place to eat out. Competition often stimulates greater success for everyone in a market.

The idea that businesses should cooperate rather than fight all-out wars was developed by Adam Brandenburger and Barry Nalebuff. They proposed the value net model, which puts a company in the centre of its universe with four forces surrounding it. These forces are:

- **Customers:** every company needs people who buy its products and services.

- **Suppliers:** these are the companies that provide materials, equipment and software that enable a business to create products and services.

- **Competitors:** these are companies that provide similar or alternative products and services.

- **Complementors:** this is where the model becomes interesting and different from others. Complementors are organizations that offer something that makes a business stronger. In the case of restaurants competing in an area of town, there may also be bars that people can drop into before their meal. The bars are complementary and they strengthen the offer of the restaurants to people dining out. A company that makes computers may load its products with software, which enhances the value of its computers. The software is a complementary product and, together with the computer, makes a more attractive offering.

In developing their model, Brandenburger and Nalebuff were inspired by game theory. They saw that game theory focuses on the most pressing forces, which in turn lead to clearer strategies and decisions. In a situation with a number of interdependent forces, game theory breaks these down into key components and helps explain a proposed strategy. Game theory shows how it is possible to change the direction of a business so that there is no absolute winner or loser in the market. With the right strategy, companies can coexist and there can be more than one winner.

The game is played by moving different levers – components in the value net tool. These components are referred to as PARTS, an acronym for players, added value, rules, tactics and scope:

- **Players:** these are all the different companies that operate within a market. For example, a business could find additional suppliers of raw materials and so reduce its costs. It could look for new companies that could add value to its product. In looking for opportunities amongst new players, questions need to be asked such as 'What could this company bring to the party?' 'Who would win or lose if they joined?'

- **Added value:** these are the things that add value. Improved products and services add value and, as a result, are likely to generate increased loyalty. Value can also be added by co-operators. Working with complementary businesses adds value to both organizations as well as customers. Back in 1986 a few large manufacturers of mud flaps lobbied for legislation that eventually resulted in spray suppression regulations requiring all heavy goods vehicles to have brushes and flaps fitted to each axle. Every manufacturer of mud flaps across Europe benefitted from the efforts of the few who pushed for the legislation.

- **Rules:** all games are played with rules and businesses similarly have rules and regulations that become accepted practices. Rules may be introduced by one player and eventually become accepted by all others. They can range from health and safety rules through to credit control, warranties, service backup and the like.

- **Tactics:** these are the messages communicated within a market that influence the actions of others (assuming that they are legal). A market leader raises its prices and it becomes a signal for others to follow suit. A company sets up an alliance with a co-operator and this encourages other companies to form similar alliances.

- **Scope:** businesses do not act in isolation. They are linked in numerous ways. Legislation in a completely different market may trigger companies in another market to believe they should pursue something similar. A downturn in a certain industrial sector may force companies to look for business in another sector or region.

Consideration of these PARTS as forces in the market will help a planner develop likely scenarios of change. Each of the components of PARTS is a tool that can transform and change the game. Understanding how these levers work within a market is fundamental to the model because it allows a company to play a game its own way – in a way that benefits the business specifically.

The origins of the model

Academics and consultants have for many years recognized the importance of strategic alliances. Strategic alliances, or networks, are the foundations of the value net framework.

It was not until 1996 that the term value net was used and the theory was expounded. Adam Brandenburger and Barry Nalebuff described the theory in their book entitled *Co-Opetition*.[1] In the book the authors acknowledged how they were influenced by game theory. Specifically they talked about game theory developed in the Second World War and later turned into economic theory by John von Neumann and Oskar Morgenstern in *Theory of Games and Economic Behavior*.[2]

Developments of the model

The concept of creating value through companies setting up interdependent value nets and collaboration has quickly caught on. The original concept of collaboration has been added to by numerous authors who emphasize the use of technology and sharing information in the value nets. Emphasis is placed on the final customers as a key driver in the value nets.

Michael Porter described the value chain within a company as a sequential process in which raw materials move through and are transformed into higher-value offerings (see Chapter 58). The value net model is different in that it is not sequential and value is added through the network as a result of cooperation and interconnectivities between the various players within the market.

The model in action

An article by Anni-Kaisa Kähkönen published in the *British Food Journal* (2012) and entitled 'Value net – a new business model for the food industry?'[3] describes how the value net model can be applied to the food industry in Finland. The Finnish food industry, like other food industries across Europe, has changed dramatically in the last few decades. It has turned from a traditional industry of farmers and processors with a myriad of retailers to an industry with a small number of very large retailers, large food processors and farming groups. There are still many small companies in the industry but they tend to follow the lead of these larger groups.

In the past, the food industry had players who operated in isolation. Today, the players are tightly linked and collaborate. Applying the value net model we can see the following characteristics:

- **Customers**: the market is highly tuned to the needs of customers. There is recognition that different segments of customers want different things. Some look for bargain prices, others for new food experiences, yet others may demand high levels of service. Large retailers are sensitive to the different needs of the customers.

- **Competitors**: the three largest grocery retailers in Finland have a combined share of nearly 90 per cent. They play a dominant role.

- **Suppliers**: the food industry in Finland is modern and high tech, using fast-developing technologies. Food is the fourth largest industry in Finland in terms of its gross value of production. It is now characterized by a small number of very large players with a tail of many small and medium-sized companies.

- **Complementors**: at the heart of the value net model is the concept of players working in networks in which they add value to their offers. Driven by consumer demands, retailers listen carefully to their customers' requirements. These they share with the food processors, informing them of changes in taste, requirements in packaging, needs for healthy eating and so on. Technology plays an important part in sharing this information and reacting quickly to it. These links pass all the way through the value chain of the industry and, through collaboration, value is added. The ultimate goal is to create value for the end customers and this cannot be achieved by one group of players alone. All the large groups have joint product development projects with different suppliers and are constantly finding new areas of co-development. Relationships between companies in the value chain are long established, some of them more than 20 years old.

The analysis of the industry provides an illustration of how collaboration adds value to all the players. The value net model is similar to Porter's five forces in that it examines the forces that shape a market. It provides additional insights by exploring the effects of collaboration and networking.

Some things to think about

- Managing your business in a highly competitive environment does not mean that you have to hit competitors head-on. There may be opportunities for collaboration with different players in the market that will add value to your offer. This requires a deep understanding of what your customers want and need. What would enhance your offer to your customers and how could you achieve this through collaboration with other suppliers in the market?

- Sharing knowledge is a good start to collaboration. Attending conferences and industry seminars and writing papers on the subject would position your company as collaborative.

Notes

1 Brandenburger, A and Nalebuff, B (1996) *Co-Opetition: 1. A revolutionary mindset that combines competition and cooperation. 2. The game theory strategy that's changing the game of business*, Currency Doubleday, New York
2 von Neumann, J and Morgenstern, O (1944) *Theory of Games and Economic Behavior*, Princeton University Press, New Jersey
3 Kähkönen, A (2012) Value net – a new business model for the food industry?, *British Food Journal*, **114** (5), pp 681–701

Value-based marketing

61

Adding value to products and services to improve profitability

What the model looks like and how it works

There are many definitions of marketing, one of which is 'marketing is concerned with getting the right product to the right people at the right price'. The emphasis in this oversimplistic definition is 'at the right price'. The right price from a customer's point of view might be a very low one. The right price from the marketer's point of view might be a high one. The price of the product is in theory the level at which two parties are prepared to execute a bargain. However, the price can be manipulated higher if the seller has a strong value proposition – that is, if the seller is able to convince the buyer that it is worth significantly more than might be apparent at first sight. Product-focused companies are not good at selling value; they are good at selling products. They make a product, they work out the cost and they add what they believe is a reasonable margin. In this way they arrive at a price. The customer is presented with the product together with its price and invited to make a purchase.

The value-based marketer produces a product, considers the benefits to the customer and how they will use it, and sets the price accordingly. The cost of manufacture plays no part except the price must more than cover all costs. The customer is reminded by the seller of the many good reasons why the price is justified. Value-based marketing is all about understanding the needs of the customer and ensuring that the product, together with its benefits, is positioned at the right price to collect the maximum amount of value.

Value-based marketing (VBM) also recognizes that not everyone has the same needs and values. Some people will appreciate the features and benefits of the product more than others and be prepared to pay for them. Segmentation is important in VBM. The value-based marketer targets only those customers who really do want and value their product.

Obtaining value in a market requires a model with five steps (Figure 61.1):

Figure 61.1   The value marketing pentadigm (after DeBonis, Balinski and Allen[1])

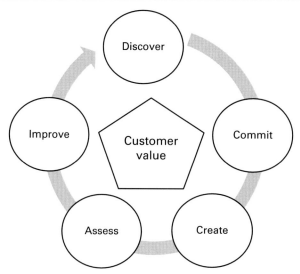

SOURCE After DeBonis, Balinski and Allen (2002)

Discover

The discovery phase is about understanding the customer. It involves defining and mapping the market; understanding exactly who the key players are within the market and who will be targeted. It also takes in the exploration of customer value expectations – what customers want from a particular offering, how they find a company that supplies the offering and how they decide which offering they will buy. This leads to the discovery of value segments; groups of customers aligned with the product offering.

Commit

It is at this stage that the company begins to take aim at segments that value its offer. The company may want to modify its offer to ensure that it has superior features and benefits over those supplied by the competition. It is important that everyone within the company understands the targets and the standards of the products and services that will be supplied. KPIs will be set to ensure that standards are met.

Create

Value marketing companies know the importance of delivering an excellent customer experience. From the top of the organization there must be a commitment to provide value to customers, not only with the product itself but with the service that supports it. The company will have an appropriate culture but it will also have a structure that ensures that the delivery of the product and the experience is consistent.

Assess

A VBM company is a listening company. It takes into account feedback from customers to understand the reason for complaints. It knows why customer orders are lost and what improvements customers want. The company is rigorous in assessing its performance against customer expectations and constantly seeking to improve customer satisfaction.

Improve

Following on from the assessment and customer feedback, the VBM company will be aiming to spot gaps between expectations and delivery and will close those gaps wherever it can. The company will aim to be proactive in understanding customers' needs and, wherever possible, anticipating them so that it is one step ahead in delivering them.

The origins of the model

Good salespeople have always attempted to sell value. If they don't sell value, the customer may regret the purchase and only buy the product once. If they sell value, the customer will return for a lifetime of purchases.

The notion of value marketing is not new. In Theodore Levitt's seminal article published in 1960 entitled 'Marketing myopia',[2] he made the following observation:

> Selling is preoccupied with the seller's need to convert his product into cash; marketing with the idea of satisfying the needs of the customer by means of the product and the whole cluster of things associated with creating, delivering, and finally consuming it.

Levitt did not use the word 'value' but he implied it by saying that the marketer seeks to satisfy needs by more than just the product, indeed the whole cluster of things that surround it.

In the 1980s and 1990s articles were written by McKinsey consultants on value marketing. In 2002 Nicolas DeBonis, Eric Balinski and Phil Allen wrote a book entitled *Value-Based Marketing for Bottom Line Success: 5 steps to creating customer value.*[3] These five steps are the value pentadigm that is illustrated in Figure 61.1.

Developments of the model

The five-step model of discover, commit, create, assess and improve can easily be manipulated to suit any condition.

Most of the developments in VBM have come from the market research tools that are used to explore what people really value. Traditional methods of asking straightforward questions as to what people value have proved limited. People do not always know what they value or cannot articulate it. They answer from the head and not the heart, explaining that they want a good product at a low price with fast delivery. In fact, they may be driven by emotional factors such as the brand, relationships, security and other such factors that come from the heart.

Conjoint analysis (see Chapter 16) is a tool that attempts to understand how people value products and services. Here the customer is asked to review a series of 30 or so combinations of features, benefits and the price, and say which they would choose and which they would reject. From an analysis of the results the researchers are able to determine the utility (the value) attached to the different features and benefits and which is the optimum combination for a certain group of customers.

The model in action

A supplier of packaging materials wanted to understand how customers valued its offer. The market for packaging materials is fragmented. Almost every company buys boxes, tape and wrapping paper while others, such as online retailers, suppliers of fast-moving consumer goods and foodstuffs, spend a small fortune on packaging materials. The needs of buyers of packaging materials are very different. Furthermore, the packaging materials

Figure 61.2 A SIMALTO grid for measuring value

Services	1	2	3	4
1. Face-to-face visit from salesperson	We never receive a visit from a salesperson 0	We spend up to 30% of the time on added-value work-related activities 5	We spend 30–60% of the time on added-value work-related activities 10	We spend 60–100% of the time on added-value work-related activities 15
2. Knowledge of sales staff who visit you	They know next to nothing about the products and the industry 0	They have a basic understanding of their products and the industry 5	They have a good understanding of their products and the industry 10	They are experts in their products and the industry 15
3. Authority of the sales staff who visit you	They have no authority and everything is referred back to their head office 0	They can make minor decisions without referring back to their head office 5	They are able to make most of the decisions on their own and without referring back to head office 10	They have the ability and authority to make all the decisions themselves without referring back to head office 15
4. The understanding of the sales staff who visit you of your business	They have no interest or understanding of my individual needs 0	They have a basic interest and understanding of my individual needs 5	They have a good understanding of my interest and individual needs 10	They have an expert understanding of my interest and individual needs 15
5. Keeping you up to date with the new packaging ideas	They seldom if ever have anything new for me to consider 0	Every now and then they introduce new packaging ideas or materials 5	They frequently suggest introducing new packaging ideas and materials 10	They are always suggesting and introducing new packaging ideas and materials 15
6. Frequency of face-to-face visits from sales staff	No contact at all 0	Quarterly 5	Monthly 10	Weekly/fortnightly 15
7. The time spent in typical meetings with packaging-material sales staff	Less than 10 minutes 0	Less than half an hour 5	Less than an hour 10	Less than a couple of hours 15
8. Proactivity of contact with the supplier	You always have to call the supplier 0	They contact you on up to 30% of the occasions 5	They contact you on 30–60% of the occasions 10	They contact you on 60% or more of the occasions 15
9. Time spent on the shop floor	Spend all meeting time in the office 0	Spend up to 30% of meetings on the shop floor 5	Spend 30–60% of meetings on the shop floor 10	Spend 60% or more of the meetings on the shop floor 15

that are purchased are only part of the offer. The customer service, ease of ordering, ability to order online, service from the help desk and quick delivery may be as important as the packaging products themselves.

The packaging company set out to understand how customers value its products and services using a market research tool called SIMALTO – an acronym for simultaneous multi-attribute level trade-off (see Chapter 51). This rather complicated name describes a simple process in which a respondent is asked to state the importance of various products and services they receive (the left-hand column in the grid shown in Figure 61.2) followed by a question that asks what level of service they receive at the present and what level they would like to receive.

Respondents were then allocated a number of points to spend to indicate how they would like to move from the level of service they are receiving at present to that which they would like to receive. Note the numbers in brackets in each box. For example, moving from level 2 to level 4 on a particular service would cost 10 points. The spending of points indicates the value attached to a particular service.

In this way, the company was able to complete the discovery phase of the pentadigm road map. The company now understood what people wanted and how much it was valued. They especially understood the unmet needs and how much these would be valued. From here they could commit different offers to different segments within the market and develop new products to meet customers' needs. Following the application of this model the company has become a market leader in the supply of packaging materials.

Some things to think about

- Many companies sell products rather than value. They set the price of their product on the cost of manufacturing and add a margin. VBM starts with the perceptions of value as seen by the customer. What do your customers value? What aspects of your offer are special, different and valued?

- How could you improve the value of your offer? What are the features and benefits that customers would like to be improved and how much would they pay for them?

Notes

1 DeBonis, J, Balinski, E and Allen, P (2002) *Value-Based Marketing for Bottom-Line Success: 5 steps to creating customer value*, McGraw-Hill, New York

2 Levitt, T (1960) Marketing myopia, *Harvard Business Review*, reprinted in July–August 2004, issue pp 45–56

3 DeBonis, J, Balinski, E and Allen, P (2002) *Value-Based Marketing for Bottom-Line Success: 5 steps to creating customer value*, McGraw-Hill, New York

VMOST 62

Defining strategies and preparing a business plan

What the model looks like and how it works

This framework was proposed by Rakesh Sondhi, an academic and business consultant.[1] VMOST, the name of the framework, is based on a hierarchy of five components – vision, mission, objectives, strategy and tactics. Imagine that these form a pyramid with vision at its apex. Vision is the starting point for developing a strategy as it leads to an understanding of the company's mission, objectives that must be achieved, strategies that will help them be achieved and tactics that will fight the various battles.

In each of the five steps in the framework, Sondhi recommends identifying what is meant by the step and analysing all aspects of it. For example:

Vision

Vision is the most critical part of the framework and it sits at the top of the pyramid. In identifying the vision for the company, it is necessary to state very clearly where it is going. Having done this, it is now necessary to analyse the vision by asking questions such as 'Will people throughout the company understand it?' and 'Is it engaging and achievable?'.

Mission

Below Vision in the pyramid is Mission. Consultants and academics might also call the mission 'the purpose' of the company – why does it exist? The mission or purpose of the company is not to make money. Hopefully it will make money by the great execution of its strategy and tactics. What we are looking for here in a mission or purpose is something that motivates people to want to work at the company.

Objectives

Next the framework moves to Objectives, which are the goals that must be achieved in order to fulfil the mission. The goals should be specific, measurable, achievable, relevant and timely (SMART).

Strategies

Goals do not just happen, they have to be made to happen and this requires strategies. The strategy is the plan of action designed to achieve the long-term aim of the company. It is the overall plan of how the company will play its business game.

Tactics

Tactics are the base of the pyramid. They are the detailed activities that will ensure that the strategy is achieved. They are the moves in the game that can be adjusted according to a changing business environment.

The power of the VMOST framework is ensuring that all the components are aligned. Do the tactics ensure the strategies will be successful? Do the strategies meet with the objectives? Do the objectives fit in with the mission? And does the mission align with the vision? If the answer is 'no' to any of these questions, it would be necessary to adjust.

The sequential nature of the framework makes it useful for structuring a business plan. It also ensures joined-up thinking.

The origins of the model

Rakesh Sondhi is an academic and management consultant who has written widely on leadership and strategic decision making. Business strategies have existed forever, though often without structure. A big danger in strategic thinking is that people jump straight into tactics. Business people are action-oriented and tactics is a demonstration of doing something. However, a good strategy requires deep thought from the outset. This is what Sondhi has brought to the table. The starting point is a vision and a mission.

Jim Collins, author of *Built To Last* (1994), is very keen on visions and missions.[2] In his view, enduringly successful companies have a clear mission. Determining this mission isn't always easy. Other management gurus such as Kenichi Ohmae believe it comes from an analysis of what a company does well, what customers value, and what the company does better than the competition.

Once the vision and mission are decided it is possible to set objectives and outline the strategy that will achieve them. It is this helpful sequencing of thoughts and actions that is appealing about the Sondhi model.

Developments of the model

The VMOST framework is a logical method of developing a strategy. It ensures consistency and alignment of the strategy to its various components. It also introduces the strategy planners to other frameworks such as PEST, Porter's diamond, and Porter's five forces. In this way the company takes a thorough look at its marketing and competitive environment.

Other strategy frameworks that have some similarity to VMOST are MOSAIC and SOSTAC© (see Chapter 37).

The success of the framework has resulted in it being used within units of a company such as departments, teams and individuals. It could be used in personal career planning.

The model in action

A company making machines for packaging food grew over a 20-year period. It prospered due to the speed and efficiency of its machines and their reliability. As the company grew, it added more product lines. They weren't all equally successful but they remained in the company's portfolio. The founder retired and the company was bought out by the management. It had begun to plateau and needed to move to a different level. The new owners applied the VMOST framework.

Vision and mission

First they determined a vision for the company. This was not easy. They struggled with the concept of vision and mission statements, believing that they overlapped. They finally agreed a simple statement which was '*to provide the most efficient packaging machines with a second-to-none service backup*'. Arguably terms like 'most efficient' and 'second to none' are open to interpretation but they evoked the spirit of always being better than the competition.

Objectives and goals followed

A detailed market study showed that the company had variable strengths in different segments of the market. They had a strong position with companies that packed fresh vegetables, fish and desserts. However, they had a relatively low share amongst companies producing ready meals and meats. They set objectives to increase their market share of machines in these neglected sectors from a lowly 5 per cent to 15 per cent within a three-year period. At the same time their objective was to maintain their dominant shares in other segments of the market as these would be key to financing growth in new segments.

Strategy

It was determined that the strategy was to grow significantly in new segments and maintain its strong position in the other segments. This would be achieved by building a strong brand as the supplier of the most efficient packaging machines with the very best service backup. The message they wanted to communicate to all segments was that their machines were leaders on efficiency, reliability and innovation.

Tactics

The company ran a tight marketing budget. It opted for PR and social media (in particular LinkedIn), which proved very efficient in communicating to a closely defined target audience.

The VMOST plan took three or four months to build. Once in place it became a vehicle for explaining to the whole company where it stood, where it was going and how it intended to get there. It brought everyone on board and it was successful because it provided focus and an alignment of the business plan.

Some things to think about

- Where would the company like to be in three years, five years, ten years? This is its vision.

- What is the mission for the company? What does the company do? Where is it going? And what are its priorities? These are its principles.

- What are the objectives for the company? These are specific aims (hopefully measurable and achievable) for the next year or two.

- What is the strategy for the company? This is the roadmap by which it will achieve its objectives.

- What are the tactics for achieving the strategy? These are the detailed means by which the strategy is carried out.

Notes

1   Sondhi, RK (1999) *Total Strategy*, Airworthy Publications
2   Collins, J (1994) *Built to Last: Successful habits of visionary companies*, Harper Business

Weisbord's six box model   63

Assessing the efficient functioning of an organization

What the model looks like and how it works

Organizational development is the study of systems within an organization with the goal of improving them in some way. Marvin Weisbord, a consultant, proposed a framework with six boxes that describe the efficient functioning of a company. An analysis of a company's performance in each of the boxes shows where improvements are needed.

Surrounding the company is an environment made up of customers, regulations, neighbours etc. It is within this environment that the six boxes have to operate.

Each of the six boxes plays a role in the performance of a company. The boxes have things feeding into them such as resources and money and feeding out of them such as products and services. Within the boxes there are likely to be formal ways of doing things and these may contrast with the day-to-day informal ways of making things happen. It is necessary to look at each box in turn and determine how efficiently it is working:

- **Box 1. Purpose:** The starting point of the assessment is to determine what business the company is in and whether there are any expected changes in the future. In effect, this is an examination of the vision and mission for the company. A company may have a purpose or a goal and it could be expressed as a vision or mission statement. However, staff may not fully understand and support the organization's purpose. Weisbord would see this as a disconnect that needs attention.

- **Box 2. Structure:** Next Weisbord looks at how the company is organized. This part of the analysis covers who does what in the various departments of the organization. Nearly every company has an organogram which lays out the formal hierarchy of who does what and who answers to whom. And yet, most companies have informal networks with members of staff knowing who they should speak to in order to get things done. Again, the framework looks for disconnects that need fixing.

- **Box 3. Relationships:** Companies are made up of people who have relationships with their colleagues, customers and suppliers. Relationships with colleagues include those in the same department and those in other departments. There are also relationships between people, customers and the technologies and systems they use. These relationships are vital to a company's success. There can be conflict in these relationships which must be sorted out if a company is to work efficiently.

- **Box 4. Rewards:** People need to be motivated by appropriate rewards not just in money but in the recognition they receive for the job they do. A workforce receives remuneration and this is the formal part of the system. However, they may not feel and act as if they are rewarded adequately. Weisbord makes the point that it is necessary to convert the reward theory into organizational practice. By this he means having the right salary and benefits that motivate people and which are considered fair.

- **Box 5. Leadership:** This is another vital component of every company. Leadership styles can be defined in theory. Some are autocratic, others democratic. Some are task-oriented, others are relationship-oriented. A leader must understand the organization and its requirements and adjust leadership qualities to suit. A key task of leadership is to scan the six boxes to see where there are misfits between the formal and informal ways of doing things. The leader's job is to sort this out.

- **Box 6. Helpful mechanisms:** These are the 'lubrication' that helps an organization operate efficiently. They include all the policies, procedures, meetings and systems used within the company. They also include all the technologies such as the software programs that knit the company together. Other helpful mechanisms are the processes of planning, budgeting, controlling and measuring what goes on within the company. In analysing the efficiency of the company it is necessary to see if it has formal mechanisms that are helpful and work.

The origins of the model

Marvin Weisbord is an American consultant specializing in organizational development. Organizational development drives improvements in a company by aligning all its component parts – strategy, structure, people, rewards and management processes.

Weisbord came to the six box model after years of consulting in which he tried to work out the relationships between various bits of data he observed. He built up 'cognitive maps' of organizations and their component parts. This resulted in the six boxes to which he attached labels. The boxes did not sit in proud isolation but related to each other. Therefore a blip in one box would have an effect on other boxes. The key to managing company improvement is to take each box and determine how efficiently it is working.

In 1976 Weisbord published his theory in a paper entitled 'Organizational diagnosis: Six places to look for trouble with or without a theory' in the *Group & Organization Studies* publication.[1]

Developments of the model

There is much flexibility in the Weisbord framework. Boxes can be looked at in isolation or as a system that drives the efficiency of the company. A quick analysis of each box may point to an aspect of the business that needs a deeper dive.

In 2008 Robert Preziosi developed a questionnaire to be used with Weisbord's framework. This questionnaire asks members of staff to agree or disagree with 35 statements. The answers show how well each box performs and where improvements are needed.

Today there are a number of online templates that make the application of the six box model relatively easy. Nevertheless, there is much work to do in obtaining the data for each box.

The framework recognizes that a company sits within an external environment. However, there is no guidance as to how to analyse the relationship between the company and these external forces. This is where alternative frameworks such as PEST analysis and SWOT analysis could be useful.

The model in action

The Weisbord framework has found considerable appeal amongst consultants. It is a tool to systematically analyse what needs fixing within an organization. It can also be used by managers within the company, considering the company as a whole or just looking at the efficiency of individual departments.

The key to Weisbord's framework is recognizing that companies have formal systems and these are necessary because they show what work has to be done and what system should be used to do it. Each of the six boxes will have formal systems. As we all know, company rules and formal systems are frequently modified by staff who have their own informal and sometimes better ways of working. The gap between the formal and informal systems is important, especially if the work to be done is not being done properly. For example, a company may have a human resources department that has laid out lines of authority showing who answers to whom. There will be times when the lines of authority don't work because somebody isn't available. Companies have ways of working round such blockages. This is all well and good and may work most of the time. It is important, however, to ensure that it doesn't become the norm, especially if in doing so quality, safety or some other important measure is compromised. Weisbord is always looking to see the degree of fit between the formal system and the informal system within the company.

Organizational change is now the norm. Sometimes it is obvious that change is required. Maybe things just aren't working. Sometimes it isn't so obvious. Staff may be constantly locked up in too many meetings and actions are being delayed. This may suggest that there is a gap between the formal systems in an organization and the informal systems that make things happen and present an opportunity for a Weisbord analysis.

External forces may also demand organizational changes. Regulatory changes in the market, new competitors, or developments in overseas markets may all require management to look at the organization and make changes.

Some things to think about

- Does your organization feel like it needs a health check?
- Are there particular areas of your organization that can readily be identified as needing attention?
- How are the failings or weaknesses in one part of your organization impacting on other parts?
- Who should carry out the analysis of your organization – should external people be brought in to do the job?
- Would the Weisbord six box framework be appropriate for the analysis?

Note

1 Weisbord, MR (1976) Organizational diagnosis: Six places to look for trouble with or without a theory, *Group & Organization Studies*, **1** (4), pp 430–47

INDEX

Printed and bound by CPI Group (UK) Ltd, Croydon, CR0 4YY

08/03/2024

14467465-0001